Praise fo

D1315875

"Curates the best advice f   :male
leaders.... Whether you are   ، ng to
advance, or are an established leader seeking to improve, *Become
the Fire* will inspire you."

— from the foreword by **Mary Dillon**,
former CEO and executive chair of Ulta Beauty

"What if every challenge you faced was fuel, or fire, to make you
better in business and in life? *Become the Fire* is a motivating read
that will help anyone overcome their hurdles and chase their am-
bitions. It's a great read for those searching for inspiration and
proof that dreams can come true."

— **Kara Goldin**, founder and former CEO of Hint, Inc.,
and *Wall Street Journal* bestselling author of *Undaunted*

"Elisa Schmitz knows what it takes not only to overcome life's
fire but also to let it forge the inner strength, vision, authenticity,
and resilience needed to turn challenges into success. By sharing real-life lessons learned by her and other courageous women
leaders, Elisa shows that success is something you can define and
create for yourself, no matter your circumstances. In fact, as Elisa
shares, it's the failures that you think of as fatal, and the differences that make you, you, that can be the superpowers you need
in order to succeed. The book's interactive component enables
you to apply the lessons so that you, too, can make a difference
and 'become the fire.' An engaging read that will inspire you to
make, or expand, your own mark in the world!"

— **Kaira Rouda**, *USA TODAY* bestselling author of
Real You Incorporated: 8 Essentials for Women Entrepreneurs

"Elisa Schmitz has that rare ability to write with intelligence,
heart, and confidence without veering into ego. And without
making unrealistic promises. Every chapter in *Become the Fire*
takes you deep into the thought processes and decision-making
of elite, proven, and highly relatable women. You'll want to have

a pen and notepad handy, as this book will ignite a wealth of your best ideas. I have always looked for role models to inspire my daughter. This exceptional book, fueled by Elisa's enthusiasm, is among the best I have read."

— **Daniel Joshua Rubin**, author of *27 Essential Principles of Story*

"Elisa Schmitz's *Become the Fire* takes you on inspirational journeys of women who seized the fire within them to achieve remarkable success. Every pathway has many twists and turns, but they prove that being true to your vision at every turn ignites the fire within."

— **Kay Koplovitz**, founder and former CEO of USA Networks and chairman of Springboard Enterprises

"I moved to Hollywood with no connections or knowledge of how to 'make it' — but I know now, and frankly, it's all in this book. As Elisa Schmitz so eloquently encourages readers: be courageous, embrace your differences, use failure to your advantage, persevere, and — the most important rule of Hollywood — good lord, *read the room*. But this book isn't about Hollywood, and *anyone* looking to have a successful and, more importantly, *fulfilling* career should read *Become the Fire!*"

— **Janae Bakken**, Emmy-nominated executive producer and TV writer of *Scrubs*, *Baby Daddy*, *Anger Management*, and other shows

"Elisa Schmitz's own story is one of resiliency in the face of personal and professional obstacles. In *Become the Fire*, she pairs her firsthand experience with stories and advice from ten inspirational women who were willing to be brave, gritty, and uncomfortable to pursue their dreams and impact the world. It's essential reading at a time when so many capable women are leaving the workforce and silencing their voices."

— **Alexandra Levit**, *Wall Street Journal* columnist and internationally bestselling author of *Humanity Works*

"Elisa Schmitz's *Become the Fire* is an engaging and informative look at the stories of women, including herself, who were trailblazers and pathmakers. Readers will find the answer to the all-important question 'How can I do it?'"
— **Christie Hefner**, former chairman and CEO of Playboy Enterprises

"Elisa Schmitz's special gift to the world has been to spark imagination into possibility. Now she's given us the tools to kindle that flame into a bonfire of opportunity."
— **Amy Millman**, founder of Springboard Enterprises and StageNext.vc

"Through the life stories of many inspiring women — including her own — Elisa Schmitz has written more than a must-read book. *Become the Fire* is a call to action and a helpful guidebook for every woman who wants to achieve success, create a positive impact, and leave a lasting legacy in the world. The journeys of these strong, authentic, and resilient women are inspiring for anybody who occasionally doubts her ability to persevere and thrive. The power and vulnerability disclosed by these leaders show that happiness and success have different meanings for different people and that there are multiple ways to achieve your vision and reach your goals, whatever they may be. *Become the Fire* is a necessary resource for current and aspiring leaders, and a fantastic gift from a terrific one."
— **Ana Dutra**, global board director and former CEO of Korn Ferry and the Executives' Club of Chicago

"*Become the Fire* is not a 'lean in'–style exhortation for women and BIPOC executives-in-the-making to emulate the loathsome posturing of the good ol' boys of the business class in order to elbow their way into the C-suite. Instead, it implores those whose gender, race, and class have historically been barriers to the boardroom to draw from the wellspring of personal experiences that have shaped their lives to fuel their goals and build better, more successful operations that reflect their values. *Become the Fire* is an inspirational reminder that some of the wisdom and skills needed for success in business are not necessarily acquired in elite institutions but are often developed along a path that may seem unconventional."

— **Charles F. Whitaker**, professor and dean, Medill School of Journalism, Northwestern University

"Wow! What a great read this book is! Elisa Schmitz's stories are so engaging, and her Sparks, Flames, and Blazes are so simple and inspiring that you just want to keep reading to find out what's next! But my advice is to slow down and savor not only the stories but the insights and the wisdom. Give yourself time to think about *yourself* as you read each chapter. And if you do, by the time you get to the end of the book, you will have ignited the flame of your own future success — and embraced your own 'outsiderness' as one of the greatest gifts of your life."

— **Candy Deemer**, coauthor of *Dancing on the Glass Ceiling* and managing partner / executive coach of Growth Leaders Group

"I've watched Elisa Schmitz build and grow 30Seconds into a successful business against all odds. I greatly admire her vision, hard work, and persistence. *Become the Fire* makes the case for how hard work, vision, and authentic experience increase the surface area for lucky outcomes. Read Elisa's story and those of other amazing women about how they overcame obstacles to create trailblazing success. A must-read for every woman entrepreneur!"

— **Lauren Flanagan**, managing partner of BELLE Capital USA and CEO of Sesame Solar

BECOME
THE
FIRE

Jacquie,

Thank you for helping me
step outside my comfort zone
and realize "Become the Fire."
You make life better with your
own fire. Thanks for the
inspiration!

Elisa

BECOME

THE

FIRE

*Transform Life's Chaos
into Business and
Personal Success*

ELISA A. SCHMITZ

FOREWORD BY **MARY DILLON**

New World Library
Novato, California

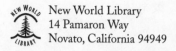

New World Library
14 Pamaron Way
Novato, California 94949

Copyright © 2022 by Elisa A. Schmitz

All rights reserved. This book may not be reproduced in whole or in part, stored in a retrieval system, or transmitted in any form or by any means — electronic, mechanical, or other — without written permission from the publisher, except by a reviewer, who may quote brief passages in a review.

The material in this book is intended for education. No expressed or implied guarantee of the effects of the use of the recommendations can be given or liability taken.

"Become the Fire" is a registered trademark of Become the Fire, LLC.

Text design by Tona Pearce Myers

Library of Congress Cataloging-in-Publication Data

Names: Schmitz, Elisa A., author.
Title: Become the fire : transform life's chaos into business and personal success / Elisa A. Schmitz ; foreword by Mary Dillon.
Description: Novato, California : New World Library, [2022] | Includes bibliographical references and index. | Summary: "A Latina entrepreneur shows readers how to turn obstacles into fuel for fulfillment, accomplishment, and success, with special emphasis on issues affecting women and BIPOC in the corporate world"-- Provided by publisher.
Identifiers: LCCN 2022027996 (print) | LCCN 2022027997 (ebook) | ISBN 9781608688104 (paperback) | ISBN 9781608688111 (epub)
Subjects: LCSH: Women executives. | Minority businesswomen. | Success in business. | Career development. | Women--Vocational guidance.
Classification: LCC HD6054.3 .S36 2022 (print) | LCC HD6054.3 (ebook) | DDC 650.1082--dc23/eng/20220701
LC record available at https://lccn.loc.gov/2022027996
LC ebook record available at https://lccn.loc.gov/2022027997

First printing, October 2022
ISBN 978-1-60868-810-4
Ebook ISBN 978-1-60868-811-1
Printed in Canada on 100% postconsumer-waste recycled paper

 New World Library is proud to be a Gold Certified Environmentally Responsible Publisher. Publisher certification awarded by Green Press Initiative.

10   9   8   7   6   5   4   3   2   1

For my children,
and for all the dreamers who want to be doers,
and the doers who want to do more.
I hope you'll be inspired to make life better with your fire.

Contents

Foreword

I t's all too easy for smart, diligent women to believe success is out of reach. Even when they work hard and play by the rules, many women say the American dream can feel unattainable. Layer in differences, or challenges outside the mainstream — including socioeconomic status, ethnicity, religion, sexual orientation, language barrier, disability, disconnection, or illness — and the climb seems that much more daunting.

In today's world, that is a tough reality to accept, but I'm here to show that it's not always the case. In fact, after you read Elisa Schmitz's encouraging book, you'll discover that success comes in many forms. *Become the Fire* will empower you to create your own definition of success and then go for it.

Success *can* be achieved despite differences, and I'm living proof. Growing up on the South Side of Chicago, the daughter of a steelworker and stay-at-home mom to six kids, I didn't know much about business, and I certainly never thought I could become the CEO of two major corporations. I had no connections, no corporate role models, and no financial safety net. To be successful in the business world, I had to do it on my own.

As a first-generation college student, I worked as a house cleaner, bank teller, tutor, and waitress to put myself through school at the University of Illinois Chicago, one of the city's most diverse four-year universities.

My corporate career began in brand management at the Quaker Oats Company. I ascended through the ranks at Quaker's parent company, PepsiCo, where I consistently relied on consumer insights and strong leadership skills to grow popular brands like Gatorade. Ultimately, I became president of the Quaker Foods Division. From there, I joined McDonald's as executive vice president and global chief marketing officer. My role took me around the world to grow the McDonald's brand. I'm most proud of how my team and I focused on delivering healthier Happy Meals for children globally.

I became CEO, for the first time, at UScellular, the Chicago-based mobile network and telecommunications company. When I later became CEO at Ulta Beauty, America's leading beauty retailer with more than 90 percent female associates, I felt my experience would bring unique perspective to help take this diverse company to new levels of sales and job growth.

With my world-class team, I transformed the Ulta Beauty business through the lens of guest insights, brand and service offering expansions, exceptional omnichannel and digital experience development, and a well-nurtured culture focused on diversity, inclusion, and respect. I'm proud to say that, during my tenure, Ulta Beauty's revenues doubled, and its market capitalization more than tripled. Ulta Beauty currently has one of the most gender-diverse boards of directors in the Fortune 500.

Having learned from some of the greatest mentors and leaders, I've brought grit and determination to every role. As a result, I've been honored as one of *Fortune* magazine's Most Powerful

Women, *Barron's* Best CEOs, and *Fortune's* Businesspeople of the Year. I also serve on the boards of directors for Starbucks and KKR, as well as nonprofit and civic organizations, including Save the Children and the Economic Club of Chicago.

I remain proud and thankful for my very modest upbringing. My journey hasn't always been easy, but it's been incredibly rewarding. I share this because it's important to understand that hard work and being driven really do pay off. You don't need to be on the "inside," have great connections, or be at the top of an Ivy League class to achieve career success. Anything is possible, and if I can do it, you can, too.

Over the past twenty years, I have watched Elisa's drive and passion. I was impressed that she was able to see around the bend when creating iParenting — such a transformative business! — from the ground up. She and her team built a business that offered so much value that one of the world's biggest media companies, Disney, bought it. Naturally, when she started her second business, 30Seconds, it came as no surprise that she once again anticipated the landscape and brought to life a game-changing business to help consumers and brands alike.

With only 2 percent of venture capital funding supporting female founders — despite the knowledge that gender diversity in business leadership yields higher financial returns — clearly there's a long way to go to close the funding gap. So, when Elisa was looking for a trustworthy investor, I proudly stepped into the role of angel investor.

But more and more women entrepreneurs are finding great success. And when one of us succeeds professionally, we help pave the way for others to follow and grow. We're creating runways together. I'm excited to see progress, but I recognize that much more needs to be done to ensure women from all walks of life can achieve success.

Become the Fire addresses just that. By sharing their inspiring stories, Elisa and ten other diverse, successful women demonstrate that success isn't limited to insiders. On the contrary, success is something that you can make yourself.

In *Become the Fire*, you'll learn ten lessons for succeeding in career and life — lessons shared by "outsiders" who unlocked their own secrets to success. The trailblazing women you'll meet in this book include Desirée Rogers, CEO of Black Opal Beauty and the first Black woman to serve as social secretary for the president of the United States; Laura Desmond, who was one of the youngest CEOs when she took the helm of advertising behemoth Starcom MediaVest and became the highest-ranking woman in the advertising industry; and Paula Boggs, the US Army Airborne paratrooper who was the first openly gay executive at Dell and later became chief legal officer and board secretary of Starbucks.

Taking the time to learn the stories of these women and what they believe it took to get to the top, whether they're successful company founders or in the highest ranks of the corporate world, is time well spent for all driven businesspeople.

Become the Fire curates the best advice from some of the world's top female leaders. Use it as a reference, a guide, or inspiration from women who have walked the road to success. These bold, dynamic women shine a light on their individual paths while championing the larger community of established and pioneering leaders so we can all learn — and achieve — too.

Whether you are just starting your career, are trying to advance, or are an established leader seeking to improve, *Become the Fire* will inspire you. I've been in your shoes, so I know you can succeed — and I'm rooting for you all the way.

Mary Dillon
Former CEO and Executive Chair, Ulta Beauty

Introduction

If you're like me, you may have grown up thinking that big success in business and life can't be achieved by outsiders. That thought passed through my mind more than once as an "outsider" myself in Puerto Rico, Lebanon, and suburban Chicago.

That thought may have been part of my worldview right up until the moment I was sitting in my tenth-floor office overlooking Lake Michigan and downtown Chicago, getting ready to read through the piles of paperwork that would finalize the sale of my business, iParenting, to the Walt Disney Company.

I reviewed the legal documents laid out across the expansive maple desk, seeing that there was a clause to cover every potential situation the media giant and its newest employee — me — could encounter. I squinted at the pages as the words began to blur and saw the first of several little red arrows flagging where I needed to sign my name, agreeing to the terms of the deal. That's when my mind drifted back to my childhood, to the family trip we took when I was nine years old to Walt Disney World, and to the first time Disney transformed my life.

I'll never forget sitting on that Disney-bound train from Chicago to Orlando; it took *days*. Sometimes it sped along like lightning. Other times it barely moved. The smell of peanut butter sandwiches blended with the stink of locker-room sweat. Crying babies drowned out the drone of the conductor's voice, a constant presence in the hot, crowded car. People of all ages, colors, and abilities talked and laughed, rocked back and forth, swayed side to side, sat down and stood up, sometimes stumbling in the aisles — and into each other — as the train jerked on its tracks.

Wriggling in my coach seat, I tuned it all out as I tried to get comfortable. I nudged my sleeping sister to the side to make more room. I glanced at my dad, his nose buried in the newspaper. I watched my older brother walk back and forth to the dining car. *Mi madre* wasn't with us, yet again.

This time, her absence meant the four of us fit perfectly into a pod of four seats facing each other. But the cozy quarters were feeling more and more cramped as the miles dragged on. In my mind, I urged the engineer to Move. This. Train. Faster. I had places to go, people to see — or one magical place to go, with treasured characters to see.

With nothing but a book or two to keep me occupied across the twelve hundred miles, the window became my world. I watched town after town roll by: smirking boys on bikes, too close to the tracks; a determined mother carrying a tired toddler, crossing a street; men in hard hats holding thermoses, taking a coffee break; teenage girls popping their gum and flipping their hair, laughing at nothing and everything. It all looked so calm — so normal.

I wondered who they all were and what their lives were like. Had they moved all over the world? Survived a war zone? Been left behind with relatives for weeks at a time? Did they have parents who spoke different languages, came from faraway countries, and screamed at each other all the time? Probably not, I thought, because I couldn't imagine that anyone had lived through the kind of chaos I had.

That's why the trip was so important to me: *Normal* kids went to Disney World. *Normal* families went on vacations like this. I wanted to feel what it was like to belong in that world, even for just a few days.

When we finally walked through the gates of the Happiest Place on Earth, I felt a moment of pure elation. From giggles to tears to a big old "Whoa," I took it all in: the stately elegance of Liberty Square; the throaty whistle of the steam train; the heady aroma of popcorn and chocolate wafting across Main Street, USA; the blurred tapestry of smiling faces posing with their favorite Disney characters; and the royal dreaminess of Cinderella Castle.

I was *there* — and after thinking about all those people I'd seen from the train, I believed that no normal kid could feel the magic that I felt. The magic felt so *real* to me, which was my first glimpse of understanding how much sweeter the rewards are when you have to struggle so hard to achieve them.

Back at my fancy, grown-up desk in my Chicagoland office, the little red arrows on the pages in front of me seemed to come alive, almost blinking like neon signs drawing my attention to the task at hand. It was time to focus and finish. I opened the top drawer of my desk and found my favorite pen: a sleek black ballpoint emblazoned with the Disney logo. Following each blinking red arrow, I signed the documents with a flourish.

I remembered every part of the journey that brought me to that point: having the vision for iParenting, creating the concept, doing the research, taking the first timid steps, answering the naysayers, backing up gut instinct with hard data, toiling through long days and sleepless nights, pitching investors and clients, building out two offices, hiring (and firing) employees, raising a business while raising a family, celebrating the joys and nursing the heartaches, riding the emotional and physical roller coaster — living the chaos.

As I set down my pen, the moment of pure elation returned. From giggles to tears to a big old "Whoa," my mind was ablaze. How blessed I was to have such an opportunity to sell the business to a brand that meant so much to me! How sweet it was that I had fought through everything I had to arrive at this day! I was ready to make an even greater impact on the world, and being the new director and executive editor for the Disney Interactive Media Group would allow me to do that.

Making *your* impact on the world is what I am here to help you with, and the first step is to understand the nature of what makes you an outsider.

You, too, may have bought into the myth that big success is reserved for those on the inside, which is to say, people who are born to it or who easily fall into it. That's because we have been told — either directly or indirectly by employers or bosses, by investors or our own friends and families, by the media or even whispers on the street — that success is for those with the "right" gender or skin color or religion or sexual orientation or socioeconomic status or abilities or connections. Since that is not us, it's easy to believe success is not for us.

But this is just not true. Life-changing success *can* be achieved by people like you and me.

All my life, I have felt like an outsider — someone who didn't quite belong. Maybe it's because *mi madre* came from Puerto Rico and spoke with a heavy accent. Or perhaps it was because my father immigrated from the former Yugoslavia and kept that Old World mentality alive in our immigrant household.

Then there's the fact that my first memories are of living in Puerto Rico, followed by living in a war zone in Beirut, Lebanon; and my next memories are of being bullied for not fitting in at my Catholic grade school in suburban Chicago. I was white-passing but not "white enough"; American but not "American enough." And I was left to mostly fend for myself because my parents were consumed with their work and their own fiery relationship.

I was married at age twenty-three, was pregnant at age twenty-seven, then became a divorced single mother working through the chaos of raising three children while battling serious health issues. You know that box labeled *other* that appears on various census, job, school, health, and insurance forms? Yeah, I often checked that box. And if you've picked up this book, my bet is that you have, too.

Despite being on the outside and frequently fighting the chaos that comes from challenging life circumstances, I made it to the top as an entrepreneur. With my talented team, I built a business called iParenting — a "Best of the Web" digital media company reaching millions of parents — and sold it to the Walt Disney Company. I was a Disney executive for two years, then built a second business, 30Seconds, that I love and that is thriving.

I know so many things now that I didn't understand when I started out in my career, and one of the most important is that our societal narrative about success is wrong. I have met many women who, like me, have had lives filled with friction, or who are different in some way, yet who are wildly successful. We are living proof that success doesn't come just to insiders who have a smooth path through life. Success is something you make yourself; and if we can do it, you can, too. I'm here to show you how, so you don't have to wonder if it's possible or if you're up to the task. It's absolutely possible, and you are more than up to it.

How can I say that when I don't even know you? The secret

is that you are up to it precisely *because* you are an outsider. You have been made strong by your experiences.

This is especially true for women and for those who are Black, Indigenous, and People of Color (BIPOC), who often have to work much harder than their male or white counterparts in order to get the same opportunities. For example, according to the 2021 "Women in the Workplace" study by McKinsey & Company and the Lean In organization, there is still a "broken rung" at the first step up to manager: "Since 2016, we have seen the same trend: women are promoted to manager at far lower rates than men, and this makes it nearly impossible for companies to lay a foundation for sustained progress at more senior levels.... Women of color continue to lose ground at every step in the pipeline — between the entry level and the C-suite, the representation of women of color drops off by more than 75 percent."

This is unacceptable, and drastic change is needed to achieve parity. Yet the unfortunate truth is that this is our current reality. That's why the purpose of this book is to help you navigate society as it is *today*. This means that while we work toward equality and making the same opportunities available to women from all walks of life, you can learn — and leverage — what has worked for me, for the women in this book, and for many other successful women I know.

We will continue to face fires and obstacles as we navigate our lives. That's why we can't just wait for the system to change. We need opportunities and strategies for success, right now. The good news is we can use the strengths and skills we have learned as outsiders to our advantage. We can learn to shift the power dynamic in our favor — and *Become the Fire* will show you how.

We all experience chaos, challenges, friction — whatever you want to call it — in our lives. However you label the chaos, it happens to all of us in some way or another. Although it shows up in unique and personal ways (racism, ageism, sexism, abuse, illness, disease, disability, divorce, disconnection, inequality, injustice, and more), everyone deals with chaos. But women who are *other* experience it even more intensely.

When chaos keeps coming at you from every direction, you develop certain skills, such as situational awareness. Not only can you read the room (or the street or the person or the threat or the opportunity) faster and more accurately than other people, you also may see things other people don't see. This gives you the type of vision that ultimately allows you to see what's around the bend — an incredible gift. You have this strength, though you may need to exercise your muscle a bit before you're able to fully use it. *Become the Fire* will help you build that muscle.

I have a code word for the chaos, challenges, and friction. I call it *fire*.

Why *fire*? Because throughout the years, there have been many times when the chaos of my life was so bad, it felt as though I had been thrown into a fire. Flame after flame the chaos came, unrelenting in its desire to singe and sear. But by battling each blaze, I became stronger and wiser and less afraid. By rising up to face that fire, and not allowing the flames to engulf me, I took on their strength and engulfed them instead.

Through this process of overcoming, I learned that fire has an energy that can be destructive or constructive. It's a powerful force that can burn you or forge you. As I tried to avoid getting burned, eventually I simply stopped trying to get out of the fire. Instead, I figured out how to *become* the fire.

What does this mean — *become the fire*?

It means not allowing yourself to be *in* the fire, getting burned, but instead using the fire's energy to ignite your motivation and drive, passion and grit.

It means not waiting for a lucky break, but instead making your own luck by preparing for and creating opportunities.

It means not focusing on what you *don't* have or *can't* do, but instead leveraging what you *do* have and what you *can* do.

It means that your mindset matters; your choices matter; what you focus on matters; what you do with your time matters.

It means that instead of letting the fire burn you, you harness the flames within and use them as opportunities to grow stronger, wiser, braver, and more resilient.

It's about seeing the fire as fuel to propel your success.

Become the Fire: Transform Life's Chaos into Business and Personal Success is for anyone who wants to start something, grow something, build something, or become something they have always dreamed of being — but who fears that their outsider status or chaotic life might hold them back. It's for the dreamers who want to be doers, and the doers who want to do more. And I've met so many women who fit this description.

In fact, it was while serving as a mentor with the Council of One Hundred, a mentoring organization made up of Northwestern University's leading alumnae, that I first started to realize the need for this book.

At one of our on-campus mentoring events, I was hosting an overflowing table of female students and young alumnae interested in pursuing careers in journalism, media, communications, or entrepreneurship. After listening to my story, it was time for Q and A. And the first question was, "How did you do it?"

The others at the table nodded in agreement and eagerly leaned in to hear my response. That's when I realized the question wasn't unique to the young woman who posed it. That question is what they *all* wanted to know.

I paused and took a moment to reflect. How did I do it? There were so many ways to answer the question — there was just so much to say. How could I answer the question in a way that would be immediately understandable and actionable? That would enable them to follow in my footsteps yet chart their own personal paths to success?

I ended up talking about ideation, passion, hard work, perseverance, resilience, and more hard work. But it took so much more — and was far more nuanced — than that. And I realized that to really answer the question, to do it justice, I would have to spend a lot more time thinking about it and putting together a comprehensive, actionable answer. That's how the seed for *Become the Fire* was planted.

Over the years, I thought about the question "How did you do it?" and how the answer would be unique to me — which may not be as helpful as what they were *actually* asking. What they *really* wanted to know was, "How can *I* do it?" And to answer that question would require much more than just telling my story. It would require understanding the skills and breaking them down into lessons — an actionable road map — so they (and you) could do it, too.

This book is not everything I've ever been through, not by a long shot. But it explains a lot of what made me, me. It shares the skills I developed, and the lessons I learned from my experiences, that enabled me to go from being burned by the fire to becoming the fire.

This book tells my story, but I was curious to learn and share the skills that guided other successful women on their paths. Just as I wondered if any of the people I saw outside of that Chicago-to-Orlando train car window were anything like me, I now wondered what other women's lives were like and if their stories were anything like mine. Did women with differences that made them feel they were *other* have similar skills or experiences? Did they view their diversity as a weakness or a strength? Did they visualize their fire as fuel to help them succeed? I wanted answers so I could speak to any woman who, like me, grew up in chaos or still lives in fear but refuses to let that stop her.

That's why I also tell the stories of ten other women who have risen to the highest ranks of their careers, using many of the same mindset shifts and skills I relied on to take control of my own transformation. These are women at the top of their game whom I have connected with or befriended over the years — and they are all as inspiring as they are unconventional.

Whether because of their ethnicity, religion, health challenges, sexual orientation, socioeconomic status, lack of connections, lack of direction, or something else — in one way or another, they are outsiders. They achieved extraordinary success even though they may not have known the *right* people, been the *right* gender or color or creed, or even had a clue what they wanted to do with their lives. They, too, battled chaos and came out stronger. They, too, used the fire as fuel to propel their success. That's how they, too, became the fire. You will see their stories appear in each chapter under the heading "Flame."

As these women revealed their secrets to me, similar themes kept emerging. It became clear that these women shared many of the same skills, honed through years of becoming the fire. I analyzed their revelations and formulated mindset shifts and skills that I then integrated with my own experience. I put it all together to create ten comprehensive lessons that will teach you to manifest the life you want, no matter your circumstances.

You will see each skill identified in *italics* in the opening paragraph of each chapter, so you can quickly identify the skill that leads to the lesson for that chapter. For example, in chapter 1, you will see that the skill of *situational awareness* leads to the lesson of being visionary.

It took years to organize my thoughts, gather the perspectives of the ten women, and develop the lessons. But *Become the Fire* is my ultimate inspiration, my deepest dive of mentorship and paying it forward. Going far beyond whatever I could tell you at a guest lecture or over a cup of coffee, this book provides mentorship on a broader, more comprehensive scale.

By telling you what I know — and what these ten inspiring women know — I hope you will realize that you can do it (whatever *it* means to you) and that you will find the motivation and the inspiration to make it happen.

As more women succeed, it paves the way for even more of us to succeed. As more women from all walks of life manifest the lives they dream of, the world becomes a better place.

To help you kick-start your transformation, throughout each chapter, you will see questions labeled "Spark." These are prompts to help you engage with the material you have just finished reading. Each Spark will inspire you to think of things you may not have considered before or in ways you may not have thought of, or to finally put your ideas down on paper, where they become real and actionable. The Spark serves both as a reflection and as a call to action to work on your own *Become the Fire* journey.

At the end of each chapter, you will see a series of intentions specific to that lesson; they appear under the heading "Blaze." Each Blaze is an affirmation of the material you have just finished reading: a mantra to help reinforce the message. The Blaze can be a catalyst as you shift your mindset to align with the theme of the chapter. You can use any Blaze that resonates with you, at any time, no matter where you are on your journey.

Become the Fire shows that success in career and life is not dependent on how smooth a path you have. It's all about mastering your own transformation — from being thrown into the fire to becoming the fire — every single day. By channeling the fire into your passion and purpose, you can literally change your life.

So, right now, I'd like you to set some intentions with me:

I will stop thinking of myself as lacking or unable or undeserving of success.

I will stop thinking of my differences as weaknesses or traits that hold me back.

I will stop thinking that being an outsider is preventing me from achieving success.

I will stop thinking that the fires in my life are burning me.

Instead:

I will think of myself as equipped and deserving and capable of achieving success.

I will think of my differences as strengths and assets to help me move forward.

I will think of my otherness as a vital tool to help me achieve what I want in life.

I will think of life's chaos as flames helping me become stronger and more resilient.

I will see myself engulfing those flames as energy to fuel my success.

I am not being burned by the fire.

I *am* the fire.

Now, are you ready to *become the fire*?

1

Be Visionary

To become the fire, you need to be visionary. Using your experiences to tap into your senses, you rely on the skill of *situational awareness* to read the room, see possibilities, and envision what's ahead. This acute level of knowing enables you to see around the corner, where opportunity awaits. By improving your situational awareness, you become more visionary — which leads to greater success.

One of the key skills in any successful job or business or venture is being able to read the room and to envision what's next and what's possible. If you can see what's *really* happening and what's not *yet* happening, you can create solutions or find better ways of doing things. Someone who has this skill is often called a visionary.

When you think about visionaries, you may picture big thinkers who manifested their ideas into grand realities that touch us all — people like Oprah Winfrey or Steve Jobs. Thinking of vision at such scale can make it seem out of reach, almost impossible to achieve. But the truth is that if you are living in a challenging or chaotic situation, you are likely already a visionary, or on your way to becoming one.

That's because being visionary happens in everyday moments, by everyday people, doing everyday things.

Children show vision every day, whether by making up their own games or coloring outside the lines.

Teenagers show vision every day, whether by starting a club at school or coming up with a creative term paper.

Moms show vision every day, whether by finding ways to support their kids' teachers or creating recipes to nourish their picky eaters.

Dads show vision every day, whether by organizing a soup kitchen or developing a summer reading program for their children.

Employees show vision every day, whether by enhancing an existing company product or pitching an idea for a new one.

Entrepreneurs show vision every day, whether by starting a side hustle in their area of interest or developing a better solution to a problem they see.

Although being visionary looks different from person to person, visionaries of all kinds share a certain set of skills. Chief among them is their use of situational awareness to see and create opportunities. Visionaries then transform those opportunities into realities that make life better.

Right about now you may be thinking, "But I'm not visionary, and I'm not sure how to be." That's OK, because cultivating vision takes practice and awareness. But I'll bet you often scan the room, interpret all that is happening around you, see opportunities, and imagine ways to make life better. That's because dealing with challenges, chaos, and fire teaches you to have vision — sometimes without your even knowing it.

Instability, friction, and fear are excellent teachers of how to be visionary. In this chapter, I will show you why that is true, then teach you how to channel the skill of situational awareness into making big moves in your career and life — so you can achieve more success.

Situational Awareness Is Key to Becoming Visionary

The key to being visionary is having strong situational awareness, which means two things: (1) being acutely aware of yourself and what your senses are telling you, and (2) understanding how that relates to being acutely aware of what is happening around you. This skill is also known as being able to "read the room" or "take the temperature of the situation."

For example, I was once pitching a marketing proposal to a big consumer packaged goods company. Representatives from several brands were in the room to see if my ideas fit into their marketing plans. To improve my chances of success, I tried to make the proposal relevant to all the brands in some way.

As I presented, however, I watched for reactions from each representative. I noticed the one who yawned; I saw the one who kept checking the clock; I made a mental note of the one who was copiously taking notes; and I felt encouraged when I saw one person nod almost imperceptibly in response to points I made. Their reactions informed the rest of my pitch.

On the fly, I adapted my presentation to focus on elements I thought would appeal most to the one who had nodded and the one who had been taking notes. Instead of trying to force a connection with each of the people in the room, I instead directed my energy toward the representatives who seemed more engaged, to build on the strength of the connection I seemed to be making. I ended up winning a contract with the one who had been taking notes, leading to a valuable client relationship.

Some people don't seem to do this. They plow ahead with their agenda — often appearing to be tone-deaf — without taking a measure of the mood or the vibe in the room. This means they can mistake the need, misread the level of interest, or overlook opportunities. This may be because they were never forced to be aware of their surroundings, as many of us outsiders have been forced to.

For me, it started when I was living in Beirut, Lebanon, in 1973, when that country was a powder keg before its civil war. One day in particular stands out for me. I was not quite five years old. My siblings and I were on the sidewalk in front of our apartment building, walking with my father toward school. We had recently moved from Chicago to Beirut, where my dad worked as chief architect for a global engineering firm. I was still getting used to the new culture — for example, women dressed head to toe in flowing black, their faces carefully hidden behind fabric — and the unfamiliar language that was so different from the Spanish and English we spoke at home.

Ahead on the sidewalk, two women approached — dressed in that traditional garb — but their eyes kept darting to the rooftops. Then they started to run. I saw the fear in their eyes and felt a chill down my spine. In the next instant, I heard gunshots coming from the rooftops. Gunfire was something new, but you don't have to be very grown-up or knowledgeable to know that it means danger. I felt the hair on the back of my neck prickle and a wave of fear crash over me as the snipers shot at a yellow VW Beetle on the street.

That chill and that tingling on my neck — intensified by the sound of gunfire and the sight of women running in response — screamed *danger* to me. I didn't know what to do or where to go, but I knew I was not safe. I felt a grown-up hand yank me hard as my dad hauled us back to our apartment.

But even there, I felt that something wasn't right. My dad called his office to let them know he wouldn't make it in that day, and *mi madre* paced the living room, tears streaming down her face as she cursed *en Español*. The tension roared into my stomach like a raging forest fire. That's the first time I can remember such a strong physical punch of fear in my body, but it certainly would not be the last.

Later that night, shots rang out again. I ran to hide in the windowless bathroom with my older brother and younger sister. It scared me that they were afraid, too — especially my older brother, whom I thought of as being braver than me. We huddled until the gunfire ended, then crept back to our beds — but I stayed up all night, terrified the gunfire would start again. I remember thinking that if I was the one to be awake and first hear the shots, I could warn everyone. I thought my being aware could help keep us safe.

Those moments of fear might have been just a dramatic childhood story. But as the chaos kept coming — physical, emotional, and social — it became a pattern in my life. Chaos is like that. It's rarely just one thing. It's often a lot of things that keep piling up, all on top of each other. Not long after the night of gunfire, *mi madre* ended up leaving Lebanon abruptly when her mother, *mi abuela*, died. My dad didn't want her to go — I remember their fight. They screamed at each other in Spanish and English and slammed doors.

Regardless, *mi madre* returned to Puerto Rico, where we had lived when I was a toddler, and left my father in a Middle Eastern war zone with us kids. I later learned that being in Beirut triggered my dad to remember the pain of his own childhood, when his family was forced to flee war-torn Yugoslavia. But at the time, all I knew was that my dad was often sad. I would sing and dance or tell jokes to try to get him to smile. I was learning how to read the room, how to adapt, how to turn the situation around. Situational awareness.

Mi madre never returned to Beirut. I later learned she believed that by not returning, she could force my father to bring the family home. She apparently believed that if she returned, we'd all be stuck there in a volatile, dangerous tinderbox. With *mi madre* as the catalyst, my dad had to be courageous and take action to ensure we made it out safely.

Because we kids had flown over from the United States on our mother's passport (which had left Beirut with her), we needed new documents to fly back home. After weeks of sorting things out, my dad was able to get us on one of the last flights out of Beirut before the conflict forced the airport to close.

SPARK

Do you feel that you have strong situational awareness? How do you survey your environment and adapt — to protect yourself or to improve a challenging situation? Think of two ways to enhance your awareness of what's going on around you.

Being an Outsider Teaches You to Become Visionary

The instability of my childhood continued when I started attending a Catholic grade school in our Chicago suburb. This was a different kind of chaos than the physical fear I had experienced in Beirut or the emotional fear I felt when my parents fought. This was social chaos. In this situation, I was on the outside looking in, trying to be accepted.

Spanish was my first language, but when we got back to America, my dad decided English should be our primary language. As an immigrant, he was proud to raise his three children as Americans. To him, that meant speaking only English. Letting go of my Spanish was a difficult process. There were times when I would sit in class mentally translating what the teacher was saying. Eventually, English took over, but not before a lot of damage was done to my social life.

Despite trying my best to fit in with my suburban, mostly white, English-speaking classmates, having a mom of color who spoke with a heavy accent made me a target. I dreaded the days she had lunchroom and playground duty, which was expected of all the Catholic school parents. Kids would intentionally mispronounce my name or mimic her right in front of me, exaggerating the way she spoke. "I'm frrrrom Puerrrrto Rrrrrico!" they would shriek, trilling the *r*'s like a motor. I tried different approaches to make them stop. Sometimes, I laughed alongside them; other times, I told them to knock it off. It didn't matter how I responded; their taunting continued.

To make matters worse, I never seemed to have the right clothes. We all wore the same green plaid uniform, but I had only one uniform while my classmates seemed to have many. On days when we were allowed to wear "nonuniform" clothing, things got even worse. It seemed like all the other kids had trendy Dickies pants and Izod or Polo shirts, and I didn't. I went to my parents and asked for a trendy shirt — but that did not go my way. My parents didn't think having an expensive Izod alligator or Polo pony on your chest was important, so they declined to buy it for me.

As the youngest of thirteen children, *mi madre* had grown up wearing hand-me-downs. As an immigrant who had survived World War II, my dad was grateful for the clothes on his back. Because they had been through so many real problems, neither had much sympathy for their daughter's "keeping up with the Joneses" problems.

With their gritty, tough-it-out mindset, my parents meant

well. But this just made me feel more ostracized. My parents simply didn't understand (or seem concerned) that in this corner of America, the label of your shirt mattered. The result of all this friction — the language, the bullying, the clothes — was that I had few true friends at school, and I was rarely invited to my classmates' houses to play.

But intentionally or not, it turned out that my parents had given me a gift, because I learned what to do on my own: I used situational awareness. I studied my environment for ways to keep safe from the bullies. I found that the school library was a sanctuary. I figured out that if I spent my lunch hour with my new *Nancy Drew* mystery, the day would go better. It was not that different from hiding from the gunfire or disappearing when my parents fought.

As I moved into the middle grades, I was always watching my back — and front and both sides — to be able to anticipate when a challenge, surprise, or danger (chaos) was around the corner. Using my senses, I learned to fine-tune my awareness of my surroundings and detect any potential threats. I started to listen to my body and look for its cues. If I got a funky feeling in my stomach or the hair on my arms stood up, I paid attention to what was happening. What was my gut trying to tell me? When I learned to focus on these sensations, I found that they were often warning me or preparing me to deal with some impending fire.

Those instincts — that knowing in your body — connects to being able to see opportunity. That's

SPARK

Are there areas or challenges in your own life, or in your work, where you wish there were solutions or a better way? Think of two opportunities you may have to make life better.

what I mean about being visionary. You feel with intensity, you examine your environment for information, and you see opportunities that others often don't. For me, the first big opportunity I saw happened in fifth grade, when I finally figured out how to get myself an Izod shirt. This is not just the story of an enterprising ten-year-old; this is the story of a person learning how to become visionary.

Situational Awareness Helps You See and Create Opportunity

After school each day, I raced home and let myself into the house using the key I wore on a string around my neck. *Mi madre* had started work as an elementary school teacher in the Chicago Public Schools, and she came home an hour or two after I did. When she arrived, she went straight to bed for a *siesta*, for at least an hour or two. "Pretend I'm not here," she would say.

We kids knew not to ask for or expect anything from her until she was ready for the family portion of her day. If we disturbed her, she might get upset or start arguing with our dad when he came home from work. We had to tiptoe around her in the house, but outside, we had the run of the neighborhood for hours every day.

I enjoyed spending time with the neighborhood kids, and I was especially good with the little ones. When I was in Beirut, they had no space for me at the American school, so I was relegated to being a "teacher's assistant" at my younger sister's preschool. I painted the preschool windows and helped the little ones settle in for snacks and naptime.

Taking care of younger kids in my neighborhood gave me a sense of purpose and fulfillment, as it had in Beirut. I really enjoyed caring for children and easing the load on their parents:

making a crying baby laugh, holding a toddler's hand to cross the street, drawing hopscotch squares for a preschooler, playing tag with a kindergartner. Those were some of my happiest memories in a childhood that was often chaotic.

On a sunny afternoon, one of the moms came up to me. "Have you started babysitting yet?" she asked.

The quick answer would have been no, I had not. But a spark ignited in my mind, the same way it would years later when I started a pregnancy magazine and years after *that* with creating content for moms on mobile phones. I could feel the excitement in my gut — similar to fear, in a way. It's a kind of knowing, and I tuned in to it — fast.

I recalled that a couple of older girls down the street had gotten paid for babysitting. Now it was my turn, and I had an epiphany: if my parents wouldn't buy me the clothes that would enable me to better fit in with my classmates, I could buy them myself. I saw the whole thing playing out. I became *visionary*. Sensing opportunity, I replied, "Not yet, but I would love to!"

Just like that, I was hired. And that job fueled my ability to make my Izod dreams come true. The first Izod I bought was a little striped number with the legendary green alligator above the left breast. I loved that little shirt so hard, I think I wore it out. I wore it so often that I started to get teased for wearing the same shirt all the time. But situational awareness kicked in. I quickly realized my mistake and got back to work so I could buy a second Izod (and then a third). Being visionary led to being aware, which led back to being visionary: a virtuous cycle.

Word spread about my babysitting. Pretty soon, I had two clients, then four, then more. Nothing made me feel better — and worse — than having a mom call me for a babysitting job after I'd already accepted one for the same night. "You're my kids' favorite babysitter — I should've called you sooner!" was something

I often heard. I felt recognized, appreciated, and seen. Work became my refuge, the place where I felt special.

On top of all that, it was exciting to control what I wore and how I expressed myself through clothing. No longer left to my own devices, I had a sense of purpose and structure. Life felt less chaotic, and I felt more empowered.

It was important to me to keep that feeling, so I have been working ever since — working my way through school, working while on pregnancy bed rest, working through my divorce, working while I was seriously ill. Work always has been, and always will be, a rewarding part of my life.

Through it all, I continued to grow my ability to read the room and see possibilities. I would tune in to my senses, figure out what they were telling me about the situation, trust those instincts, and act on them. That's how I became visionary in business.

SPARK

How have you experienced vision, or seeing around the bend, in your own life? Think of two times you envisioned ways to make life better, no matter how big or small.

Visionaries Recognize Opportunity and Act on Their Visions

I experienced my first big entrepreneurial vision during my first pregnancy. An entrepreneurial vision is the moment when you survey the landscape of a certain niche area and see a way to make something useful or provide a solution in that space — to see around a corner. It's the same skill as having situational awareness in a chaotic environment: you look for what is there and what is *not* there; you look for a safer or better way forward.

I had recently graduated from the Medill School of Journalism at Northwestern University and had launched my career as a journalist. Trying to report stories and hit deadlines while battling morning (and noon and night) sickness, hormones, aches and pains, and other maladies I had never experienced before was a new challenge. More and more often, I found myself focusing on this new being growing inside me. Instead of a knowing in my gut, there was a *life* — and I was so curious about it! What was going on in my belly? Why did I sometimes feel butterflies fluttering? What was the baby doing in there? How big was he *right now*? And how many more times could a woman go to the bathroom throughout the course of a day, for goodness' sake?

I had so many questions, yet there were so few places to turn for answers. My midwife? I could call her only so many times. *Mi madre*? She didn't really remember the details. My friends? I had gotten married at age twenty-three and was among the first to get pregnant. And reading the book *What to Expect When You're Expecting* over and over again could get me only so far. I found myself wanting something *more*. I wanted timely information about what was happening with my body and my baby, and I wanted it delivered to me regularly.

My insatiable curiosity drove me to look for a pregnancy magazine, but the only one I could find was a quarterly publication about pregnancy fitness. Huh? Where was the stuff I *really* wanted to know about, like whether it's normal to crave turkey sandwiches and lemonade? I just couldn't shake the desire for this type of insight and the feeling that there could be an opportunity. That's what being visionary initially looks and feels like — then you take action.

I asked every professional I knew in the "expectant mother" world what they thought about this lack of timely pregnancy information in the market: my midwife, my obstetrician, my childbirth educator, my salesperson at the baby boutique. Everyone seemed to agree that there was no pregnancy magazine out there and that, indeed, it looked to be a gap in the marketplace that needed filling. My gut instinct was telling me I was onto something, and the response from professionals was backing it up. A spark ignited in my mind: maybe I could create a solution.

The idea kept gnawing at me. If I felt this lack of information was a problem, maybe other pregnant women did, too. I had only a couple of friends who'd already been pregnant, so I asked them what they thought about the idea of a pregnancy magazine. The first one gave me her vote of confidence, but it was the second one who really shook me.

"Why would you want a pregnancy magazine when you've got *What to Expect When You're Expecting*?" she asked. "It seems like a lot of work and kind of redundant when a book already offers that kind of information." Wow, my first naysayer (out of a polled audience of two). As confident as I was, she made me question myself.

I thought long and hard after that conversation. Was I just trying to reinvent the wheel? Or was I right that there was a need in the market for something fresher, more vibrant, more timely, and from various voices? These are the moments when people — especially women and BIPOC — may back down from their ideas. A few words of opposition and they get scared. But visionaries don't give up easily, especially when they feel something in their bones.

As focused as I was on my work and my pregnancy, I decided to take another step toward this idea that just wouldn't let go: asking other pregnant women for their feedback. Becoming visionary means acting on your concept and gathering resources to support your case — in this circumstance, data. I had to consider that maybe I was an anomaly. Being a journalist, perhaps it was only natural for me to want to dig into a magazine about my current topic of interest. Would other pregnant women feel the same?

There was only one way to find out, and fortunately, I knew exactly how to do it because during and right after college I had worked in market research. To get an in-depth picture of what expectant moms thought, I designed a survey that was easy enough to fill in — if I could find the right people to interview.

And boy, did I find them. Toting a stack of surveys and ballpoint pens with me at all times, I talked to expectant moms at my doctor's office, at my childbirth preparation classes, in stores — pretty much anywhere I went. I would approach them with a smile and, being pregnant myself, would explain that I was thinking of creating a pregnancy magazine and would love to know what they thought. Every one of the moms I asked filled out that survey.

Before I knew it, I had reached my goal of one hundred completed surveys. Excluding the early naysayer, ninety-eight out of the one hundred women I surveyed said yes, they would subscribe to a pregnancy magazine like the one I described. Those other two? One wanted the information, but she would not subscribe because she had no discretionary income. The other was saturated with pregnancy information through her family and friends.

But 98 percent was more than I could have hoped for. I wasn't an anomaly, after all. Other pregnant women wanted this information

SPARK

Look around at your friends and family, your customers, your boss. What do they need? How can you serve them better? Are there tools or resources that would make life better, easier, simpler?

just as much as I did. As I reviewed those surveys, the excitement
grew. My gut instinct had been backed up by data gathered from
experts and consumers in the space. I had found a legit hole in the
market, and now I had to decide what to do about it. The spark
had turned into a flame, and I had *become the fire*.

Being Visionary Means Going All In on Your Vision

Long before the word *entrepreneur* was sexy — or even really
a thing — I knew a bit about building a business. My paternal
grandparents had started theirs from nothing. They had come to
America to escape the Nazi and Communist regimes in Europe
with only a few dinars to their name. Settling in a small Illinois
farm town, they built a custom cabinet business that became well
known in the Midwest and highly regarded for quality and crafts-
manship. They based their business on a simple formula of hard
work and word-of-mouth referrals.

Then there was *mi abuela* in Puerto Rico, a descendant of
the island's Taíno Indigenous people. She managed the family
farm — growing coffee beans, oranges, bananas, and plantains —
and ran a side business of making clothes for people in their
pequeño pueblo, all the while raising her many kids (including *mi
madre*) mostly on her own.

Even though I was nervous about taking the huge leap to
start my own business, I could not stop smiling. I'd been able to
anticipate the market by seeing around the bend and thinking a
couple of steps ahead. I was apprehensive, but I was ready.

Your Pregnancy, which was more like an in-depth printed
newsletter, launched in 1996. This was the very early days of
the internet, which I had started using in grad school and in my
work as a journalist. It seemed like putting up a complementary
website would be a good way to build an audience and get more

subscribers. Then, moving *Your Pregnancy* online would be an effective way to reach many more moms. I could just see around the next corner to what *wasn't* there, or what *could be* there, and knew there was a better solution to providing pregnancy information on a larger scale.

The foundation of the business was great content. Using expert sources like obstetricians, midwives, lactation consultants, doulas, childbirth educators, and prenatal fitness professionals, and sharing interviews with a variety of pregnant moms, the novel website began to grow. As the audience grew, so did the realization that the website was becoming the bigger opportunity. That's when it started making sense to phase out the printed newsletter and focus on growing the website.

One of the best early decisions was investing in a great domain name. A lot of time was spent ideating on intellectual property (IP), carefully considering what should follow the "www." What should the website be called, and why? What would appeal to the target demographic of expectant moms who wanted timely information delivered to them, as I'd wanted? What would be easily searchable and findable — and memorable — using key words? And would that name be available?

After creating an exhaustive list and undergoing a domain search, the name Pregnancy Today emerged as the winner. Pregnancy Today evolved into a robust online destination that not only regularly published great content but also enabled expectant moms all over the world to communicate with each other via message boards and email lists. At the time, these things were very new; we were among the first organizations to use our website in this way.

Years before Facebook and the proliferation of social media, Pregnancy Today had an interactive community element that connected pregnant parents by the month their baby was due, location, childbirth preferences and needs (e.g., natural childbirth or cesarean delivery), and more. If it wasn't offered, all people had to do was ask, and we could create a new channel, message board, tool, or resource.

I was excited to see more and more users sign up, comment on articles, interact on the message boards, and email feedback. It meant we were making a difference in the lives of expectant moms. A handful of users rapidly grew to hundreds, followed by thousands and growing — all while I was adjusting to life as a new mom myself.

But as Pregnancy Today continued to attract new pregnant users, I began to see a problem: pregnant users eventually were not pregnant anymore. Having delivered their babies, they no longer needed pregnancy information, inspiration, and connection; they needed *baby* information, inspiration, and connection. I needed a second website — and suddenly, I had a vision for a larger company with greater reach that would help more moms.

The question then became, how would I fund it? Pregnancy Today was making money, but not the kind of money that could launch a whole new website. I needed a way to raise the revenue it would take to be able to launch a whole new platform — one that would pick up where Pregnancy Today left off.

Considering different ideas, I realized that I'd received a press release about car seat safety from a big automotive company. To promote their brand, they wanted Pregnancy Today to write about tips for installing car seats to keep babies safe.

This was a typical request for "editorial coverage," which means the publication writes about the topic and brand as a news or feature story, rather than the brand buying an ad. What I saw, however, was that this automotive company would be a perfect sponsor for my new Babies Today website. I could reach the exact

SPARK

Do you dream about a
better world or making
a positive difference?
What does that look like
to you? What can you
do to bring part of this
vision to life now?

audience they wanted to communicate with, and they could provide revenue to help make the website a reality.

I designed a sponsorship proposal on the back of a napkin — how much content we would create, and for what kind of fee. Then I picked up the phone and called the number on the press release. By the time I was done negotiating with the car company, we had agreed on the terms of the deal that would make them a sponsor of the upcoming Babies Today website. The money arrived the following week, and Babies Today was born.

Being Visionary Means Growing Your Vision

What sets visionaries apart is their ability not only to see opportunities but also to create them — then grow them. It didn't take long before I realized I was going to have the same problem again in another year or so, when my users with babies would no longer have babies — they would have toddlers. That's when the vision for the iParenting.com network came fully into focus.

The idea was to have a separate site for each stage of the life cycle — from preconception to raising teenagers and everything in between. By the time we finished building, there were more than forty sites in the iParenting network, with a library of about five hundred domain names that protected both our iParenting IP as well as other ideas we were considering. Not unlike the Wild West, where pioneers were staking their land claims, protecting the vision and preserving future ideas on the internet (via those important words that follow the "www.") was the goal.

My vision for the business continued during my second pregnancy — this time, with twins. Trying to work while chasing an active toddler, coupled with a high-risk pregnancy, created more than double the chaos. With contractions starting already at week twenty-four, I ended up on bed rest at home for four weeks. At week twenty-eight, I went into active labor, and my doctor sent me straight to the hospital.

To prevent my twins from being born twelve weeks prematurely, I was given emergency levels of medications designed to slow or stop labor, which was painful but effective. I was put on hospitalized bed rest, hooked up to a continuous IV drip of magnesium sulfate, and given regular steroid shots to help mature the babies' lungs — for *six weeks*. I worked in the hospital with a laptop astride my bulging belly, and that was when an entrepreneurial spark ignited yet again.

By that point, the iParenting community had grown to include parents from all over the world who had gotten used to hearing from me about my family and pregnancy and what was new on the site. I wrote about these things on community board posts, on email lists, and in my regular Editor's Letter. I had become the voice of the brand, so people noticed my absence. I began to receive email after email from expectant moms checking in on me. I responded to every message, letting them know I had been hospitalized with the twins and was hoping to keep the community updated.

But responding to every email became a lot to manage, and we realized there had to be a better way. The spark struck hard and fast: what about an online diary? The vision was to turn my pregnancy journal entries into an open forum accessible to our users, similar to a series of articles, where they could leave comments for me rather than send an email. A hybrid between articles and message boards. And that's how — long before anyone had heard of the word *blog* or understood the massive power of the online mom community — our online diaries were created.

As my online journal (blog) grew in popularity, many of our users asked if they, too, could publish their own journals that people could comment on. With families and friends spread out across the miles, and still long before Facebook or other social media, it was a transformative way for our users to share their pregnancy and parenting updates with their own circles as well as with our wider audience.

Our innovative online diaries enabled parents all over the world to chronicle their experiences. We were excited to be among the first companies to share user-generated parenting content around the globe — and that fueled our growth.

SPARK

How can you act on the opportunities you see around you? Come up with two ideas — things like starting a side hustle, connecting with someone in the field you're interested in, or volunteering for a cause you're passionate about.

I ended up giving birth six weeks prematurely. My preemie identical twin daughters spent a couple of weeks in the hospital but were otherwise healthy, a fact that I celebrated with our online community when I shared their birth story. Then I got back to the business of building the iParenting network while raising my family. The vision for my next business, 30Seconds, would come later. But by then, I had honed the skill for seeing around the bend.

The Virtuous Loop of Being Visionary

To become the fire, you need to be visionary. Being visionary means you tap into your senses and rely on situational awareness to read the room and envision ways to make life better. This knowing inside enables you to see around the corner and into opportunities, then take action to bring the possibilities to life. The more situationally aware you are, the more visionary you can be. And the more visionary you are, the greater your success can be.

This pattern played out for me again and again. Situational awareness helped me envision ways to make life better (for myself and for others), see business opportunities, and then take action to bring the visions to life. The more situationally aware I was, the more visionary I became. The more I grew my vision, the more success I achieved.

Let's break down that formula with what was going on for me in the early days of Pregnancy Today.

Being visionary means you rely on situational awareness to envision ways to make life better. During my pregnancy, I noticed a lack of timely pregnancy content. I envisioned new ways to create pregnancy information, to fill a void in my own life and in the lives of other pregnant women.

Seeing opportunities to make life better, you take action to bring your visions to life. Seeing the hole in the pregnancy market as a business opportunity, I took steps toward bringing the vision for a pregnancy publication to life: doing market research, securing IP, creating content and tools. These actions took Pregnancy Today from an idea to a reality.

The more you grow your vision, the more success you can achieve. As the website grew, we had more and more ideas for how to expand content, tools, and audience. By going all in on the vision, we transformed Pregnancy Today into iParenting.com — achieving greater success.

This basic formula applies no matter where you are in your journey to become the fire. Use it when you need help envisioning your ideas, when you want to jump-start your situational awareness, or when you need encouragement to act on an opportunity. What will you envision? The world can't wait to see!

FLAME • Jules Pieri

First Jobs: Babysitter, janitor
Education: BFA (industrial design, graphic design, French), University of Michigan; MBA, Harvard Business School
Personal Life: Married, mother of three
Board/Civic Roles: Board member, University of Michigan Alumni Association; entrepreneur-in-residence emeritus, Harvard Business School
Key Takeaway: "Enjoy the process of figuring out the destination, seeing the big picture. Make a mark."

Jules Pieri is a self-described "girl from the wrong side of the tracks." In Jules's family, no one had gone to — or was expected to go to — college, and one of her brothers died of a drug overdose. Growing up in a working-class neighborhood of Detroit, where her father was an autoworker, Jules dodged drugs and violence daily at her rough-and-tumble public school. For many of her peers, staying out of jail was considered "exceeding expectations."

Jules's escape was reading. This was her situational awareness kicking in. She learned that if she kept to herself, she was less likely to get caught up in other people's troubles. Instead of hanging out on the street or in the parks, she could be found for hours at a time lost in biographies about Abraham Lincoln and Juliette Gordon Low, founder of the Girl Scouts. "I wanted to live a life worth writing about. I wanted to do something important," she says. "My childhood was about becoming a self-starter and independently seeking inspiration." Her reading habit helped open her mind — and her world — allowing her to imagine a different path for herself.

This is when her situational awareness served her a second time. Jules noticed that there was a teacher, Patt Morency, who paid extra attention to her classwork. Ms. Morency asked Jules about her reading and encouraged her writing. Instead of ignoring or rebuffing the teacher's attention and support, Jules trusted her instincts and accepted Ms. Morency's help.

Jules felt like the teacher was offering her a lifeline, a way out of her circumstances. Soon, that was literally the case. Ms. Morency suggested that Jules apply for admission and a scholarship to an elite boarding school — an opportunity that would remove Jules from the violence and drug dealing that posed a constant threat at the public school.

Jules was fortunate to have a teacher who noticed her, looked out for her, and actively helped her. Many other kids aren't as fortunate. Whether they're perceived as "not wanting to learn" or they're not provided with the tools and support they need to succeed, the "system" fails them. Much societal work must be done to ensure equal opportunities for all students.

But someone who is visionary *sees* these opportunities and takes the risk of being open to them. Many people don't make that leap from being aware of options to acting on them, but Jules did. At age thirteen, she imagined a different life for herself — a life in a school where students cared about their future and worked toward doing the important things she dreamed of; one where she didn't have to fear for her physical safety; one where she could create transformational concepts — like the people she read about in books.

With Ms. Morency's help, Jules secretly applied for admission and a scholarship to the boarding school. After she got both, Jules seized the opportunity to change her life. Looking back, Jules laughs about the abrupt change that came with moving to the upscale northern Detroit suburb of Bloomfield Hills, where one of her classmates was the daughter of Lee Iacocca, CEO of Chrysler. "Suddenly, I wasn't in Kansas anymore," she says. Her new world was as fanciful as Oz.

To keep up with her boarding school classmates, who made her head spin with tales of what they owned, what they did, and where they traveled over summer breaks, Jules became "the most popular babysitter" to neighboring families so she could earn enough money to buy a Schwinn Varsity bike. "Being the number one babysitter means you're reliable, you're not the social butterfly. You're a dweeb with a bank account, and you can control your own destiny."

Always scrappy and industrious, Jules also worked "under the table" as a janitor at a florist shop. Again, she didn't just do her job: she looked around for opportunity. Jules studied the environment to find ways she could contribute more to the business. When she noticed that terrariums had become a very big seller, causing the supply to "dry up," she found what she calls her big break. She talked to the owner of the shop. The next thing she knew, she was reverse engineering the ones they had sold in the shop, literally making terrariums from scratch. "And mine sold just as well," she says with a laugh. This is situational awareness at its best. Soon, she wasn't just sweeping the shop; Jules was a key player in its product development.

Those terrariums were not just a high school gig: they were the beginning of an entire career path for Jules because they taught her something important about seeing a need and designing solutions to fill it. Jules knew she didn't want to be as strapped as she had been growing up, or to live in that kind of hopeless neighborhood ever again. So she looked for a college major that would enable her to be well compensated for her business and design skills.

Jules landed on industrial design, which she saw as a collision between art and business. She seized the opportunity to go on a design internship in Paris, which "rocked my worldview." Living and studying in Paris showed her how big the world was and how much opportunity there was in her field.

Jules added French and graphic design as second and third majors and graduated with the highest of honors. She followed her undergraduate degree with an MBA, after which she went to work for product design start-up Continuum.

As her career advanced — working in executive roles for companies like Stride Rite and Hasbro, and even serving as a "top lieutenant" for Meg Whitman, CEO of such companies as eBay and Hewlett Packard — Jules saw an opportunity to make innovative products available to the masses and help launch them to greater success. Industries like music and publishing were democratizing and leveling the playing field to help small businesses, so why not consumer products?

Jules is a believer in the mind-body connection, especially when it comes to acting on entrepreneurial visions. "Everyone feels fear about a risky choice or hard decision. Success means getting past the physical sensations of butterflies or a churning stomach. I always look at things sideways." Instead of analyzing a situation head-on with simple data or a pros-and-cons list, she looks around at her environment for information and then looks more deeply inside herself. "I look in the mirror for my own counsel. I developed this skill as a kid because there was no one I could ask." Trusting her instincts enabled Jules to push past the fear, act on her vision, and make the leap to entrepreneurship.

In 2008, she cofounded The Grommet, an online platform dedicated to the maker community — which comprises independent do-it-yourself (DIY) technologists, inventors, crafters, designers, and hackers — and ran it as CEO for twelve years. During that time, the company discovered and jump-started such products as Fitbit, SodaStream, and OtterBox, helping to make these products into household names.

In 2017, Jules sold a majority stake in her business to Ace Hardware, the world's largest retailer-owned hardware cooperative, and in 2019, while still running The Grommet, she published a book, *How We Make Stuff Now: Turn Ideas into Products That Build Successful Businesses.*

In June 2020, Ace fired Jules and her cofounder, Joanne Domeniconi, from their roles at the company over clashing visions for the company's future. Although being fired is typically considered a failure, for Jules, her Grommet experience can only be considered a success. "Grommet was the culmination of my life's work — and Joanne's. We share a deep satisfaction and priceless legacy with the many talented and committed individuals who made it all happen."

While Jules's vision for The Grommet has come to an end for her, a visionary always has another idea. Jules is currently an investor, so it will be interesting to see what opportunity she sees — and seizes — next. One thing is certain: it will involve being visionary. "Enjoy the process of figuring out the destination, seeing the big picture," she advises.

Reflecting on her career and life so far, Jules feels good about the difference she has made. "Life is short. I try to live with no regrets, be a good person, and make a mark. That's what success is to me."

BLAZE

I am situationally aware.

I read the room (or the person or the opportunity).

I envision ways to make life better.

I see opportunities all around me.

I transform ideas into realities. I bring possibilities to life.

The more visionary I am, the more success I achieve.

2

Be Your Authentic Self

To become the fire, you need to be your authentic self. Getting clear on who you are; knowing your fears, needs, desires, and values; discovering what you believe in — that's self-awareness. People who hone the skill of *self-awareness* know what they're good at and what they're passionate about. That self-awareness leads them to be their authentic selves, which results in more success.

To be highly successful, you have to be really good at what you do. Realizing what you're good at, or becoming really good at something, often takes time, repetition, and a lot of exploration — both of the inner self and the outside world. Someone who has done the work of exploring their interests, beliefs, and talents and has aligned them with a successful career path or business idea is likely pursuing what they're good at and what they're passionate about. They're self-aware, and they follow their passions as they climb life's ladder.

They recognize their weaknesses and play to their strengths. They know what drives them, and they're comfortable in their own skin. They take as many reps as possible in the areas they want to improve and grow. Secure in and true to who they are, there's no need to put on a facade or to mask their true personality. They're being their authentic self. They own their authenticity.

Many of us may think it's better to be someone other than our true selves. The differences that make us feel we are outsiders may lead us to believe that adopting a persona that aligns more closely with insiders — people we see as successful — will help us succeed. But the truth is a well-kept secret: the very things you fear might hold you back are the superpowers you need to succeed and move forward. The differences that make you, you — that's your authenticity. Own that, because being your authentic self is a key to success.

By having to deal with so many challenges, by walking through all that fire, you have developed certain skills, abilities, preferences, and passions. You know what you feel good about and what you don't. You know your character and what motivates you. You know your strengths and weaknesses. Dealing with friction has a way of exposing your raw self.

This means you are on your way to honing the skill of self-awareness, if you haven't already. In this chapter, I will show you why self-awareness is important, then teach you how to own your authenticity so you can find success by being who you truly are.

Self-Awareness Is Key to Being Your Authentic Self

Being your authentic self requires self-awareness, which means two things: (1) having intimate knowledge about your inner self (your passions, talents, and vulnerabilities), and (2) having intimate knowledge about how your inner self interacts with the outside world (how your passions, talents, and vulnerabilities align with career paths, business concepts, educational and social opportunities, and even other people). *Self*-awareness is different than *situational* awareness because it is so highly personal. It's *you* getting to know and understand *you* by observing *you* in the world.

Self-awareness means knowing what you're good at and what you're not good at. What you like and what you don't like. What motivates you and what bores you. What other people praise you for and what they criticize you for. What bosses promote you for or demote (or even fire) you for. All those things can help you become highly self-aware. Once you have that level of awareness, your authentic self can shine.

There have been many times in my life when I had the thought, "I wish I were normal." To me, "normal" meant not a child of immigrant parents, not someone who lived in a war zone, not someone with an unpronounceable name, not someone who didn't have the right clothes, not someone in a hospital on an IV for six weeks, not someone who's a divorced single mother, not someone with a rare disease — the list goes on. But what is "normal," anyway? I have come to understand there is no normal; there is only our own authenticity. Normal is simply a mirage that distracts us from the beauty and strength of our authentic selves.

Many of us are labeled as some type of *other* at some point in our lives: Person of color? Single parent? LGBTQ? Differently abled? Immigrant? Health-challenged? Religious (or not)? Assault survivor? The list goes on. To many people, being *other* might be considered a limitation, a weakness. But not to me. Instead, I believe it is a strength.

Starting at birth, I racked up label after label as the world tried to define me. Although the labels the world has given me may conveniently slot me into some category or another, for some purpose or another, they don't tell my story.

Because I know myself best, the only labels that really matter are the ones I give myself. Those are the labels that define the authentic me. So, I label myself as kind, courageous, strong, passionate, innovative, thoughtful, hopeful, and resilient, to name a few. These labels provide a foundation for how I stay true to who I am and to the me that I strive to be every day.

Being self-aware can make or break you. When I was building out my business teams, for example, I knew that I lacked certain knowledge — about IT, finance, and legal matters, among other things. While an entrepreneur must wear many hats, there are certain tasks that require you to fill in gaps in your knowledge with people who know more than you. That's why I partnered with, hired, or outsourced tasks to coders, accountants, and lawyers, among other professionals. I learned to work with and manage team members who had a core competency in an area that I did not. I didn't feel that I had to be the "smartest person in the room" about everything or all the time. Because I put the business and its team first, there was no place for a fragile ego.

Bringing bright minds into the mix ensured the company would have expertise in all key areas. I learned to listen more than I spoke. It's amazing what you can learn when you just let people talk or, even better, ask them what they think. Surrounding yourself with diverse people who know more than you is a sign of strength. Successful leaders listen to their team members and incorporate their advice into the decision-making process. And that can make the difference between failure and success.

SPARK

What labels has the world put on you? Do they represent the authentic you? Come up with at least five of your own "labels," words that describe who you are or who you want to be.

Some leaders may not realize this. They like to hear them-selves talk, or they want to be the smartest person in the room, despite not understanding the nuances of a situation. Conse-quently, they overlook things, make mistakes, or don't maximize their opportunities. I have come to believe this is because they are more self-*involved* than self-*aware*. Becoming self-aware is a process. For me, it started in childhood.

You Have to Try and Try Again Along the Way to Becoming Self-Aware

Developing self-awareness means exposing yourself to a variety of experiences and putting yourself out there in order to find the authentic you. Every up and down and good and bad experience you encounter when you try — it all matters.

I was one of those girls who grew up thinking she just wasn't good at math (another thing society often incorrectly tells us). But that wasn't really true. I was actually pretty good at math until I got to algebra. That was when math didn't seem to make sense anymore; or at least, that's when I stopped trying to make sense of it. I started telling myself I just wasn't good at it, and some-how that became a self-fulfilling prophecy. I didn't try very hard to learn it, doing just enough math at school to get an average grade.

On the job, it was a different story. While I was telling my-self that I wasn't good at high school math, I had a part-time job working at a large retail clothing store. I was promoted from the sales floor to cashier, from cashier to service desk, from service desk to cash office manager. Because the cash office job involved a lot of math, I thought I wouldn't be good at it, and for that rea-son, I was leery of accepting the role. But because the job came with a raise, I decided to try despite my reservations.

My promotion didn't sit well with some of the other store employees — especially the ones who had been there for much longer than I had. Some expressed their frustration with a mean look, while others went as far as stealing my food from the break room refrigerator and tossing it into the garbage. It was the first time I'd dealt with workplace jealousy and resentment.

It was pretty uncomfortable. Those resentful employees made me apprehensive about going to work, not knowing what to expect. I did the only thing I could think of doing: smile and do my job. By taking the high road and focusing on what I could control — my own reactions — and not responding to fire with fire, I gave them less to work with.

Eventually, the temperature of the situation dropped. They left me alone, or set aside their resentments because we had to work together, and a couple of those coworkers became friendly with me. The situation made me more self-aware. I realized that, despite my best intentions, not everyone is going to like me — and that's OK. I can't beat myself up if some people don't respond favorably to the authentic me — those are simply not my people.

In addition to the resentful employees, there was an assistant manager at the store — I'll call him *the predator* — that I dreaded working with. Long before the #MeToo movement, the struggle of being a female in the workplace was real, and like many women, I was regularly rebuffing advances.

"How about I give you a ride home, sweetie?" the predator would ask, touching my hair, putting his arm around my shoulder, or even brushing a kiss across my cheek. "I can help make things better for you around here."

My self-awareness kicked in, and my inner voice told me loud and clear that I did not want or need this type of "help" at work. I would continue to earn promotions and the respect of my colleagues with hard work and a good attitude.

Having my own transportation became a new priority, though, so I finally convinced my dad to help me buy a car for my brother and me. But I cringed when Dad pulled up to the house in a faded blue 1968 Chevy Nova that he'd paid a friend $250 for. This was a "three-on-the-tree" stick shift beast of a vehicle that clearly had seen better days. My brother took one look and said, "That's OK — she can have it," and walked back into the house. Sensing opportunity, I quickly got over my embarrassment and said, "Thanks! Will you teach me how to drive it?"

Motivated to have my own wheels, I put in the reps and mastered the beast, which turned out to be quite reliable. Affectionately called the "Blue Bomber" by my friends, the car was a game changer in terms of getting to and from school and work. When my brother saw how much independence I had, he decided to learn how to drive it, too.

Once I had transportation, I was able to avoid the predator more easily. I was always "in a hurry," rushing from one job task to another or hurrying home to study — leaving no downtime.

Being in the cash office meant I was responsible for the accounting of six or eight cash register tallies at the end of the night and making sure all the cash, checks, and credit card totals balanced out — for the entire store, for the entire day — down to the last penny (and back then, there were lots of actual pennies). Even as a high schooler who dreaded the math homework she had to do after getting home late from work, I did the cash office job successfully. "Now this is the kind of math I'm good at," I told myself.

At school, I was telling myself a story about what I was or wasn't good at. At work, the promotions affirmed that I was good at what I was doing. There, my authentic self was shining.

I worked throughout high school and college, becoming a manager at women's clothing stores, a tanning salon, and a market research firm. I worked as a hair model for hair-care companies and sold spring break trips to fellow college students. The income I made supplemented the student loans I took out to help pay for my education.

My parents had urged me to attend their alma mater, the University of Illinois Urbana-Champaign. But my heart was set on the fashion design program at the University of Wisconsin–Madison. Because I chose Madison over Champaign, my parents told me I'd be responsible for paying the significant difference between the in-state tuition at U of I and the out-of-state tuition at UW. Believing I could work my way through any financial obstacle, I agreed.

In college, I loved making my own decisions. But that meant I made plenty of mistakes, and got into dicey situations, on my way to figuring out who I was and what I believed in.

Some situations were personal: peer pressure and under-age drinking led to being put on "disciplinary probation" at my dorm. Some situations were social: going to parties and visiting fraternity houses put me in precarious situations. One night, my friends and I were at a fraternity party when I found myself on a tour of the frat house with a guy I liked. The tour ended in his room, and that's when the make-out session started. (I'm about to describe an incident of sexual assault. If this could be triggering for you, please skip the next five paragraphs.)

What started out as a few innocent kisses quickly turned into an attack on my mouth. I remember the smell of beer on his breath as he moved things along much faster than I wanted, and my inner voice warned me this was not a good situation. As he slid my shirt aside, exposing my neck and shoulders, the flip-flop of "knowing" in my belly told me this was going very wrong. I told him no, and to stop. But he pretended not to hear me. He pushed me onto his bed and pinned me down.

That's when the make-out session turned into a full-blown sexual assault. "It's OK, your friends are doing it down the hall, so you can, too," he whispered into my ear, trying to convince me. The hair on the back of my neck prickled. I didn't care what anyone else was doing. I just knew I needed to get out of there before something *really* bad happened.

Since the word *no* wasn't working, I tried physically pushing him away, but he lay down firmly on top of me — all six feet of him. His hands were everywhere: unhooking my bra, unbuttoning my jeans. I felt powerless, and that's when I started to feel sick. Worried sick, which gave me an idea. "I'm going to throw up," I told him, gagging. He didn't believe me, or maybe he didn't hear me or care. His hands were pulling on my underwear, pushing me toward full-blown panic. I retched loudly, now truly ill, and then once again — even louder.

That's when my voice must have pierced through his fog. His eyes popped open, stunned. He rolled off me, and relief flooded my body. I jumped up, ran out of the room, then out of the house — buttoning myself up on the way out. Deeply shaken, I took it as a lesson in self-awareness: deciding what felt right and what didn't, listening to my inner voice, being the authentic me, not someone who needed to fit in. In short, I learned the importance of staying in my power.

But the effects of that assault stayed with me. I realized that I had been lucky to get out before I was raped but that many other young women would not be that fortunate. I knew that, somehow, I would do something to help other women become aware of situations like these: situations in which you think you like someone, and that maybe they like you — but then things change in a split second, turning into sexual violence. In other words, date rape.

I was discovering that the process of becoming self-aware

can be painful. But a seed had been planted: a desire to make a difference for young women like me. (I share what I did about it in chapter 9.) I was coming to understand that making a positive difference is a vital part of who I am.

Academically, I struggled to find my major, trying three before finding the one that felt like "me." Although I had grown up with my Old World grandmother doing needlework of all types, and *mi abuela* had run a side business making clothes, I found that fashion design wasn't what I wanted after all.

I transferred into the art department, but when I looked at what my classmates were creating, I started to convince myself that my work just didn't measure up. It came to a head for me when my class was assigned a project that involved showing motion. I made a little wooden dog on a rocking-horse base that had a spring attaching its head to its body. When you rocked it, its head would bob up and down. I thought it was clever until I saw that my classmates had created huge contraptions involving light, wind, and propulsion.

I realized that even if I felt I had the flair of an artist, I likely did not have the talent or mindset needed to excel in that world. The fact that I had designed what was in essence a child's toy said much about my past and, ironically, where I was going in the future. Kids had been, and would continue to be, very important to me. Since my self-awareness radar was up already after one failed major, I decided this second failed major was another lesson learned, and I moved on again.

SPARK
What are your weaknesses or vulnerabilities? Which ones require more reps so you can improve or grow? Think of two ways to work on them.

I started taking more courses in the Communication Arts department, falling in love again with expressing myself through writing. I also discovered the world of media and landed on the radio, TV, and film major. Putting together film and video packages lit me up, and I decided to pursue media as my professional direction.

Unfortunately, all the time I had spent figuring out my major had set me back. The process of becoming self-aware had cost me both time and money. When I finally rang the bell and graduated, a semester late, I was exhausted and broke. But I was a happy UW alumna.

Finding the Win-Win as You Become Self-Aware

After graduating, I continued working in management roles at a market research firm and a retail store as I looked for my first job in media. Working in a high-end mall, managing a women's clothing shop, I was approached one day by an executive from a trendy national clothing retailer. Her territory included the mall where I worked. In addition to checking in on her company's location there, she had been watching me manage my store — even visiting as a "customer" a couple of times.

Which is why it was a surprise when, at her next visit to my store, she offered me a job. "I think you'd be a great addition to our executive training program," she said, inviting me to their corporate office to learn more about it.

Working for her company would mean more money, more prestige, and more opportunity. But my heart just wasn't in continuing to climb the retail ladder. My self-awareness told me I'd never forgive myself if I didn't fulfill my goal of landing a job in the highly competitive Chicago television market.

Soon after, I caught a break in the media space. *Mi madre* was active in the Chicago Latinx community. As president of the Chicago chapter of the National Conference of Puerto Rican Women (NACOPRW), a nonprofit promoting the economic, social, and political participation of Hispanic women in the United States and Puerto Rico, *mi madre* made her mark. One day, after being interviewed for the nightly news on the local Telemundo affiliate, she struck up a conversation with the television station's director of operations (I'll call him *el jefe*) and learned he had a job opening. *Mi madre*'s eyebrow raised, and she passed along the tip to me.

I called right away. After discussing my work experience in management coupled with my communications degree and Spanish language skills, we agreed it seemed like a good fit. I had an interview with *el jefe* at the TV station, and within two weeks, I had started my new job as assistant director of operations. And. I. Was. So. Excited. It felt like a job that would allow me to be my authentic self.

Working on the operations side of a television station was frenetic, but I learned so much. Speaking *Español* nearly as often as English, I was the liaison between management and the production crew, which consisted of union employees.

There was always tension between the two sides, and different stressors daily, so it took every management technique and relationship skill I'd learned over the years to keep the precarious balance. Whenever possible, I strove to find compromises that allowed each side to feel that they had won something (or at least not lost everything).

One helpful discovery was finding the win-win: when both sides got something they wanted on the way to accomplishing the common goal of a great newscast. My favorite win-win situations were when I was living my authenticity — making life better for employees by expanding their horizons. If we were missing a camera operator, for example, I would ask someone with that skill to fill in for the missing person, and in exchange, I would schedule training for the helpful employee on another piece of equipment they wanted to learn.

I found that if I was constantly looking for opportunities to expand our employees' skill sets, it made it easier to fill holes in the production schedule. The win for station management was having more cross-trained employees. The win for the employees was having more skills to add to their repertoires.

It all came down to communication — the "how" of the communication was sometimes more important than the "what" of it — and that was something I was finding I was good at, not only in school but also out in the real world. I was becoming more self-aware every day, and that was the ultimate win-win.

SPARK

What have bosses praised you or promoted you for? What have they said needs improvement, or what have they demoted or even fired you for? Writing even a few thoughts about these experiences can help you become more self-aware.

Take Every Opportunity to Become More Self-Aware

In addition to the management and production teams, I connected with nearly everyone else at the TV station — from the receptionist to the custodian. I got to know the news director, reporters, and anchors. Whether we sat next to each other in the lunchroom or just chatted in the hallway, they were all generous with their time and experience.

It was because I made it my business to know them and try to help when I could that I got my first opportunity to go "out in the field" with a camera crew. One afternoon, all the reporters were out on assignment, and the news director needed some B-roll (supplemental video footage) and a couple of sound bites (short interviews) for a story. He needed someone to coordinate and hold the mic, so I raised my hand, and suddenly, with the blessing of *el jefe*, I was a field producer.

Being out with a camera crew and doing interviews (*en Español*, no less), I felt that I was making an important contribution to the newscast and, ultimately, helping viewers. Seeing my interviews on the news, I got my first taste of the power of journalism — and I liked it. My self-awareness bells were ringing big-time.

Without losing sight of my primary job in operations, I started looking for opportunities to support the news director and broadcast team. A highlight was serving as a production assistant on a live nighttime shoot of *Nochecita Guadalupana*, a holy mass honoring Our Lady of Guadalupe. Helping to make the broadcast a success, and wearing my "TV Crew" hoodie while on site in the church and in the live truck, felt really good. I was tired, but my curiosity and growing self-awareness kept me going. I was learning every day, and that kept me inspired.

Although I worked very well with *el jefe* and had the respect of my colleagues, the desire to become a journalist started to take over. I researched ways to advance my career in journalism and discovered Northwestern University's Medill School of Journalism, right in my own backyard.

I thought long and hard about the choice I had to make:

play it safe and stay at the station, where I was recognized and appreciated and had career momentum, or take a risk and start over by going to grad school, taking on more student loan debt, and embarking on an ultracompetitive new career path. I was warned that, after New York and Los Angeles, Chicago is the third largest media market. Competition is fierce, and for newbie reporters or producers, it's incredibly tough to land a job.

But I learned something important about myself: I'm good with taking a calculated risk, especially when I feel passionate and believe the potential reward will be worth it.

SPARK
What gaps in your knowledge would hinder you along your desired career path or business launch? How can you fill in these gaps (either yourself or with help)?

When I told *el jefe* I wanted to go to grad school full-time, he frowned. I let him know that while I loved my work at the station, I was passionate about sharing information that helped people. I wanted to become a journalist. As a former reporter himself, he smiled in recognition. Despite his preference that I grow my career at the station, he wrote me a letter of recommendation that helped me achieve my goal of admission to Northwestern, a path that would change my life yet again.

Be Agile as You Discover Your Authentic Self

From our Chicago and Evanston newsrooms, my Medill classmates and I covered breaking news and a range of other stories that taught us the fundamentals of reporting and writing. We learned how to identify news; find and research stories and sources; conduct comprehensive interviews; write crisp, impactful copy; present information in a variety of forms; and conduct ourselves with high standards.

And I fell even more deeply in love with writing. There was just something about communicating in that way that worked for me. I was never as smooth or articulate a communicator as when I was writing. I came to realize that it was because I was living my truth. In journalism, I had found my professional passion.

By being agile on my journey — exploring options, peeking down different paths, trying on various roles, helping in unexpected ways, connecting with everyone I could — I discovered what felt right and what didn't.

The friction felt uncomfortably hot sometimes. But by working through it, I discovered my abilities, preferences, and passions. I got to know my character and what motivates me. That fire showed me my strengths and weaknesses and exposed my raw self. I let the real me out to play, and I learned what makes her shine. And once I showed up as who I truly am, there was just no stopping me.

SPARK

How can you enhance your self-awareness? Start with two ideas to help bring out the authentic you — things like trying something new, connecting with someone you may not have thought of, taking a class, or even journaling.

The Virtuous Loop of Being Your Authentic Self

To become the fire, you need to be your authentic self. People who are their authentic selves are more likely to succeed because they are self-aware. That self-awareness drives them to do what they're good at and what they're passionate about. Because their self-awareness leads them to do what they are good at and what they love, they're more likely to succeed.

This pattern played out for me again and again throughout my career. Self-awareness led me to understand my talents and passions. I leveraged my strengths on the job and to start businesses that helped people. I succeeded because I did what I was good at and what I was passionate about. I succeeded because I was being authentically me.

Let's break down that formula with what was going on for me when I started my businesses.

Being your authentic self requires you to be self-aware. Over the years, I had taken a hard look at myself — *me* getting to know and understand *me* by observing *me* in the world — to the point where I knew my biggest career strength would be using my communication skills to help others.

Being self-aware leads you to do what you're good at and passionate about. I followed my passion for journalism, and then later for pregnancy information, to start a company to inform and inspire expectant moms.

The more self-aware you are, the more likely you are to succeed. The website drew the attention of an engaged audience, brand customers, and major media companies — ultimately being acquired. I then followed my passion and skills again to build a second media business.

This is a simple formula you can follow no matter where you are in your journey to become the fire. Use it regularly to check in with your self-awareness or as a reminder that one of the most important things you can do to be successful is just be yourself. Taking the time to get self-aware, to get clear on who you really are, will pay off when the authentic you is allowed to shine!

FLAME • Sarah Hofstetter

First Jobs: Mother's helper, deli worker
Education: BA (sociology, journalism), Queens College
Personal Life: Married, mother of two
Board/Civic Roles: Board member, Profitero; board member,
   Campbell Soup Company; associate national commissioner,
   Anti-Defamation League
Key Takeaway: "Look at who you are in your totality, then create
   your own authentic style."

Sarah Hofstetter has always been unapologetically herself. Her parents divorced when she was thirteen, then both remarried, creating a blended family. Her three younger siblings called her their "second mother — but not in a good way," she says, reflecting on her frenetic childhood on the South Shore of Long Island. There, Sarah could be found picking up after the younger kids and even helping to balance the family checkbook, all the while constantly packing bags to bounce between her parents' homes.

A grounding influence for Sarah was her grandparents, whom she calls her greatest role models. Three out of four of them were originally from Europe. Her maternal grandfather emigrated before World War II, arriving in America with literally nothing. "He built himself up from rags," Sarah says of her self-made grandpa, a rabbi who spoke seven languages.

Her paternal grandparents, who just recently passed away in their nineties, were survivors of the Auschwitz concentration camp. They met each other just after liberation — her grandmother was on a death march, and her grandfather had fled the camp nearby. "They were lost and hungry," Sarah says. "My grandfather found sixteen women on a death march, and the seventeen of them banded together to try to get back to civilization."

The couple made their way to America, where they started their own insurance brokerage — a family business that is still thriving today. "Life wasn't easy. Their story is one of perseverance."

Guided by her grandparents' example, Sarah has been keeping kosher and observing the Jewish Sabbath her entire life, as well as striving to stick to the 613 commandments of the Torah. "This has meant resisting the temptations of fast food as a child, fending off rebellious friends trying to get me to sneak out with them on Friday nights, and even politely declining clients' invitations to sample products that my faith prohibits."

Although Sarah's turbulent childhood and devout religion may label her an outsider, she views her differences as assets essential to her authentic self. Her self-awareness from such a young age allowed her authenticity to shine brightly; traits that could have held her back instead propelled her forward. "You have to embrace your individuality. If you try to be somebody else, it becomes inauthentic," she says.

Sarah's first "career" job after college was working for a start-up that had gone public six weeks earlier. Net2Phone, a technology company enabling phone calls over the web, needed her to do public and investor relations, despite her not having a clue about either. Undaunted, Sarah's self-awareness allowed her to figure out what she needed to know. "I bought a book on PR at Barnes & Noble and taught myself public and investor relations."

Married by age twenty-two, Sarah had her first of two children, a daughter, by twenty-four (she also has a son). They live only about a mile away from where Sarah grew up because "my professional life is so crazy, my personal life had to be more familiar." In constant contact with her extended family, Sarah relied on her mom to relieve the babysitter when Sarah or her husband couldn't make it home from work on time.

Sarah rose through the ranks at Net2Phone to run all corporate communications. Eventually, she felt she had hit her glass ceiling and decided to leave the company — but they didn't want to let her go. She decided to start her own company, Kayak Communications, with Net2Phone as her first client. "They gave me a one-year retainer," Sarah explains, "and I trained my own replacement."

Sarah's authenticity became her calling card. Colleagues and clients alike knew what to expect from her because she was always straight with them and told it like it was. "It's about making sure you're consistent; I became a trusted adviser."

Sarah started doing more and more work for 360i, a growing Atlanta-based ad agency. By 2006, she had joined the company full-time. Armed with self-awareness and a dogged problem-solving ability, she continued to move up the ranks. Soon she was guiding company strategy, and every review cycle, her responsibilities grew.

Sarah was only in her thirties when she took the helm of 360i, first as president, then as CEO, and ultimately as chairwoman. She grew the company from thirty employees to a thousand, and from $5 million in revenue to $180 million, by continually pivoting company offerings to be aligned with changes in consumer behavior.

Sarah earned the trust and business of megabrands around the world despite not being able to take clients out for the usual fancy dinners because she keeps kosher. Instead, she turned the tables on them — by taking them out in her own way. "It's an experience to go to a kosher restaurant if you've never been to one before, so you make it into a new, cultural experience for them. It demonstrates my values, and clients appreciate that. It's about prioritization, looking at things in totality, and making choices that work for everyone."

After five years as CEO, Sarah realized that she loved marketing, but she didn't love running an agency. So she trained her replacement. Meanwhile, her former boss at 360i, Bryan Wiener, had become CEO of Comscore. When Sarah was ready to make a change, he brought her on as president in 2018.

Sarah was excited to try to turn the Comscore business around, but only six months into the job, Bryan and Sarah announced their resignations from the company, citing "irreconcilable differences with the board." Although it was a difficult decision, Sarah says, "I only had two choices: (1) execute a strategy I didn't believe in, or (2) walk away, knowing I stuck to my values."

Because sticking to her values is core to her authenticity, Sarah left Comscore with no regrets. But she had joined the board of directors of Campbell Soup Company, so there was very little downtime. "It's pulling on all the different experiences I've had in my career," she says. In 2020, Sarah became president of Profitero, an e-commerce performance analytics company that was recently acquired by Publicis Groupe, to help build a team and further Profitero's focus on helping brands win in e-commerce.

Sarah attributes much of her success to self-awareness, candor, and empathy. "I'm my authentic self. I put myself in others' shoes, and that affects how I react. Some might think that's a weakness, but I don't. I ask a lot of questions. The more curious you are, the better at problem-solving you will be."

But ultimately, Sarah says, success comes down to who you are and what you believe in. She stresses not only *having* a values system, but *living* that values system, such as "I stand for X; therefore, I do X."

Sarah's faith is a red line she will not cross, and she broadcasts that loud and clear. "Communication — knowing what to say and when to say it — is key. Everybody knows I'm completely off-line once it's time to light candles on Friday night. That's why it's OK if someone sends me an email on a Friday night and I don't get back to them until Saturday night. I am a crazy workhorse, and I dispel any notion that I won't make up the time."

To help others find success by being their true selves, Sarah says it's important to know your superpowers and your vulnerabilities — and how to stay flexible, to weather life's ups and downs. "You never know what challenges will come your way. Man plans and God laughs. Look at who you are in your totality, then create your own authentic style that works for you."

BLAZE

I am self-aware. I know my strengths and weaknesses.

I am passionate about what I'm good at doing.

I find opportunities to become even more self-aware.

My differences make me authentically me.

I let my authentic self shine.

I am at my best when I'm being my authentic self.

The more authentic I am, the more success I achieve.

3

Be Comfortable with Being Uncomfortable

To become the fire, you need to be comfortable with being uncomfortable — to tolerate that awkward feeling of standing out or being the *only* in any given situation. People who can perform through discomfort are self-confident. The skill of *self-confidence* drives them to embrace opportunities, take bigger risks, and accomplish greater goals. The more they flourish outside their comfort zones, the greater their tolerance for discomfort becomes. The more self-confidence you have, the more discomfort you can endure. The more comfortable you are with being uncomfortable, the greater success you can achieve.

Becoming successful requires confidence, a belief or knowing that You. Can. Do. This. (Whatever *this* is.) For example, some people are confident in their artistic abilities, but not in their athletic abilities. Or in their scientific skills, but not in their relationship skills. The confidence they feel in certain areas may lead them to pursue opportunities where they believe they can excel. And as we discussed in chapter 2, when you do what you're good at, you're more likely to succeed.

The self-confidence you need to excel at something is created over time, through experiences in which you can learn and grow and master a certain skill. By starting small and accomplishing achievable tasks, you build up your ability and appetite for taking on bigger challenges. The more you succeed at the smaller stuff, the bigger the challenge you can tackle. One by one, rep after rep, your confidence grows.

You learn from your mistakes, and you course correct as needed. You realize that by stretching yourself, that's where the growth is. You trust yourself to embrace opportunities, take greater risks, and accomplish your goals — even if they're outside your comfort zone. Then one day, you realize there's nothing you can't do when you set your mind to it. That's self-confidence. That's what leads to being comfortable when others may not be. And that's when you gain the advantage.

Being comfortable with being uncomfortable gives you an edge. Many people who feel uncomfortable in a situation will find a way to get out, to extricate themselves from it, just to end the discomfort. They prefer to remain in their comfort zones. If you can tolerate that awkward feeling and — even better — learn to thrive with it, chances are very good that you will succeed where others cannot. The power dynamic shifts, and their loss can become your gain.

Many of us have been trying our whole lives to fit in, just to avoid that uncomfortable feeling of being different in some way. You may stand out from those in the room, but being the *only* doesn't have to feel awkward. By focusing less on what other people think of you, and more on what *you* think of you, you will feel more at home in your own skin. By embracing your differences as your superpowers, you will feel comfortable — or be able to push past discomfort — in any given situation.

Having a different culture or religion, being raised by immigrant parents, having an alternative sexual orientation — those differences help make you who you are. Learning to own them instead of feeling like you have to apologize for them — that's how you gain the confidence you need to be comfortable, and even be a standout, wherever you may find yourself.

I'm an introverted extrovert, so there's a part of me that doesn't want to stand out. As I was growing up, I felt self-conscious and concerned about what others were thinking. I was often underestimated based on factors beyond my control, and I felt like I wasn't part of the pack. I was a tiger among lions — with awkward stripes that made me feel like I was standing out when it would have felt much more comfortable to be blending in. As much as I wanted to fade into the background, my stripes, or differences, made it feel like there was nowhere to hide.

It wasn't until high school that I started to embrace my stripes, tolerate that awkward feeling, and focus less on what others were thinking. I had learned that being underestimated could actually be a good thing. When others size you up based on superficial factors, they are often taken by surprise when what they perceive to be a weakness actually reveals itself as a strength. Their miscalculation can result in your having an advantage. So, by realizing that what I thought of myself was more important than what others thought of me, I got comfortable with being uncomfortable and allowed myself to stand out.

It turns out that a tiger's stripes are not just there for aesthetics. The stripes serve several purposes, including to help camouflage tigers as they hunt and even to confuse their prey as they blend into tall jungle grasses — appearing less powerful than they really are. Yes, even tigers can be underestimated. Unlike lions, who hunt in groups, tigers rely on their stripes — which are individual to each tiger — to help them not only survive, but also thrive. Tigers don't do any of this actively; they just do it by virtue of who they are.

As I got comfortable with my stripes, I made more friends — the kind that liked the authentic me — and my self-confidence grew. Sure, there were some people who didn't like the bold young woman who was emerging, which didn't always feel comfortable. But I learned it didn't matter, those were not my people, and there were many others who *did* like me. Most importantly, *I* liked me. By the time I got to the point of raising investment capital as a female entrepreneur and building a business as a single mom, I was so used to being uncomfortable that being uncomfortable felt just fine.

I was comfortable because I had self-confidence. Self-*confidence* is different than self-*awareness*. Self-confidence is the knowing you have inside of you that you've got this, no matter what. It means even if you make a mistake, even if you fail, you will be OK. It means even if you're underestimated — and sometimes especially when you are — you can shine. When you're confident, you have greater presence. You can own the room or any situation you are in. When you own the room, you can make anything happen.

You can develop this skill, too. Because you have your own stripes, you likely know what it feels like to stand out when you may prefer to blend in. But because you are a tiger, you need to get comfortable with what makes you, you. It's time to focus more on what *you* think about you than what others think. Prepare to own any lingering discomfort so you can use your stripes to your advantage.

In this chapter, I will show you why confidence is key to success, then teach you how to enhance your self-confidence so you can be comfortable with being uncomfortable and even own any room you are in — ultimately achieving more success.

Self-Confidence Is Key to Being Comfortable in Any Situation

A vital part of being comfortable in any situation is having self-confidence, which means two things: (1) knowing your skills and believing in your abilities, and (2) knowing how your skills and abilities can help you achieve whatever you set your mind to. Being self-confident enables you to feel secure in how your talents, successes, resilience, and grit can propel your career, business, education, relationships, and more.

We grow our confidence and self-worth by overcoming our challenges and fighting our fires: dealing with bullies; passing tests; confronting prejudice; getting hired; earning promotions; being laid off or fired; making friends; building relationships; collaborating with colleagues; dealing with resentful coworkers; rebuffing advances; surviving domestic violence or sexual assault; having and raising kids; grieving breakups, divorce, and loss; battling illness. By overcoming life's chaos, you build your strength and confidence. And once you have self-confidence, there's no awkward situation you can't handle and no room you can't own.

For me, learning to own the room started on a baseball field. As a child, I was the only girl on my local youth baseball team. It wasn't the most comfortable situation: I took a lot of teasing, and so did many of my teammates — simply because I was on the team. I was a tiger among lions, and the lions didn't like me much.

Then there were those who underestimated me. They doubted my ability, solely based on my gender and size (I was rather petite). Members of opposing teams would often size me up based on my stripes and call me out as a weak link. Whether they thought I'd be an easy strikeout or they should hit to wherever I happened to be playing because I'd likely drop the ball, extra pressure and discomfort were always there. And this is why it was so satisfying whenever I proved them wrong.

Despite the awkwardness — that omnipresent feeling of being uncomfortable — my teammates and I jelled as we played baseball all summer, winning more games than we lost. I was growing my skills and even making a friend or two. That's why I was ecstatic when we made the playoffs.

But our family vacation coincided with the city championship game. Despondent at the prospect of missing the big game, especially after the bumpy road I had taken to get there, I still had one more uncomfortable thing to do: throw myself on the mercy of the court (my parents). "I've just got to play in this game," I pleaded, even though by that point in my life, I dreaded asking my parents for anything. "Can we please leave on our trip right after it's over?"

Seeing my distress, they really listened, contrary to so many times I'd awkwardly pleaded with them for something (remember the Izod shirt that didn't go my way?). When my dad finally said that yes, since we were driving, we could leave after the game, I hugged him in relief. He smiled and said, "Go get 'em, tiger!"

The day of the big game, my discomfort was palpable. The stakes were as high as they'd ever been, and under the hot summer sun, my stripes were beacons for unwanted attention. As usual, the opposing team pointed me out right away. They snickered and I cringed. I felt like a target attracting arrows.

There was a player on the opposing team whose talent was kind of legendary, so I'll call him *the legend*. He was the cleanup hitter who usually could be counted on for a home run when it was needed most. As it turned out, it was needed in this championship game.

It was the bottom of the ninth inning with two outs, and we were ahead by a run or two. But the bases were loaded — and the legend was at bat. You could feel the tension on our side, and you could see the glee on their side. The opposing team was pretty sure they had this game in the bag with the legend's impending grand slam. "Hit it straight out to center field!" the legend's teammates yelled, smirking. Because, of course, that's the position I was playing.

That's when it started. My teammates looked at me, frantic. We were playing on a recreational park field, so there was no warning track or home-run fence. Just a city sidewalk and the busy street behind me. They waved their arms and yelled, "Get back! Further back! Even further back!"

As the legend stepped up to the plate, I jogged backward. And still, more arm waving, and more "Back! Back! Back!" As the ball was pitched, I was still jogging backward. That's when I heard the telltale crack of bat hitting ball in that "Oh, shit!" sort of way. The kind of sound that tells you the ball is going *back* — straight to center field — straight toward me.

Looking into the sky, I saw the ball barreling my way. It was coming in hot, too fast, and I wasn't in the right spot. But I believed I could get there. If I could just get myself into the right position, I knew I could catch that ball. I'd show everyone, especially myself, that I could do it.

Baseball cap on, I still squinted against the sun, my backward jog turning into a full backward sprint. My eyes, locked on the ball, constantly assessed where it was going in relation to where I was on the field. Mouth full of chewing gum, mitt raised to the sky, I went back, back, back — almost to the sidewalk — until I found the sweet spot where ball met glove. With a satisfying thump, the ball landed safely in my hands, and that is a sound I will never forget.

What came next was even more memorable. My team — whooping in victory (and relief). The opposing team — jeering the legend for being "robbed" of his game-winning grand slam victory ... by a tiny girl! Yes, a girl caught the would-have-been-a-game-winning-home-run fly ball cracked hard way out to center field. And a girl helped her team win the city championship.

After our victory, I was interviewed for the local news. I remember feeling excited and relieved at the achievement. I had owned that field, and the feeling stuck with me. It was a game changer in terms of how I felt about what I could handle, about my skills and abilities, about my self-confidence.

It hadn't mattered that I'd been underestimated. In fact, that uncomfortable feeling of being underestimated may even have helped me because what those other players perceived to be a weakness had become a strength. I'd had something to prove, and I'd proven it. It hadn't mattered that those doubters had thought I would never be able to catch that ball. What mattered was that *I* believed I could catch that ball. And I did.

That was one of my first lessons in getting comfortable with being uncomfortable. I had to push past so much discomfort to get to that winning moment: tension from my teammates, bullying from opposing team players, and even begging my parents to let me play in that game. So many little fires to extinguish. Getting comfortable with being uncomfortable isn't the most pleasant experience, even though it sounds so simple. Being the *only* isn't easy.

Being the *only* — whether in baseball or business — can be very uncomfortable, which is often enough to stop us in our tracks. But just because something feels uncomfortable doesn't mean you shouldn't do it. Feeling different — whether because of ethnicity, sexual orientation, religion, ability, gender, size, or anything else — doesn't have to be a disadvantage. In fact, your difference can be your superpower.

That's because what makes you different can be the core of what makes you uncomfortable. The key is to understand and embrace that feeling. Female? Fabulous! Short? Super! Latina? Lovely! BIPOC? Beautiful! First-generation? Fantastic! Whatever your stripes say about you, own them. Get comfortable with what makes you different — what makes you, you — and you will get comfortable with being uncomfortable.

In my baseball situation, because the doubters underestimated me (because I was a girl and I was petite — a couple of stripes), I was like a tiger camouflaged in tall grasses. They just didn't see me coming until it was too late. My difference became not only *my* super-power, but also one for my entire team. Catching that ball, owning that baseball field, set the stage for my self-confidence propelling me forward.

SPARK

Have you been underestimated? How did that work out for you? Think of two ways that your greatest differences can become your greatest strengths. (Get comfortable with your differences, and you'll get comfortable with being uncomfortable.)

I decided I liked being a tiger. I decided to own my stripes. I learned to just be myself and to be confident in who I am. The confidence that came from owning my differences has made the difference, countless times, between failure and success.

Building Confidence Stripe by Stripe
Leads to Feeling Comfortable

True self-confidence isn't something that comes easily. It is painstakingly built — rep by rep, stripe by stripe — and it's the key to feeling comfortable with being uncomfortable. Building self-confidence is the internal process of watching yourself succeed or solve problems by taking baby steps that lead to bigger steps — until, finally, you're undaunted by giant leaps. The more leaps you take, the greater the likelihood you'll achieve big success.

Being self-confident can lead you to make decisions that result in life-changing experiences. One of the best decisions I made as I built out the minimum viable product (MVP) of the website for my second business, then called 30Second Mom, was to first launch its social media presence. For example, even before 30SecondMom.com was live on the web, @30SecondMom was live on Twitter.

Because I was confident in my knowledge of parenting and my abilities as a mom, I would tweet about parenthood, mom tips, life hacks, food ideas, or just something that happened to me during my day as a single mother of three. Through social media, I grew a following for 30Second Mom even before it was a live website, and this audience would become invaluable when it came time to launch the site.

One of the other benefits was being recognized as an "influencer" in the mom space. I was invited to be a founding member of Friends of Ricki, a then-groundbreaking social/TV community to raise awareness of Ricki Lake's relaunched TV talk show, *The Ricki Lake Show*. I attended events and show tapings in Los Angeles, and with other business travel in California, I was flying to and from LA on a regular basis — a four-hour flight from Chicago.

I don't love to fly. I deal with the discomfort of it because I have to, in order to get where I want to go. I used to love to fly, until one trip to visit family in Puerto Rico. The flight home was bumpy, which was OK — until we started experiencing turbulence so severe that it caused the plane to suddenly drop. Yes, it literally dropped what felt like a mile, but was probably only a few hundred feet, according to one of the flight attendants.

But it was enough for food and drinks to fly into the air, hit the ceiling, and fall back down with a crash. Enough to make other passengers scream in terror. Enough for me to develop a fear of flying. The plane dropped a couple more times before we landed, and flying would never be the same for me again — which is really uncomfortable when you fly as much as I do!

But I didn't let the discomfort hold me back. To help me get more comfortable flying to and from LA, I researched which airlines would give me the best flight experience for the best price, and I found Virgin Atlantic. Not only did Virgin have nice planes with cool lighting, comfortable seats, and other fun features, but it also offered an easy way to upgrade your seat for a nominal fee. At the time, if you bought a regular coach seat, you could see if a first-class seat was available twenty-four hours before your flight. If it was, you could upgrade to first class for less than a hundred dollars (and sometimes much less than that).

For an uncomfortable flier like me, this was a godsend. In first class, I would have extra attention from flight attendants, easier access to a bathroom, more room to pull out my laptop and work, watch a movie, enjoy a meal, and try to sleep — especially if I got a window seat so I could prop myself against it. All those distractions helped me get through the string of four-hour flights. I would set an alarm on my phone for the exact moment I could attempt to upgrade, and sometimes I was rewarded with a more comfortable flight.

That's how I found myself in first class, booked in my favorite window seat, on a Virgin flight home from LAX to ORD. I happily boarded the plane, stowed my luggage in the overhead bin, and went to sit down in my coveted seat by the window — but this time, it was occupied.

A woman wearing sunglasses was propped against *my* window, fast asleep. Awkward as it was, I did the only thing I could think of doing — sat down in the empty aisle seat next to her. I snuck another glance. She looked so familiar. I knew her somehow. I racked my brain — was it someone I knew in real life, someone I knew as part of my ever-growing online world, or someone else altogether? I knew I knew who she was, but I couldn't figure out how I knew her.

As the flight attendant made his rounds to ensure we were all buckled in before takeoff, he leaned over me to tap her on the shoulder. "Sorry to disturb you, but I just need you to fasten your seat belt," he whispered apologetically. Startled, she removed her sunglasses and looked at him in surprise. "Oh, thank you," she said, fastening her seat belt and putting her glasses in a sleek case.

That's when I got a good look and was slammed with immediate recognition. I knew who she was: a top executive for a major media company, the force behind a popular TV show. She wasn't a celebrity; she wasn't the face of a brand; she wasn't someone that just anyone would recognize. But if you were a builder of media businesses (as I was), or you knew anything about who heads up hit TV shows (as I did), or you were a fan of successful women in business (as I am), she was an icon — so I'll call her *the icon*. And. She. Was. Sitting. In. My. Seat.

Talk about awkward! So, what did I do? I let her have the seat, of course. I felt none of my usual nerves upon takeoff. I was so preoccupied with thoughts about how to handle the fact that the icon was sitting next to me that I barely noticed we were airborne. When I stole another glance, she was fast asleep again (this is why window seats are so helpful!). Her being asleep gave me plenty of time to decide whether I would try to talk to her.

On the one hand, I didn't want to be one of those chatty airplane people that annoy those who don't want to talk to strangers on airplanes. On the other hand, *hello!* The icon was sitting right next to me. If I didn't take the opportunity to tell her how much I appreciated her leading the way for women in media, I would never forgive myself.

By the time the flight attendant came around to ask what we'd like to eat and drink, waking her again gently, I had made up my mind. I would push past my discomfort, say one little thing about how much her work meant to me, then leave her in peace for the rest of the flight. And so, after we placed our orders, that's exactly what I did.

"Excuse me, I don't mean to intrude, but I just have to let you know that I think you and your show are amazing. Thank you for all you do for women, and especially for women who are in media." The words tumbled out and she looked at me in surprise. It was clear she was not used to being recognized. "Thank you for saying that. It means a lot," she replied, smiling. "You obviously know *my* name, so tell me, what is yours?"

That's how our three-hour conversation started. Over cocktails, then dinner, then dessert, we shared our professional histories, reflections on the media industry, and even some of our future goals. I was thrilled when she invited me to her corporate offices for a meeting with her team. By the time our flight touched down in Chicago, I realized that I hadn't felt uncomfortable at all during that flight — not from the flying, and not from the situation.

SPARK

Think about a time when you felt uncomfortable but pushed past that feeling to move ahead or to improve the situation. How could it have gone even better? How can you continue to stretch yourself and grow?

My usual feeling of discomfort when flying had led not only to one of the most comfortable flights of my life, but also to a life-changing experience with someone I truly admired. I had stretched and I had grown. That awkward plane situation led to a business meeting about collaborating with a major media company. And that led to more confidence in myself and in my business. It was another validation that I was on the right track — the feeling that "I've got this."

Self-Confidence Requires More Than Just "Fake It 'Til You Make It"

When it comes to self-confidence, you may have heard the phrase "fake it 'til you make it." This means that if you don't feel confident about something, pretend that you do, and eventually you will become confident — and successful.

To a certain extent it makes sense, but you can fool yourself — and other people — for only so long. And for many situations, pretending that you're good at something or that you know about something or that you're someone you are not, just won't work. It's also a good way to develop or exacerbate "impostor syndrome," the feeling that you are a fraud or a phony unworthy of success. Why do that to yourself?

Take my encounter with the icon. If I had tried to fake my way through that conversation, it never would have worked. There's no way to fake the industry knowledge and experience I had in order to: (1) know who the icon was, and (2) hold down an in-depth, three-hour conversation about our careers, thoughts on the business of media, and our goals. Pretending to have self-confidence would have broken down immediately. A "fangirl" moment is not the same as a peer-to-peer discussion leading to mutual respect and opportunities.

I've had a few fangirl moments, and it's hard to know what

to do when you see a celebrity. My rule of thumb when spotting an actor, musician, or other public figure is simple. Be kind, deferential, and respectful. If you're a fan, calmly let them know. Being nice and speaking from the heart always go a long way. Something good may happen if people respond to the authentic you. Authenticity is something you just can't fake.

That's also why "fake it 'til you make it" isn't a viable career or life path. You have to do the work of building confidence, accomplishment by accomplishment, to actually become self-confident. To get there requires plenty of reps, lots of varied successes, and the achievement of myriad goals.

Some people think faking it 'til they make it will get them where they want to go. They pretend to know what they're talking about, or they project a persona or confidence that lacks the substance to hold it up. When you try to dig deeper with them, you hit the shallows quickly.

People who lack depth or credibility can never be truly comfortable because they're presenting a false veneer. Like the traveling fortune teller Professor Marvel, who pretended to be the all-powerful wizard in *The Wizard of Oz*, things aren't always as they seem. That's why it's important to look behind the curtain, and it's why making sure you don't need a curtain is key.

SPARK

Have you ever tried to "fake it 'til you make it"? How did that work out for you? Looking back, what would you do differently?

Self-Confidence Means You Can Be a Tiger among Lions

The need for self-confidence and getting comfortable with being uncomfortable really hit home for me during the early years of iParenting. As we pitched investors to help the business grow, I was often the only woman in the room. Surrounded by men in suits, my stripes were glaring. Being sized up and underestimated yet again, I felt like a tiger in the lions' den.

Yes, it was daunting, but I had prepared exhaustively. I knew my subject matter. I knew my market. I knew my customer. I knew my clients. I knew my data. And I had stats to back everything up. All that preparation and knowledge gave me confidence, the belief that I could do this.

Still, I could have felt uncomfortable — especially when it became clear that these investors were used to talking to other men about topics they understood much better than pregnancy and motherhood. And as the ones controlling the bags of money, with plenty of options for where to invest it, they had the advantage.

I saw the skepticism on their faces. You didn't have to be a mind reader to know what they were thinking: Where was the money in pregnancy? What was the return on investment (ROI) on being a mom? How would they double, triple, quadruple their investment dollars by funding a nebulous concept like parenting? It wasn't as clear-cut as, say, healthcare, energy, transportation, or real estate.

Because I was the founder and the only one who had ever: (1) been pregnant, (2) given birth, (3) been a mom, (4) been a journalist, (5) written about these topics, and (6) worked with other moms, experts, and brands in the space, all eyes were on me for answers — and I felt the weight of their stares. Yes, all those *only*s made me different. And those differences could have made me uncomfortable. Instead, those differences became my superpowers, and they fueled my confidence.

I knew what I was talking about. My depth of knowledge — about being pregnant, being a mom, being a journalist, being an editor, being a publisher, being a marketer — gave me credibility. I told them about the size of the market and the four million births each year in the United States alone. I shared the fact that moms control the majority of household spending and influence most purchasing decisions. I explained why brands need to develop relationships with moms as early as possible to establish brand loyalty and increase market share.

As I spoke, I saw the stares turn into glints of recognition in their eyes. Maybe they were thinking about their wives or sisters or mothers or daughters — a critical connection between moms and money had been made. And that's when the power dynamic shifted.

Intrigued, the investors leaned in to learn more about the power of the mom market. By the time we shared the business plan and let them know that competitors were already calling about potential collaborations, their skepticism had transformed into belief. The glints of recognition had turned into dollar signs in their eyes.

That's when we gained the advantage. That's when I owned the room. With the investors on board, iParenting was poised for continued growth, enabling it to serve even more parents around the world with the best information and resources. And that's what mattered most to me.

SPARK

Think about a time when you owned the room — or any space you were in. This can be any situation in which you felt that you had an edge or the advantage. Even if you're not sure, what does owning the room look like to you? How could it play out in your own life?

The Virtuous Loop of Being Self-Confident

To become the fire, you need to be comfortable with being uncomfortable. People who are comfortable with discomfort are more likely to succeed because they are self-confident. That self-confidence drives them to embrace opportunities, take bigger risks, and accomplish greater goals. The more they flourish outside of their comfort zones, the greater their tolerance for discomfort becomes. This ultimately enables them to be comfortable in situations where others may not, resulting in life-changing experiences.

Because they have put in the reps, accomplishment by accomplishment, they have built their skills, knowledge, and credibility. That feeds their confidence, so they feel they've "got this." Self-confidence leads them to feel comfortable even when others underestimate them. Because they can thrive through that awkward feeling, they own the room — and believe they can achieve whatever they set their minds to. And that leads to more success.

This pattern played out for me again and again. Overcoming challenges, fighting my fires, enabled me to grow my skills and abilities. Owning my skills and abilities, and leveraging them to achieve bigger goals like growing a business, led to greater confidence. Self-confidence enabled me to be comfortable with being uncomfortable, owning the room — or whatever situation I was in — and achieving success.

Let's break down that formula with what was going on for me when I was talking to the icon and pitching the investors.

Being comfortable with being uncomfortable requires you to be self-confident. Over the years, I had solved problems, worked through challenges, and succeeded by taking small steps that led to giant leaps. Getting comfortable with my differences and believing in myself helped me grow strong and confident — even when outside my comfort zone.

Being confident leads you to flourish outside your comfort zone. I pushed past discomfort to get where I wanted to go — until feeling uncomfortable started to feel just fine. By focusing less on what other people thought of me and more on what *I* thought of me, I felt at home in my own skin. I built my knowledge and credibility to the point where I could engage in experiences that others may shy away from.

Thriving through discomfort leads you to greater success. Because I could thrive in situations that others perhaps could not, the power dynamic shifted. I leveraged my knowledge and experience to own any room — or baseball field or airplane — that I was in. Eventually, I believed there was nothing I couldn't achieve once I set my mind to it.

This simple formula applies no matter where you are in your journey to become the fire. Use it when you need to work on your self-confidence, or as a reminder that it's OK to feel awkward or uncomfortable. Just don't let discomfort stop you. It may take some time to feel like you can stretch beyond your comfort zone, but the more you do, the more you can succeed!

FLAME • Laura Desmond

First Jobs: Lifeguard, sports marketing intern
Education: BBA (marketing), University of Iowa
Personal Life: Widowed (from wife Marylyn)
Board/Civic Roles: Board member, DoubleVerify; board member, Adobe
Key Takeaway: "Embrace every challenge and be willing to do things there is no road map for."

Every year on Laura Desmond's birthday, her father would take her out for a drive in the family station wagon. "You can be anything you want to be, Laura," he would say. "The sky is the limit." Her father's words were a prophecy.

Born in Chicago to two "type A" parents from middle-class

beginnings, Laura, alongside her brother, grew up believing she could do whatever she set her mind to. Her father, the first in his family to go to college, was a strategic thinker who encouraged Laura to dream big. Her mother, a nurse turned homemaker, was the one who helped execute on the dreams and make things happen. "Mom was the roots, and Dad was the wings," Laura says.

Laura was also a child of the Equal Rights Amendment, the women's liberation movement, and Title IX, a federal law that prohibits discrimination on the basis of sex. Growing up surrounded by these cultural shifts that helped empower women and girls, she felt her opportunities were unlimited.

Laura's confidence started with her passion for athletics. From an early age, she found herself drawn to team sports because she "loved to win and hated to lose." In high school, she was a three-season varsity athlete, competing on the volleyball, basketball, and softball teams. "I thought I would play college sports, but I was not Division I-level good. My dad thought it was more important for me to go to a good school and focus on my career."

Athletics played a big part in Laura's career development, too. In college, she worked as an intern in the University of Iowa's sports marketing department. There, she was part of a team whose mission was to drive attendance at women's basketball games. One of her favorite memories is her team getting twenty-two thousand fans to attend the Iowa versus University of Connecticut women's basketball game, a milestone achievement. Setting goals and then achieving — or blowing past — them became a hallmark of Laura's life.

It was also at the University of Iowa where Laura discovered her love for marketing. For a school assignment, while flipping through *Life* magazine, Laura spotted an ad for Crest toothpaste. From her perspective, it was a great example of a brand doing helpful things for people. "I thought fluoride, healthy teeth, healthy gums — advertising fuels growth that fuels R & D, and this is all good for the world."

It turned out that Laura was the only one in her class of twenty students who believed that advertising was good. Although it may have felt uncomfortable to be the *only*, that's when Laura decided to embrace her passion for marketing and advertising. That's also when she began to realize that being the *only* wasn't necessarily a bad thing and that she'd better get used to it — because it would end up happening repeatedly throughout her life.

During her senior year, Laura interviewed for jobs with major brands and ad agencies. She became one of only twelve associates to be offered a job by Leo Burnett, a legendary Chicago-based ad agency with many Fortune 500 clients. That was the first step on her journey to becoming CEO of the company that would become Starcom MediaVest, the world's largest global media agency.

Armed with self-confidence and an insatiable curiosity, Laura charted a fearless path through the corporate jungle. When one of her early bosses asked her what she wanted to do with her career, Laura replied in the simplest terms she could. "I want to wake up in the morning and be challenged. I want to always be moving forward." And once the higher-ups knew that about her, there was no holding her back. "They gave me the freedom to make things happen. After each accomplishment, I would look at them and say, 'What's next?'"

As Laura describes it, when her bosses gave her more rope, she would accomplish more and more, so they gave her even more rope. This became a virtuous cycle of increasing self-confidence, which led to further promotions and success.

Laura notes that while big companies can be slow and stifling, she kept things moving by having an entrepreneurial mindset. She was always looking for new ways to learn and solve problems. Laura learned that clear, authentic communication was key — as was leading with empathy. "I would think about what my colleagues had going on at work and at home, what they were going through as a team and individually. Having empathy for others helped me get teams fired up to reach higher, to go through walls."

Laura achieved all this despite being a tiger among lions. She got used to being the youngest person in the room, the only woman in the room, and the only gay person in the room. She learned to make her mark without feeling awkward about being the *only*. "From early on, I got comfortable with it," she remembers. "I didn't notice it. I was like a fish in water."

Laura quickly climbed the ranks at the agency because she was always being handpicked to work with senior leaders around the country. "I just loved the game. I was always like, 'Put me in, Coach!'" Her can-do attitude enabled her to show others what she was made of.

By age twenty-seven, Laura was transferred to the company's European headquarters in London, where she found herself constantly traveling to help run the Europe business. Despite confronting plenty of potentially uncomfortable language and cultural barriers, she succeeded. "I was comfortable no matter what, so they would say, 'Send her in; she can handle it.'"

That transformational experience led Laura to important global roles. She then became CEO of the Latin American division, and she built that business from zero to $35 million in just two years. That success fueled more success. Laura earned top leadership roles as the CEO of MediaVest in New York City, at the time a floundering business that she and the team turned around, and as the CEO of Starcom MediaVest Group Americas, a pivotal promotion that put her in the running for the global top job.

The next thing she knew, she was offered the top CEO spot, becoming one of the youngest CEOs when she was appointed in 2008 to lead the eight-thousand-employee subsidiary of Publicis Groupe. "Not one of those promotions made me feel like, 'Now I've made it,'" she says. "I saw each promotion as a bigger stage, a bigger mandate, a bigger opportunity. It certainly gave me confidence, and I loved every minute of being on top of the hill. But the way I see it, each move forward only earned me the right to do more."

All the while Laura was building a booming business, she also was building a diverse and inclusive company culture. Long before diversity and inclusion were priorities for corporate leaders, she helped the company set a strong tone. That's why she and her partner, Marylyn, together for more than twenty-five years and married in 2014, integrated their personal and business worlds. "I wanted to resolve any mystery and be honest about who I am. At business dinners or events, I would introduce Marylyn and say, 'This is my partner.' Everyone was comfortable and accepting." When clients got to meet Marylyn, they were so charmed that Marylyn soon became known as "Laura's secret weapon."

Because Laura made being *other* so matter-of-fact, it became no big deal — and it even inspired other people to come out at work, too. "It was important to make it cool and be a nonissue, because it truly is a nonissue."

As CEO, Laura grew the Starcom business from $525 million to $1.4 billion, weathering the great recession and then leading the way as a digital disrupter. With her guidance, the company transformed from a traditional ad agency to a digital-first media agency with data at its core. With clients like Procter & Gamble, Coca-Cola, and Microsoft and partners like Facebook, Twitter, and Google, who all believed in her vision, the opportunities became endless. "We were the first to tackle the digital divide. We made our own luck."

During her watch, the company earned more honors and recognition than any other media agency in the world. Under her leadership, Starcom was the number one media and marketing services agency globally for five straight years.

Laura earned her own accolades, including being named *Mediaweek*'s Media Executive of the Year, Chicago Advertising Federation's Ad Woman of the Year, and one of the World's Most Powerful Women by *Forbes*. Mayor Rahm Emanuel even proclaimed an official "Laura Desmond Day" in Chicago.

But Marylyn started to experience health challenges, and Laura wanted to be there for her in a way she could not as a global CEO. "I felt that after ten years as CEO, and twenty-eight years in the ad business, there was another chapter in my life to write. I didn't want to retire — I just wanted to figure out how to do the things I love but be more available."

When she left Starcom in 2016, Laura was the highest-ranking woman in the advertising field. "It's a nice thing to say, and it's a fantastic thing to have achieved. But I achieved that with a great team, and it only earned me the right to do even more. No matter the result, I want to know that I was as good as I could be."

Once she moved on from the agency, Laura's entrepreneurial spirit caught fire. "My reputation earned me a platform and enabled me to do everything I'm currently doing." Laura started her own consulting company and became a private equity operating partner and member of several corporate boards.

As lead director of the board (and even a short stint as interim CEO) of DoubleVerify, a leading software platform for digital media measurement and analytics, Laura had an integral role as the company went public in April 2021. "It was a feeling of great pride to be part of something early in its growth story. Also, a feeling of disbelief that you're standing on the balcony of the New York Stock Exchange, ringing the bell. It was a bucket list item I never knew I had."

Sadly, Marylyn's health battles returned. After some complications with cancer treatment, she decided to end treatment and to focus on quality of life. In December 2021, "after eight years of pushing back multiple health challenges, she died as she chose to live: gracefully, peacefully," and at home with Laura at her side.

With the grief and heartache of endings come opportunities for new beginnings. "I'm a lot more vulnerable, but also a lot more approachable. I'm like a house that has been rehabbed down to the studs."

Personally, Laura is focused on keeping Marylyn's memory alive through the legacy endowments in STEM they established in her name and the foundations she cared about. "Marylyn was courageous, and I carry that forward. Part of my legacy is taking care of her legacy. When you have resilience, somehow you're able to keep going."

Professionally, Laura describes this period of her life as if she, herself, is a start-up. "I pivoted and I'm iterating my platform. With start-ups, the platform may be the same, but the use cases change. Why not the same for people? I can be Laura 2.0 or Laura 3.0."

She encourages women to have confidence in their ability to pivot, especially during these most disruptive of times. "Had I not stepped away, I never would have had these opportunities — such as being part of an initial public offering [IPO] — along with more time with my friends and family."

Laura advises women to develop an expertise and become thought leaders by writing about what they know, getting published, speaking at conferences, and connecting with like-minded networks. "I hope I inspire women to see the different careers they can have over the course of their lifetimes."

Laura sees a key component of achieving success as learning to be comfortable with being uncomfortable. "Put yourself at the intersection of your passion and your company's purpose. Embrace every challenge and be willing to do things there is no road map for." And this, she stresses, requires confidence. "Figure out what you don't know. Realize that not everyone is on the same journey as you. Be willing to give some things up. Let go of what you think you know, to grow."

With so many accomplishments already, what does "success" truly mean? For Laura, it can mean access. "Success gives you the option to have choices." Now, with access to top talent and investment dollars to make stuff happen, Laura may, as a venture capitalist, build her own portfolio of companies. Laura notes that only a small fraction of all venture investors are women. "Yet when women are on public company boards, those companies perform better," she says. "There's so much more to think about, more to come, more to do."

But success is even more personal than that. "I define success as, 'Did I make an impact? Did I leave a long-lasting legacy?' It's gratifying for me when people tell me my leadership made a difference. That's when I feel happy."

BLAZE

I am self-confident. I know I've got this.

I can accomplish whatever I set my mind to.

I am a tiger among lions.

My stripes are my superpowers.

What I think of myself matters more than what others think.

I am comfortable with being uncomfortable.

The more comfortable I am, the more success I achieve.

4

Be Courageous

To become the fire, you need to be courageous. Fear plays a key role in decision-making and in sharpening the skill of *motivation*. But fear should guide you, not paralyze you. By learning to use fear to fuel your motivation, your courage grows — and you can achieve greater success.

Becoming highly successful is not for the faint of heart. In fact, navigating your way along the path to success can be downright scary. It requires the ability to take risks, to overcome fear, and to do the thing you think you cannot do — but that you want to do. When you figure out what that thing is, chances are very good that it will be outside your comfort zone, beyond where you feel safe and secure. That may frighten you, but that's OK. Let me explain.

You won't get where you want to go by staying in your safe place or by doing the same things you've always done. Being successful requires you to take bold, decisive action. To move beyond dreaming to doing. To act on your aspirations in order to achieve the desired outcome. And to act, you have to be motivated enough by the reward to take on the risk. Motivated enough to overcome the fear that may be standing between you and the thing you want to do.

Motivation is what drives you. It's your reason for doing the thing. It's your *why*. The stronger your motivation, the more likely you'll be able to overcome the fear that threatens to hold you back. The more intense your drive to accomplish your goal, the more likely you are to push past your fear. That means having courage. And there is no real success without courage.

Being courageous is a mindset. To have courage is a choice you make. Unlike bravery, which is more of an inborn trait — either you're brave or you're not — courage requires you to decide to move forward even if you're afraid. Whereas people who are brave act because it's in their DNA, people who are courageous act because they believe what's on the other side of their fear is worth the risk, stress, or anxiety. Their motivation to achieve the thing they want is more powerful than the fear they feel of not achieving the thing.

When faced with the choice of holding back because of fear or moving forward despite fear, courageous people move forward. And because it's a choice, anyone — including you — can be courageous if motivated.

Motivation is a powerful force. Whether in your personal or professional life, once you identify your why, motivation can ignite a fire in you. That fire can help you accomplish the thing you feel driven to do, even if you're afraid. Keep in mind that the thing you want doesn't have to be as specific as trying for a promotion at work or as ambitious as building a business. Many times, your why may be as basic as seeking peace, avoiding harm — or simply staying alive.

The key is not letting fear hold you back. If you let your fear rule your life, you will stay stuck. And as we talked about in chapter 3, remaining in your comfort zone is a great way to *not* grow and to *never* become comfortable with being uncomfortable.

But don't get me wrong: fear serves an important purpose. Fear can be your friend, and it can be your guide. That's because when you pay attention to it and give it the respect it deserves, fear can be an indicator that helps you identify and analyze risks and threats. Fear can even help keep you alive. By being attuned to the fight-or-flight response in our nervous systems, we not only increase our chances of surviving an attack by some outside threat but also help develop our situational awareness. And as we talked about in the first chapter, situational awareness leads to being visionary.

Being courageous means you feel afraid, but you push past that fear and act anyway. It's important to listen to your fear but not be led by it. The more action you take, the less fear you feel. By facing your fears, you become courageous and begin to fear less. When what you want drives you more than the fear hinders you, your motivation will provide the courage needed to achieve your goals. It's doing what you're afraid of that helps you build courage. And with that newfound courage, you can achieve more success.

Many of us grew up afraid, and some still live in fear. Regularly confronting challenges and fighting fires, we learned to understand our body's physical manifestations of fear. Those sweaty palms, goosebumps on our arms, butterflies in our belly — and so many more discomforting sensations — warned us that chaos was coming or burned us when faced with flames. There were certainly occasions when we curled up in a ball to stay safe.

But there were many other situations when we decided to move forward, despite those discomforting sensations. Over time, we learned to weigh the risk versus the reward, and depending on our level of motivation to achieve the thing we wanted, we decided to be courageous and act, whether that meant earning a promotion, building a business, seeking peace, avoiding harm — or simply staying alive.

For me, learning to be courageous started in childhood. You already know one of my earliest moments of fear. Living in war-torn Beirut, and being left there with my father and siblings when *mi madre* returned to Puerto Rico because *mi abuela* had died, I experienced intense fear as a young child.

But Beirut was not the first or the last time *mi madre* would leave us kids behind. This fiercely independent Latina made her own rules and didn't let society's — or anyone's — expectations dictate her actions, even in her role as a mother. *Mi madre* loved us dearly, but she had her own rationale for why she did the things she did. No one really understood her reasons — not even my father (despite their now sixty-plus years of marriage). *Mi madre* danced to a beat only she could hear, and we all had to learn to live with that.

But *mi madre*'s courage was plain to see. She was adept at assessing risk versus reward, weighing pros and cons, and pushing past fear to take actions she felt were best for her family or herself, despite what anyone else thought. And from what I can tell, she was often right.

Being the youngest of thirteen, *mi madre* had many brothers and even more sisters. Because she was the baby, her sisters (*mis tías*) were more like mothers to her than sisters. In fact, one of *mis tías* dropped out of school in seventh grade back in Puerto Rico to help *mi abuela* care for the younger kids. *Mi tía* courageously sacrificed her own education to ensure her siblings could continue with theirs. Her siblings' well-being became her why, fueling her motivation to be there for them.

Mi madre ended up being the only one in her family to go

to college (in the United States, no less). Although she was apprehensive about leaving her homeland, *mi madre* was motivated to keep learning. She accepted a scholarship to the University of Illinois, pushing past her fear and stepping into the unknown. Her courage led her to graduate school, then on to a successful career as a teacher in the Chicago Public Schools.

When *mi madre* took my younger sister and me on a childhood trip to visit *mi tía* and other family members who lived in New York City, we were excited to see her, along with another *tía*, and to spend time with several of our many cousins (*mis primos*). As my sister and I were getting reacquainted with a couple of *primos* in the apartment's small living room, at some point, I realized *mi madre* was nowhere to be seen. I felt my palms grow sweaty — the first physical manifestation of fear.

"*Donde está mi madre?*" I asked *mi tía*. Poor *tía*. A look of concern swept across her face, but she quickly tucked it away.

"*Ella está en la ducha,*" she responded. *Mi madre* was in the shower? Okaaaay.

A couple of hours passed with no sign of *mi madre*, so I asked again. *Mi tía* looked noticeably annoyed and uncomfortable. I felt goosebumps on my arms — the second physical manifestation of fear. And still, *mi tía* replied that *mi madre* would be back soon. I gotta tell ya, I didn't really believe her. Between the look on her face and *mi madre*'s track record of leaving us behind, my Spidey sense was on high alert.

With my little sister looking to me to see how she should react, I tried to be strong, to show her all was well. We played (well, mostly fought) with our *primos*; we ate dinner; we pretended nothing was amiss. But with increasing urgency, I continued to ask an irritated *tía* about *mi madre* — until the moment I'm sure she'd been dreading finally arrived. At the end of her rope, an exasperated *tía* decided to tell us the truth. I felt butterflies in my belly — the third physical manifestation of fear, telling me I was about to face the flames.

In blunt, broken English, *mi tía* explained that *mi madre* had returned to Puerto Rico for a while, so we were going to be staying with her in New York. It was unclear for how long, but we needed to stop asking questions and "just be good." That meant we had to stop pestering her and to stop fighting with our *primos*.

Mi tía's revelation was a shock to the system. Forget sweaty palms and belly butterflies — this was a hair-standing-on-end full punch in the gut. As much as I tried to hold back my tears, I just couldn't help it — I started to cry. And once my sister saw me crying, she started wailing. We loved our *madre*, and when she was gone, there was a palpable void.

But it wasn't just that we missed our *madre*. It was that trust had been broken — again. Not only because poor *tía* had lied to us multiple times. More significantly, *mi madre* had once again left us behind, without even letting us know — without even saying goodbye. *Mi madre* had simply disappeared — leaving someone else to explain her absence — just as she had left us in Beirut with our father. It was a scary thing for anyone to deal with, but especially for a child.

Did I want to curl up in a ball? Yep. Did I decide to curl up in a ball? Nope. I remember feeling a sense of responsibility to rise up and show my sister that we were going to be OK. I knew in my heart that how I reacted was going to make the difference between a successful outcome and a total disaster.

If I decided to retreat into myself where it felt safer, I would be abandoning my sister at a time when she needed me. If I continued to cry and act out, poor *tía* would be pushed to her wit's end. And that would not be good for any of us. My motivation became clear. Our safety and well-being became my why, and my motivation to achieve it overrode any fear.

So I chose to be courageous. I began to reframe my thinking. Maybe *mi madre* had a very important reason for needing to be in Puerto Rico. Maybe being left at *mi tía*'s was OK after all. I decided to view *mi tía* as a no-shit-talking, older, and wiser version of *mi madre*. And I learned that, under her roof, if you behaved, life could actually be pretty interesting.

For example, *mi tía* made amazing Puerto Rican food — even better than *mi madre*. And when not eating her homemade ethnic dishes, we got to experiment with foods we'd never had before, like tuna salad.

We even had our first-ever free lunches from the Meals on Wheels–type food truck that occasionally appeared out front near her apartment building. Waiting in line with other families from the block, my sister and I were surprised when we each received a sandwich of American cheese on white bread and a small carton of milk. *Mi tía* reminded us that we weren't allowed to drink our milk until after we'd finished our food. When we asked why, *mi tía* answered that there wasn't enough milk for seconds, so we had to wait to quench our thirst until we finished eating.

As we ate our lunch curbside with *mis primos* and other kids from the block, I thought about how different my life back in suburban Chicago was from theirs. Even though I got bullied for never having the right clothes or shoes, at least back home I always had food to eat and milk to drink. The experience delivered important lessons in gratitude and food insecurity — realizing that those who faced it needed support, which sometimes came in the form of meals from a welfare truck.

It was during this time with *mi tía* that I grew to love her as a second mother. I was struck by her courage, taking in and caring for her sister's children — along with her own children and grandchildren — despite her challenges.

I realized how very fortunate my family was. Even through

my lens as a child, the economic disparity between *mi madre*'s family and my father's family — and our own nuclear family — was striking. *Mi tía*'s cramped Brooklyn apartment on a crowded block of old apartment buildings was a drastic departure from our modest house on a tree-lined street abutting a neighborhood park. For *mis primos*, the block was their world. In their world, opportunities were drastically different than the ones in the world my immigrant parents had created for us. Their world required enormous motivation and courage to navigate.

The experience with *mi tía* taught me that courage is perseverance despite obstacles. It's when you feel something so strongly in your bones or heart that you know you have to do it, despite your anxiety. You're making a choice, the decision to act — despite those uncomfortable physical manifestations of fear. Courage is having heart and fortitude in the face of flames.

Mi madre was being courageous in taking care of her own needs or those of others in her homeland. *Mi tía* was being courageous in helping her sister and her nieces, despite her own hardships.

And I was being courageous — because I was motivated. The motivation to be strong for my sister (who also was being courageous) and to "be good" so it was easier for *mi tía* to manage while *mi madre* was away, became my why. Our well-being became the thing to accomplish in the face of fear.

It's when you decide to push through the physical manifestations — and emotional challenges — of fear that you are being courageous. And when you have courage, you are more likely to succeed. You, too, can become courageous. In fact, you already are. You have likely pushed through your fear countless times. Now it's time to kick your motivation up a notch so you can be even more courageous, because the more courageous you are, the more success you'll achieve. In this chapter, I will show you why motivation is key to courage, then help you enhance your motivation so you can be more courageous in your pursuit of success.

Motivation Is Key to Becoming Courageous

To be courageous, you must sharpen your motivation, which means two things: (1) knowing what drives you (your *why*), and (2) using your why as fuel to push past the fear that stands between you and your goal (the *thing*). Being motivated enables you to assess a situation and then to decide to act because you believe what's on the other side of your fear is worth it.

We enhance our motivation by identifying what drives us, what makes us jump out of bed in the morning, what we're passionate about, what we want or need, what makes us feel secure or proud, or what brings us joy. By identifying our thing, one thing at a time. Once we know what the thing is, we can assess the risk involved in trying to achieve the thing versus the reward of the thing. If we really want or need the thing, chances are good that we'll decide to go after it, even if we're afraid of what it will take to get it.

Many of us are used to the feeling of risk or fear because of all the fires we have faced. And the more we push past those feelings successfully, achieving one thing after another, the deeper our motivation becomes. Once you have tasted the sweetness of the reward that results from your motivation, the more motivated you become to achieve even more. The greater your motivation, the greater your courage. And the greater your courage, the greater your success.

All of us can be courageous, but it takes work. Like a muscle, courage needs exercise. Exercising your courage muscle will help it get stronger. Similar to self-confidence, which is created over time through experiences in which you learn and master a certain skill, courage is created as you take calculated risks, push past your fear, and achieve your goals.

By starting small and accomplishing things outside your comfort zone that are scary but doable, you slowly build up your motivation and courage to achieve bigger goals. The more you succeed at the smaller things, the bigger the things you can achieve. Thing by thing, rep after rep, your courage muscle strengthens.

I continued to exercise my courage on another trip to New York City with *mi madre*. Early in my high school years, this trip was pitched as another visit to see *mis tías* and *mis primos* — but this time, it would be just *mi madre* and me.

I found myself in a different Brooklyn apartment, the home of a different *tía*, and yet I experienced déjà vu when *mi madre* ended up disappearing — again. My state of mind? Scared, yes. Disappointed, yes. Surprised, not so much. When it came to her sudden departures, I learned to never expect straight answers from *mi madre* or *mis tías*.

I believe *mi madre* was afraid that explaining she was leaving, or just saying a proper goodbye, would create a scene she wasn't emotionally prepared to deal with. Maybe the potential drama of a tearful separation was too much for her. Looking back, I wish *mi madre* had shown more courage in this situation.

Yes, it would have been difficult, but being courageous often is. Maybe each time she told me she had to leave, and explained why, it would have become easier — for both of us. But indirectly, *mi madre* taught me that I can do hard things. Hopefully, as a mother myself, I taught my own children the same — in a more direct way.

Whatever the reason for *mi madre*'s departure, on this trip to New York City I often found myself alone with different, older *primos* in Brooklyn because *mi tía* was busy at work. This time, though, there were more serious things to worry about than fighting with *primos* or a lack of milk. One *primo* had a drug habit that made me terribly afraid. He carried his stash around in a brown paper lunch bag, setting it down on the kitchen table — or wherever he happened to be.

I'll never forget the time he drove me to the home of yet another *primo*. High as a kite, he set down his stash on the console between the car's two front seats. I stared at the brown bag warily. To put as much distance as possible between the bag and me, I leaned into the car door as far as I could, but the drugs were still too close for comfort.

As we navigated the busy Brooklyn blocks, people were everywhere — walking on foot, riding on bikes, sitting on stoops, standing on curbs. *Mi primo* seemed to know many of them, waving or laughing or nodding in recognition as we drove past. A friend waved him over, so he pulled up to say *hola*. The friend peered into the car and noticed my stripes — lighter skin, lighter hair — right away. *"Wassup, amigo? Quién es la gringa?"*

I was not surprised to be referred to as *la gringa*, a slang term referring to Americans, or fairer-skinned or lighter-haired people. Among *mi madre*'s tan- and brown-skinned Puerto Rican family, my lighter features made me a tiger among lions. Even in my own family, I was often the *other*.

Laughing in response, *mi primo* let his friend know that I was his cousin from Chicago. The friend's eyebrows shot up in disbelief, and the two shared another laugh. But the *gringa* moment passed, and I exhaled my tension. Then, as they spoke in Spanglish, the friend handed the joint he was smoking to *mi primo*, who took a hit. Shrinking further into my seat, leaning harder into my car door, I tried to disappear. Still, *mi primo* leaned over, offering me the joint as his friend looked on expectantly.

I guess the "cool" thing, and maybe the easier thing, would have been to nonchalantly take the joint and give it a try —

especially since I was trying to fit in. But quickly assessing my situation, I decided that even if they were insulted or labeled me an outsider because I wouldn't smoke with them, I had to stick to my values and what felt right to me. So rather than going along with what may have felt easier in that moment, I instead replied with a baffled look and a simple *"No, gracias."*

Mi primo shrugged his shoulders, as if it were my loss. After a few cringey moments of them puffing away while I pretended I wasn't there, we drove off. *Mi primo* turned to me and, noticing my worry, gave me a sad smile. "Don't worry, cuz. I take my drugs seriously. *No problemo.*"

I just shook my head, but inside, I was shaking in fear. I realized that while staying with *mis primos*, I would need to rely heavily upon my motivation to be safe, to continue making decisions that would lead to successful outcomes, even if it felt intensely uncomfortable. What was on the other side of that fear was my why: my health and well-being. The thing was self-preservation.

I declined the unnerving string of invitations from *mi primo* and stuck as close as possible to *mi tía* — or just kept to myself — until it was time to return home. I was once again grateful for how fortunate I was. For some in my own family, those busy Brooklyn blocks shaped their worldview.

When opportunities for drugs are more accessible than opportunities for a good education or job, your why can become cloudy. Drug dependence and addiction can be destructive and deadly. Societal change is needed to ensure that help, tools, support, and opportunities are more readily available. It takes motivation and vision to be able to see beyond the street, and even more resources and courage to manifest a life beyond the block. We need to shine a light so others can see a path out.

Mi primo would never know how big of an impact he had on me. I wrote my college application essay about the experience and how it impacted my motivation and the choices I made then and afterward.

Being in that fire taught me that while saying yes may lead to new experiences, sometimes the more courageous choice is to say no. Unknowingly, *mi primo* helped me become more aware of my surroundings, better understand my values, and use that sharpened motivation to build my courage and pursue my goals.

After the experience with *mi primo*, my inner voice kept reminding me to be motivated and courageous — and to not do something just because others were doing it. That doesn't mean I never dabbled in drugs or alcohol (remember my freshman year in college?). But that guarding inner voice was always with me, part fear and part motivation. I learned to listen to that voice of courage — and let it guide me along my journey.

The fear part warned me and alerted me to potential threats. The motivation part helped keep me out of harm's way and focused on my goals. I became driven. My motivation drove me to do more, to courageously achieve more — to do the thing, even if I was afraid.

SPARK

What motivates you? Think of two times your motivation led you to overcome your fear. How did that work out for you?

Clarifying the Myth of Being Fearless

When it comes to overcoming fear, you may frequently hear the word *fearless*. Being fearless sounds so intimidating, as if you literally have no fear. Between you and me, do you know many people who have zero fear? Yeah, me neither. But I used precisely that word in chapter 3 to describe Laura Desmond's journey to the top as she fearlessly navigated the corporate jungle. Was she fearless? Yes. Did she feel zero fear? No. I realize it's confusing. That's why I'm going to clarify the myth of being fearless and explain what being fearless actually means.

People who are fearless have discovered a key component to success: respecting the role fear plays in their decision-making and enabling it to enhance their motivation. They have learned to assess any given situation, listen to their body's physical and emotional manifestations, and allow their fear to guide them instead of paralyzing them.

They have done the work of growing their motivation — why by why, thing by thing — to the point where it fuels their courage. Their motivation to achieve the thing is more powerful than the fear they feel of not achieving the thing. That's why, when faced with the choice of holding back or moving forward, fearless people let their courage take over so they can keep moving ahead. And that courage is what leads them to greater success. Fearless people have simply amplified their ability to be courageous.

There have been many times in my life when I have been called fearless, whether in Beirut, baseball, or business. People who know me well — and people who don't know me at all — have remarked on the strength or bravery they believe I display. But now that you know a bit more about me, you know I'm not "without fear."

Rather, I use any fear I feel as a guide to help me navigate the world and achieve my goals. I rely on courage when making strategic decisions. Most of the time, my motivation to achieve the thing is more powerful than the fear I feel of not achieving the thing. And when faced with a choice of retreating or advancing, courage takes over so I can keep moving forward.

Life can be scary, and life can be hard. But we can do scary things, and we can do hard things. In fact, it's only by doing scary and hard things that we will achieve any meaningful success.

These truths really hit home for me when I was building my second business, 30Seconds, as a single mom with three kids. I was off to a solid start as a serial entrepreneur. My team and I had put in the exhaustive work needed to build the first iteration of our innovative website, 30SecondMom.com, and had launched it into the world.

The company had been selected as one of the "5 Hottest Start-ups" by the Digital Collective and was a finalist for "App of the Year" and "Tech Woman of the Year" in Chicago's Moxie Awards. We had received solid press coverage in *The Huffington Post*, *Fast Company*, *The Chicago Tribune*, *The Chicago Sun-Times*, *Crain's Chicago Business*, ABC-TV, WGN-TV, and more.

So, when 30Seconds was invited to be part of the Springboard Enterprises Digital Media/Technology Accelerator in New York City, a program that accepts only the highest-potential entrepreneurs, I was beside myself with excitement. Springboard accelerates the growth of women-led companies, and its portfolio companies have executed more than 225 exits to strategic acquirers and achieved twenty-two IPOs (including Zipcar, iRobot, Constant Contact, and the RealReal). I was humbled and honored to be included in their circle, and I was looking forward to great things.

Around that time, however, my health started failing. One of the first times my body's autonomic system went berserk, I was on a family trip. My kids and I were visiting cousins in downstate Illinois. Out of nowhere, my heart rate skyrocketed, and I nearly blacked out. Chalking it up to exhaustion, I got through the trip with only one or two other similar experiences.

But the episodes of what I came to learn were tachycardia, or an abnormally high heart rate, only increased in frequency and severity and were joined by other debilitating symptoms. Some days, I would experience things like migraines, joint pain, or severe allergic reactions. Other days, it was shooting and tingling pain or wild, unrelenting swings in my heart rate, body temperature, and blood pressure that caused dizziness and near fainting.

I frequently found myself being transported by ambulance to the emergency room and admitted to the hospital. These scary events would happen any time of the day or night. It even happened when I was at a scheduled doctor's appointment. The nurse taking my vital signs was concerned by the unusually low blood pressure readings she was getting, so she called the doctor in to verify what she was seeing. The doctor checked my blood pressure herself. When she confirmed the incredibly low numbers, the doctor told me it was impossible to understand not only how I had driven myself to the appointment but also how I was able to walk through the door unassisted. I was admitted to the hospital immediately — again.

Having been healthy and strong for most of my life, with no allergies or preexisting conditions, I was frightened by what was happening in my body. I remembered my six-week hospital stay, when I was pregnant with my twins, continuously connected to monitors and IV drips. The incessant sounds of machines monitoring my vitals and pumping me full of meds and fluids were both threatening and reassuring. But with the pregnancy, I understood what was happening — and the countdown to delivering my babies. With my new medical scare, there was only confusion and uncertainty.

Throughout more hospital stays than I can recount, doctor after doctor remarked on how "interesting" a patient I was. (I would much rather be a "boring" patient.) They told me that I might need everything from serious medications to IV infusions to surgery to a pacemaker.

Finally, one specialist explained that he suspected I had a problem with my autonomic system — the system in your body that's responsible for regulating involuntary body functions like your heartbeat, blood pressure, breathing, body temperature, swallowing, and digestion. He suggested I go to the Mayo Clinic in Rochester, Minnesota, for a full workup because, he said, "Mayo is where they figure out the tough cases like this one." Hmm.

The experts at Mayo leave no stone unturned when looking for answers to challenging health problems. My first visit, which lasted more than a week, involved an exhaustive examination of every bodily system. I consulted with specialist after specialist and underwent test after test. The days were filled with questions, hypotheses, pokes, prods, procedures, vials, and tubes — all in the hopes of getting to the bottom of my complicated health situation.

The results of the Mayo workup were myriad diagnoses, including a heart condition and a rare autoimmune disease. To treat the autoimmune disease and related symptoms, my Mayo doctors prescribed a treatment plan that included intravenous immunoglobulin (IVIG). Immunoglobulin, part of the blood's plasma, is rich in antibodies to help fight disease.

I was prescribed other medications and even more tests to be done by local doctors back home. Because cancer was still a possibility, I had a spinal tap and a positron emission tomography (PET) scan. Working with a team of specialists at my hospital's cancer center, the doctors concluded that IVIG was the best course of treatment. We would start with five initial rounds and go from there.

The IVIG treatment was not as easy as it may sound. I was one of those people who, ever since childhood, hated needles and injections of any kind. (To those of you who also hate needles, I apologize in advance for this part — you may want to skip the next five paragraphs!) My needle aversion was intensified by being in the hospital with my twins, on an IV that needed to be changed out every three days for six weeks — yes, that's at least *fourteen times*, not counting the times they "missed" the vein and had to try again — and receiving regular steroid shots to mature the babies' lungs.

The fact that I have very small, hidden veins that are reluctant to cooperate only complicated matters. Then there were the more recent ER visits and hospital stays that only added to my IV and injection fatigue.

Although the hospital stays and necessary needles were difficult to endure, they also helped prepare me for the process of IVIG. I found that, when it comes to fear, the more you are exposed to what you're afraid of, the less afraid of it you become. By doing the thing you fear, over time, you can build up a tolerance to it.

Much of what we fear comes from feeling out of control. So when we face our fears, we gain more control over them. It also helps to acknowledge the fear by talking or even writing about it. This helps you see it for what it is, realize it's there, and that it's OK for it to be there.

To overcome fear, support can be a lifeline. That's why, when it came time for my spinal tap and IVIG treatments, I explained my fear to a dear friend, *mi amiga*. I told *mi amiga* about my difficult veins and dread of needles. She not only listened and empathized but also worked with me on coping strategies. Best of all, *mi amiga* came with me to some of those scary appointments.

Together, we explained my reluctant veins, asked for an IV nurse specialist to insert the IVs, and requested heat packs to help draw my veins to the surface. *Mi amiga* sat through the "let's hope they find a vein quickly" drama, then the hours-long IV drip process. Every time there was a challenge, we prayed. Every time it went smoothly, we celebrated.

When the infusions were over, I was relieved and grateful. And I did see improvement in my symptoms. My doctor even remarked that she hoped my disease had been put into "remission." And it had, at least for a while.

But my health battles were far from over. I would go on to have additional rounds of IVIG — and even more IVIG treatment may be needed in the future. These are challenges and symptoms I will likely have for the rest of my life.

I tell you all this because that serious health fire was blazing in the background while I was participating in the rigorous Springboard accelerator program in New York City. While some parts of the program were done remotely, other parts required in-person participation.

Several trips to New York City were needed, including the final Demo Day showcase, when we were to pitch our start-ups to an audience of business insiders and investors — *Shark Tank* style. If I wanted to finish the program and "graduate" with my cohort, I would have to be there and perform, no matter how unwell I was.

To enhance my motivation during such a fear-filled time, it helped to visualize the outcome of not participating in Demo Day. After all, no one was *making* me do it. I didn't *have* to fly to New York, stand on a stage, and deliver a pitch — when it would have felt safer and easier to stay at home, lying on my left side to help keep my heart rate stable.

I asked myself what it would look like if I didn't act. I could let the fear win and simply drop out. How would it feel to not be there, to not graduate? Next, I visualized the outcome of taking action, despite my fear. How would it feel to fly there, be up on stage, deliver my pitch? What's the worst thing that could happen — would I misspeak, black out, drop dead? In other words, would I fail? On the flip side, what was the best-case scenario? Would I be confident, deliver my pitch, open new opportunities? In other words, would I succeed?

By visualizing what could happen either way, I assessed the risk and the reward of participating. Weighing the pros and cons, and accepting either of the potential outcomes, I could respect my fear without letting it paralyze me. And once I felt my motivation overtake my fear, courage was in charge. Once the courageous me was in control, I could be fearless in pursuit of my goals, no matter whether I succeeded or failed.

This process helped me realize that part of becoming courageous is giving yourself credit for any act of courage, big or small. Whether that means pitching your business on a New York City stage or successfully getting an IV. It's important to celebrate the wins and forgive yourself for the losses. Armed with the feeling that I would be OK, no matter the outcome, I decided to move ahead with the Springboard program and finish up strong.

SPARK

When have you let courage take over? Think about two times when you were fearless. What was the outcome?

Being Prepared Helps You Become Courageous

By now you know that being courageous means you understand the potential downsides of taking action in the presence of fear, but you act anyway. You know that courage means taking a calculated risk and moving forward, despite the anxiety you may feel. That's exactly what I did when I made the decision to finish the Springboard program.

But when it comes to courage, a key to enhancing your motivation is to be prepared. The more prepared you are, the sharper your motivation becomes and, ultimately, the more courageous you will be.

My mission was to be as prepared as possible to get up on that Springboard stage and nail my 30Seconds pitch. I worked intently with my Springboard mentors and coaches. I tried different approaches to capturing the essence of my business yet leaving them wanting to know more. I drafted pitch deck after pitch deck, and PowerPoint became my friend. My team and I created handouts and branded promotional items (swag) to give away to attendees. I rehearsed my speech in front of anyone who would listen — even if it was only the mirror. I got myself as ready as I could, until all that was left was getting there and delivering my pitch successfully.

Again, I found that support was a lifeline. I enlisted a friend/colleague to go with me to New York City. Because one of my debilitating symptoms was dysphagia, or trouble swallowing, eating food with texture was a challenge. My friend helped ensure I got enough nutrition by finding soups and shakes that I could tolerate.

While I stayed at our hotel practicing my pitch, she found a creamy butternut squash soup at a nearby Manhattan restaurant. That soup ended up fueling me the entire trip. In fact, when my friend went back for more the next day, only to learn it had been a special and not on the menu that day, she explained the situation and they made another batch, just for me. That little thing — having the right food to eat — made a big difference.

On Demo Day — powered by butternut squash soup, speech memorized, PowerPoint perfected, handouts and swag ready to go — all that was left to decide was wardrobe. What could I wear to project confidence and strength? I had brought a few choices with me — black, blue, green, red — unsure of what my mood and symptoms would be that day.

Feeling particularly bold (maybe it was the special soup), I decided on a red dress with black leather trim, paired with black leather boots. The outfit made me feel edgy and strong. To me it said, "I'm healthy. I'm ready. I've got this." I believed the look projected the assuredness — and the courage — I wanted everyone to see. All that really matters is how your clothing makes you feel. If you believe in the feeling your clothing gives you, chances are very good that others will, too.

You know that expression, "Luck is where preparation meets opportunity"? Yeah, that was me. I had prepared, down to the last detail, and I was about to make my own luck. I stepped into the Springboard Demo Day space with courage as my guide. I set up my booth, talked to fellow founders, huddled with mentors. Then it was time to pitch.

My palms were sweating, and the belly butterflies were fluttering. Those worries returned — would I misspeak, black out, drop dead? What if I failed? I took a deep breath, then another. I decided those thoughts didn't matter. I had faced so much fire to get to this moment. I had to get out of my own way, to be in the present moment — which was the only one that did matter. With a successful pitch as my why, I felt motivation overtake fear, and courage was in charge.

SPARK

When did you allow fear to hold you back? Think about a time you could have done something but were too afraid. How could you have overcome the fear?

I want to tell you my pitch came out exactly as I'd rehearsed it, but that would not be accurate. The pitch came out better than I'd rehearsed it. That's because with an audience that was interested in what I had to say, the pitch came alive. It became a living, breathing thing that responded to the vibe in the room — and to my own interpretation of what I was hearing myself say and how the audience was responding to it. I saw people nodding in understanding, jotting down notes, taking pictures of my PowerPoint slides. This fed my courage, and any remaining tension was replaced by excitement.

Talking afterward at my Demo Day booth with interested attendees, I was humbled and gratified by their feedback and the opportunities that may come from it. I had experienced the best-case scenario: I was motivated; I was courageous; I had succeeded.

The Virtuous Loop of Becoming Courageous

To become the fire, you need to be courageous. People with courage advance toward a goal despite their fear. By making both big and little things happen despite being afraid, you exercise your courage muscle, strengthening it. The more motivated you are, and the more you do what you fear, the more courageous you become — taking the risks needed to accomplish your goals and fulfill your dreams. The greater your courage, the greater your success.

This pattern played out for me again and again. My motivation helped me overcome my fear and fight my fires, which strengthened my courage muscle. The more courageous I became, the more success I achieved.

Let's break down that formula with what was going on for me when I was participating in the Springboard program.

Being courageous requires you to respect fear, enabling it to enhance your motivation. I listened to my fear and acknowledged my body's manifestations, but I didn't allow it to paralyze me. Instead, I used fear to fuel my motivation and help me prepare for success.

Being motivated leads you to discover your why and ignite your courage. My motivation to finish the Springboard program and graduate with the rest of my cohort became my why. That motivation enabled courage to take over so I could move forward.

The more courageous you are, the more success you can achieve. Because my motivation to achieve the thing was greater than the fear I felt of not achieving the thing, courage helped me deliver a successful pitch. The greater my courage, the greater my success.

This basic formula applies no matter where you are in your journey to become the fire. Use it when you need motivation, want to exercise your courage muscle, or seek to become fearless. What will happen when the courageous you is in charge? No doubt, you will make life better!

FLAME • Desirée Rogers

First Jobs: Preschool assistant, cosmetics counter representative
Education: BA (political science and government), Wellesley College; MBA, Harvard Business School
Personal Life: Divorced, mother of one
Board/Civic Roles: Board member, Inspired Entertainment; board member, MDC Partners; board member, World Business Chicago
Key Takeaway: "Don't be afraid. Go for what is in your gut."

It takes enormous courage to be the *first* or the *only* at anything. And being the first or the only is very often how Desirée Glapion Rogers's life has played out. Desirée didn't plan on being a trailblazer, and being one didn't always come easily. But her courage led the way. In fact, *fearless* is one of the first words she uses to describe herself.

As the first African American woman to run the Illinois State Lottery, the first African American woman to become president of a major gas utility, the first African American woman to serve as social secretary for the president of the United States, and the first non-family-member CEO of Johnson Publishing, Desirée has been shattering glass ceilings her entire career. "I think it's important that I try to pave the way for the next generation so they will not have to face some of the obstacles I have endured," she says.

As a child, Desirée always wanted to be "in charge." Growing up in New Orleans as the oldest of two children and as the descendant of a Creole voodoo priestess, Desirée was a natural-born leader who enjoyed "living life at my own direction." She loved to help her mother and grandmother at the daycare centers they owned in the city. Over more than forty years, three generations of families brought their children to Glapion's Academy.

It was by working at those centers that Desirée learned important entrepreneurial leadership lessons. "As a young person, I knew it wasn't so bad to be the boss," she says with a laugh. As her mother's assistant, Desirée led the kids in play, crafts, and chores. "I always gravitated toward encouraging others to do good work. I learned that the customer is always right. Even if they're wrong, they're right."

Her father was an educator and coach who rose to leadership positions in nonprofit organizations and on the city council. Desirée's parents and grandmother modeled the importance of hard work and relationship building. She describes her childhood as "disciplined but free" and attributes her strength and courage to having strong female role models. Her grandmother, with just an eighth-grade education, worked as a domestic before starting the daycare centers with Desirée's mother. "She had a strong entrepreneurial spirit. They taught me that nothing was impossible."

After graduating from high school, Desirée followed in the footsteps of cousins who had gone to school on the East Coast. Though her priority was always school, she worked part-time while in college at the Bloomingdale's cosmetics counter — foreshadowing the business she would run later in her career.

After graduating from Wellesley, Desirée worked in entry-level positions for Xerox and New England Telephone before deciding to get her MBA. After graduating from Harvard Business School, Desirée moved to Chicago to work for AT&T. After a couple of years with the corporate giant, she shifted gears to a more entrepreneurial experience, working as an executive for restaurateur and real estate developer Larry Levy. Reflecting on the difference between her corporate and entrepreneurial jobs, she notes that it all depends on who's at the top. "All companies are different, depending on the leader. Make sure you have a good relationship with whoever is in charge," she advises.

Desirée learned that she did not "have the patience for a start-up" after she launched a consulting business and shut it down in less than a year, right around the time she gave birth to her daughter, Victoria. By the time Victoria was a year old, Desirée had moved on to run the Illinois State Lottery. At just thirty-one years old, as the first African American woman to hold the position, having courage was key. "I carried myself with confidence," she says. "I surrounded myself with colleagues who knew more than I did. I was not afraid to reveal what I didn't know or to ask for help."

Over six years, Desirée built a team of three hundred employees at this "company within the government." She and her team "had a ball thinking about how to increase revenue." After growing the lottery's annual sales to $1.6 billion, Desirée decided it was time for her to move on to the next challenge. "I am curious and always want to learn something new," she explains.

Stepping into the role of vice president for a gas company, Peoples Energy, Desirée learned the ropes of a new industry despite not having an engineering degree. "I would ride around with employees working in homes to understand their jobs. I developed relationships with community leaders, who helped me understand the needs of many of our customers, including the Reverend Jesse Jackson."

After six years, Desirée was named president of Peoples Gas and North Shore Gas. She was the first African American woman, and the youngest person, to hold that position. "Don't be afraid," she says.

"Go for what is in your gut." Desirée oversaw a $463 million budget, two thousand union and nonunion employees, customer service, engineering, and a six-thousand-mile underground system. After Peoples Energy was acquired by a Wisconsin-based electric company, Desirée stayed on briefly. Then, intrigued by fresh opportunities, she was lured to a new role by Allstate Financial.

At Allstate, she was tapped to lead a new division of the company — the Allstate Social Network — that would focus on e-business and leveraging social media to engage with the company's consumers online. But after she spent a year developing the concept and leading a community of talent, vendors, and third-party alliances to build and launch the strategy, President Barack Obama came calling, and as Desirée explains, "You don't say no to the president!"

As the first African American woman to serve as social secretary for the president of the United States, Desirée was "nervous but excited" about taking on what would be her most prominent role yet. Tasked with "helping to implement the hope and the dreams" that the Obamas represented, Desirée worked to breathe new life and vibrancy into the White House — showcasing the range of American diversity while fostering inclusion and education.

As a special assistant and trusted adviser to the president, Desirée repositioned the White House as "the People's House," planning hundreds of events demonstrating its fresh vision and culture (such as hosting a performance by the actors of *Hamilton*) and partnering with more than two hundred cultural and community organizations.

The "gate-crasher" incident that led to her resignation happened during the Obamas' first state dinner. At the event honoring the prime minister of India, a Virginia-based married couple who were trying to become reality TV stars, along with another man, were able to make their way past multiple layers of security and into the party, even though they were not on the guest list.

After a lot of political finger-pointing and trying to determine who was to blame, the Secret Service took responsibility. But as social secretary, Desirée also fell on the sword. "It's politics. Someone had to leave, and it was certainly not going to be the Secret Service. I would have preferred a different exit. But you realize that life is full of twists and turns."

Desirée didn't let this incident define the entire experience. "Opportunities to create change can be the most rewarding. I was part of the original team that had the honor of working for the first African American president and first lady. It was so special to serve my country. I will always remember the White House fondly."

Back in Chicago, Desirée became the first non-family-member CEO of the iconic seventy-year-old Johnson Publishing Company. Ironically, her grandfather had told her as a child that she should be featured in the pages of *Ebony* magazine someday. Who knew that she would come to oversee the renowned *Ebony*, as well as *Jet* magazine, the Johnson Archives, and Fashion Fair Cosmetics, the world's largest Black-owned prestige cosmetics company? "Seek opportunity that speaks not only to your intellect, but also to your heart," Desirée advises.

The business was struggling financially, so Desirée repositioned it for enterprise growth and investment. Under her leadership, the company relaunched its websites, growing its audience, digital footprint, and client base. "It led me to love working in the African American and ethnic markets," she explains. "I was able to take the lessons I had learned up until that point and direct them to creating good in my own community."

To raise capital, Desirée helped with the difficult decision of selling the company's iconic downtown headquarters — the only Chicago high-rise to be designed by an African American — and its media assets. Desirée then turned her attention to the company's cosmetics business. "Through my work at Fashion Fair, I saw how important something as simple as the right foundation and lipstick could change the confidence of a woman. And we all know how important confidence is for women." But when the founder's daughter, Linda Johnson Rice, opted to run Fashion Fair, Desirée decided it was time to move on.

Desirée had discovered how much she liked the beauty industry, and especially the ethnic cosmetics space, so she decided to put on her entrepreneur hat again and pursue buying an ethnic cosmetics company. "There's always risk. You've got to take a chance. When you are afraid, there's no way you can be open."

Over the course of two years, she looked at thirty different companies. She finally set her sights on Black Opal Beauty, a twenty-five-year-old global company producing quality cosmetics for women of color. "I thought it was a great opportunity to develop and market great products for darker skin tones around the world."

Around the same time, Fashion Fair went into bankruptcy. That's when Desirée and her business partner, Cheryl Mayberry McKissack, acquired the iconic firm at auction — just two months after buying Black Opal. Now, as CEO of Black Opal Beauty and Fashion Fair Cosmetics, Desirée is focused on bringing these beauty brands to a broader market.

Desirée's definition of success is "happiness and the ability to change the world," and she's still courageously hard at work on it — one tube of lipstick at a time. "We're making Black Opal one of the beauty choices for women of color worldwide, while creating opportunities for people of color to grow their own businesses through strategic partnerships. If a little lipstick makes you happy, grab it."

Desirée maintained her courage even after hearing those three words that everyone dreads: "You have cancer." At just forty-one years old, despite maintaining a healthy lifestyle, Desirée was diagnosed with breast cancer. As with everything she does in her life, she fearlessly battled back. "I gave it everything I had. I connected with my mother and daughter on a more profound level. I noticed every little act of kindness."

Desirée decided to live each day with joy, and the disease helped her align her priorities. She not only survived but emerged even stronger. "With all the opportunities you have to say yes, also learn to say no. [Say no] when the opportunity will sacrifice your well-being or it doesn't fulfill you or it doesn't feel right. We're all so busy trying to get to the next thing. Slow down and listen to what your mind is trying to tell you. Love yourself first."

Desirée reminds women that although we all have different paths, our opportunities are unlimited if we have the courage to embrace them. "You never know where your next opportunity will come from. Keep your eyes open and always do your best work. The reason we are stopped from being great is that we worry. We think we're going to fail. We will fail, but we must keep going. Go for it, give it a try, take charge, get it done. Push forward."

BLAZE

I am motivated to make things happen.

I listen to my fear, but I am not led by it.

Being prepared helps me be courageous.

When courage is in charge, I am fearless.

The more I do what I fear, the more courageous I become.

The more courageous I am, the more success I achieve.

5

Be Friends with Failure

To become the fire, you need to have failed. To fail is human. It is by failing that we grow the skill of *resilience*, spark our curiosity, and become lifelong learners. By being friends with failure, you will learn life's most important lessons, each one teaching you something you need to know and leading you closer to success.

Failing in order to succeed? Hmm. It seems so counterintuitive, right? But it turns out that failure is one of life's greatest teachers. It is in the trying, the failing, and the trying again that we learn the lessons we need to achieve great success.

That's because failure leads to success in everyday moments, by everyday people, doing everyday things.

Children learn to walk by standing up, falling, getting up, taking a step, falling, getting up, taking another step — trying again and again until they're walking across the room.

Teenagers learn to drive by stepping on the gas, slamming on the brakes, giving less gas, easing back on the brakes — trying again and again until they've mastered the pedal pressure.

Parents learn to calm babies by rocking them, feeding them, changing them, burping them, singing to them, reading to them — trying again and again until their babies are soothed.

Employees learn to advance by pitching a client, losing a client, taking ownership, solving problems, gaining a client — trying again and again until they become indispensable.

Entrepreneurs learn to build companies by seeing opportunity, testing concepts, iterating ideas, pivoting business models — trying again and again until their start-ups are viable.

Although failing looks different from person to person, people who are friends with failure are united in the knowledge that they learn by trying. They know it's OK to fail because their resilience will enable them not only to bounce back from the failure but also to learn from the failure — bringing them that much closer to success.

Yet fear of failure often holds us back from living the lives we dream of. Maybe we were bullied or criticized as kids, which makes us reluctant to try something we're unsure we can do. Maybe we've experienced embarrassment or humiliation, which makes us leery of putting ourselves out there again. We may believe that if we can't pull something off flawlessly, we shouldn't do it at all. It's almost as if we believe we must be perfect, which couldn't be further from the truth.

But what is failure, anyway? Just as success means different things to different people, failure also has different definitions, depending on who you ask. That's because what failure means depends on how you define success.

Sometimes, success is clearly defined — it's black or white, with no shades of gray. Remember my baseball story in chapter 3? Success was black or white: catching the ball would mean success, while dropping it would mean failure. Because my success helped the team, I'm grateful to have succeeded. But in so many other situations, success is not as clearly defined.

The good news is that those shades of gray allow you to define success for yourself. For example, do you have to get an A on your term paper, or is a B also considered a success? Do you have to run a marathon, or is running a half-marathon or even a 5K good enough? Does your start-up have to go public or get acquired by a major corporation, or is providing value to your customers a winning metric? Do you have to get a job in the C-suite, or does serving in middle management suit you just fine?

If you define success as perfection, or believe it needs to be black or white, you may find yourself constantly frustrated or falling short. That's why, when defining success, shades of gray may be OK.

When speaking of perfection, I think of my dear father, the perfectionist. As a young teen, he arrived in the United States from war-torn Europe with his parents and two younger brothers. My grandfather had been a talented builder who worked on the railroad and, along with my grandmother, hunted wild game to put food on the table. During World War II, part of my grandfather's job was to rebuild sections of the railroad that had been destroyed by bombs. Watching his dad at work, my father became fascinated by the precision of the tracks, the locomotives, and all things rail related.

Given a love for the railroad that stemmed from his childhood, it's easy to understand why my dad specialized in transportation architecture. Because of his expertise, he was sent all over the world — including places like San Juan and Beirut, where we lived when I was young — to help cities improve their transportation systems.

His drive for perfection was always there, though, and because he was a perfectionist, things sometimes failed to get done. My dad may have felt that if something couldn't be done perfectly, it was better to not do it at all. To him, success was often black or white, with no shades of gray.

I'll never forget the bookcase renovation project, for example. In our living room, there were built-in bookcases with glass doors. The bookcases needed to be painted, so the glass doors were removed. After the bookcases were painted, my dad wanted to find the perfect hinges before he would reinstall the doors. To him, success meant getting that precise detail exactly right. While he looked for the ideal hinges, those doors sat in front of the bookcases, precariously propped against them. Many months went by, and other projects took his attention. The doors seemed destined to remain unattached forever — which, for a talented architect, would be a definite "fail."

For *mi madre*, however, success was not black or white. Frustrated by the doors sitting there day after day — certain that someone would get hurt or that the doors would stay that way permanently if she didn't act — *mi madre* came up with a plan to turn the failure into a success. While my father was away, she enlisted the help of a handy family friend. Within a few hours, hinges had been purchased and the doors had been hung. When my father returned, no one said anything about the fact that the doors were now securely attached to the bookcases.

The hinges may not have been perfect, but the project was successfully completed. *Mi madre* was happy, and who knows, maybe my dad was relieved that one worry was off his plate. Everyone moved on to something else because the mission had been accomplished. In that situation, as in so many others, done was better than perfect.

I realized early on that perfection can be the enemy of accomplishment. So instead of waiting until everything is just right, when I get to a place I feel is good enough, I go with it — iterating and course correcting later as needed.

Life is too short to obsess about perfection. If you wait too long, opportunities will pass you by. Whether in your personal or professional life, it helps to reframe your thinking about failure — to make good enough the new perfect.

Whether success is black or white or a shade of gray, each of us has experienced failure. But all the times you have failed — whether at work or school, with your family or partner, or in terms of what society expects of you — are times you have learned, adapted, and grown. So there's no need to fear failure. It's how we respond to failure that matters. By embracing failure as an ally, you can rise above the majority of people who let setbacks bog them down.

The key is resilience. The ability to bounce back from mistakes, stress, and fire is critical along your journey to success. Prepare to flex in response to changes, stay agile, and learn to pivot as you navigate your way to success.

Failure means you tried something that didn't happen to work. It's when you decide to learn from what didn't work, to bounce back and grow from the experience instead of retracting, that you become friends with failure. And when you embrace failure as a lesson to learn from, rather than a mistake to run from, you are more likely to succeed.

In this chapter, I will show you why resilience is key to becoming friends with failure, then help you become even more resilient so you can use your setbacks as a launching pad for greater success.

Resilience Is Key to Becoming Friends with Failure

To be friends with failure, you need resilience, which means two things: (1) having mental fortitude when you make a mistake or fail, and (2) using your mistakes and failures as opportunities for learning and growth. Being resilient enables you not only to endure and bounce back from hardships and setbacks but also to use them as teachers and course correctors along your journey.

We strengthen our resilience by realizing that, as humans, we are not perfect, by understanding that we will make mistakes, and by acknowledging that we will fail. Once we accept imperfection, mistakes, and failure as part of life, we can use those experiences as the lessons they are, allowing them to help us improve and grow.

Most of us know what setbacks feel like. And because the feeling of failure is so discouraging, we may try to avoid it at all costs, which only serves to hold us back from greater success. But we can't let the fear of failing stop us from trying. That's why we need to flip the script about what failure means. By reframing failure as an opportunity to adapt, grow, and try again, you fuel your curiosity and drive to be a lifelong learner. By pushing past disappointment and instead seeing each failure as a potential iteration along your journey, you will come to see that failure can ultimately lead to success.

My ability to be friends with failure began early on. The transition from small Catholic grade school to big public high school was as bumpy as it sounds. Like Dorothy in *The Wizard of Oz*, I found myself going from black-and-white Kansas to Technicolor Oz: the sights, sounds, and smells of the high school created an almost overwhelming visceral experience. As a dazed freshman wandering the expansive yet crowded hallways, I struggled to adapt and find my way. One thing I thought might help me fit in, feel more at home, and make friends was athletics.

The problem was, I was not in Kansas anymore. Unlike the no-cut sports in my parochial grade school, not everyone got to play on the teams at my ultracompetitive high school. With thousands of kids from diverse backgrounds, my high school boasted athletic programs that were often ranked among the best in the state, providing fertile training grounds for student athletes with college, Olympics, and even professional sports aspirations.

Pint-size kids like me rarely made it past the first level of try-outs. But I didn't know that until I went through it. Even worse, I learned that the baseball team was for boys only — girls had to play softball. I had never played softball before, and the awkward difference in the size of the ball stymied me. I found the ball sometimes hitting the edge of my mitt instead of the sweet spot I was used to.

Regardless, I gave the tryouts my best effort. When I learned I had not made the team, I felt embarrassed and dejected. I had failed. After a brief bout of self-pity, I decided to lift my head and look around. Were there any teams that did not require an embarrassing tryout? Were there any sports in which vertically challenged kids like me could blend in, rather than stick out like a sore thumb?

It turned out that there were. Even though I had never heard of cross-country, I eventually found myself on that team. Although running three miles outside, across all kinds of terrain, in all kinds of Chicago weather, as fast as I could, was challenging (and kind of sucked), I was glad to be part of a team again.

Being on the cross-country team led me to also join the track-and-field team. Although running shorter distances on an oval track, faster than I had ever run before, was also a challenge (but sucked less), I looked forward to practices and track meets. The competition I enjoyed most was against myself — to improve my own personal best race scores.

One unexpected bonus of my participation was becoming a "go-to" person for the coach. Because I was willing to try my hand (or feet) at competing in track-and-field events that others would shy away from, I was called upon to participate in such novelties as the long jump. (Yes, I was getting comfortable with being uncomfortable.)

Long jump was a strenuous event that required you to run

really fast until you hit a marker on the track, then hurtle your body as far as possible into a pit of sand, where someone would measure how far you had jumped. With coaches, teammates, opponents, and spectators watching, the pressure was intense, so I could see why it wasn't a very popular event. But because so few team members wanted to do it, there I was, a pint-size long jumper.

I'm not saying I was good at it; I experienced my fair share of mistakes in the form of "scratches" and awkward sandpit landings. But I'm proud that I did it, and I count those track team experiences not as a failure but as a success. I pivoted to something new. I pushed myself. I got stronger, physically and emotionally. I *tried*.

SPARK

When have you failed? Think about two times you hit a big bump in the road. What did you learn from those experiences? Think of how failing may have helped you along your path.

I realized that failure is just a way to keep learning and growing. Sometimes, those bumps in the road are detours that simply reroute your eventual return to the same path. Or those bumps can be life's way of redirecting you to something else you should try, taking you to a new path altogether, taking you to someplace where you may succeed. Failure is often a necessary stepping-stone to take — even if it's embarrassing or painful — as you make your way toward success.

Resilience Means Staying Agile and Learning to Pivot

Life provides constant reminders that being agile in response to challenges can make the difference between sadness and happiness, failure and success. It's your mindset, the lens through which you view the world, that sets the tone. Because when it comes down to it, how you react to life's chaos is really all you can control.

Resilience means staying agile as you deal with that chaos and learning to pivot as fire comes your way. And being resilient has served me well on my journey, most recently with 30Seconds.

You know how, when you work really hard at something, you hope it will be a huge success? Then, when it doesn't happen right away, you're disappointed, especially when you look at some people who seem to have it all and appear to be "overnight success" stories.

But behind every successful person is failure. Seriously.

There's no such thing as overnight success, and no one truly has it all. What appears to be quick success or huge success is most often preceded by years of hard work, trial and error, and iteration by people with a passion. People who just wouldn't give up. People who pivoted until they found their way.

When I started 30Second Mom, I had a goal to build an inspiring destination that would empower a positive community of moms to make life better, in the same amount of time it takes to watch an ad on TV. Using that simple metric, my start-up succeeded quickly.

But I also had a vision for what the company could be with outside investment and at scale. Think "TikTok for moms" — long before TikTok was even a thing — and you'll get a sense of my vision. The projections were impressive, and they attracted early interest from the business community.

But challenges came in the form of single motherhood, health battles, changes in the business marketplace, and uncomfortable encounters with potential business partners and investors. For example, one investor told me that, despite my track record, he would never invest in a female founder; another investor called me "baby"; and yet another invited me out for drinks after my pitch. Seriously? No, thanks.

Sometimes life has a way of shining a light on not only which path to choose but also which path not to choose. I was invited to speak at a conference for top brand marketers that was being held in a downtown Chicago hotel. Looking to showcase fresh ideas for reaching consumers on their mobile devices, the conference organizers offered me the opportunity to share 30Second Mom with what could be many potential business partners.

Backstage, I gathered my thoughts, trying to not be over-whelmed by the fact that some in the audience about to listen to me speak had the power to take 30Second Mom to the next level. Onstage, I looked out over the sea of people who may be able to alter the trajectory of my company. I reminded myself that, de-spite my detailed PowerPoint, all I really had to do was tell them about my business in simple terms. And so, I did.

Afterward, several people came up to talk to me — including one guy who told me his name and that he was a brand manager who lived on the West Coast. I'll just call him *the creep*. He was in Chicago for the week, attending this conference and having other meetings. The creep said he knew 30Second Mom was "going to be a unicorn," meaning a start-up worth at least a billion dollars. Then he said he'd look for me at the cocktail reception so we could chat.

Later, at the cocktail reception, which was intended for net-working, I was conversing with the vice president of a big ad agency when the creep appeared at my side. Draping his arm over my shoulder, he said, "You were so great up there. We need to talk."

The agency vice president excused himself, and there I was, alone with the creep. Slipping out from under his arm, I thanked him for the feedback. That was just the opening he needed to tell me all about himself and how, by working together, we could do great things. To escape, I told him I needed to find someone I had to talk to before dinner, and the creep made me promise to sit with him at dinner so we could continue our conversation.

At dinner, I scanned the grand ballroom for an open chair between two women. It didn't matter who they were; I just didn't want to deal with the creep. The plan worked, and my dinner companions were lovely. After dinner, as people again broke out into pairs or groups for networking, the creep found me talking to my dinner companions.

That's when he grabbed my hand. "This is for you, to join me upstairs so we can talk. The room number is on the jacket," he said. I looked at what he had placed in my hand, and when I saw it was a keycard for a room in the hotel, I dropped it as if it had burned me. "No, thank you," I said.

Trying not to panic, I looked at the two women I was with. While the creep bent down to pick up the key, I motioned to them that this was not going well, and they started to pay attention to what was happening. The creep stood up, key back in hand, and smiled. "I have to go to the bathroom," he said. "Hold my phone for me until I get back." With that, he pushed his iPhone into my hand and walked toward the bathroom.

These types of situations happen to women far too often. In fact, up to 81 percent of women have experienced sexual harassment. And when we're confronted by this type of behavior, we frequently go into protective mode, retract, and therefore miss out on opportunities.

Unfortunately, the creep made me feel like I was his prey and that I needed to protect myself. It was time to get out of there, but I still had to decide what to do about his iPhone. My female allies told me to leave it on the table, and they would cover for me so I could duck out. While the coast was clear, I grabbed my coat and bag, and fled into the crisp Chicago night. Looking back on this experience, I could be both angry and sad about how it turned out: an event filled with opportunity had devolved into one filled with fear and loss.

Yet that experience (and others) showed me what the road to building a "TikTok for moms" could look like. Getting my business to that scale likely would require many more speaking engagements, many more investor pitches, many more booze-fueled networking events, many more creepy come-ons.

And what would happen if I accepted those types of business deals or investment dollars? How much stress, deflection of advances, battling to prove my worth and my company's value would it take? The path I saw was riddled with more than just potholes; they were more like manholes that were missing their covers. One misstep could mean a very dangerous fall.

In that moment, it felt like all the work I'd put into preparing for that event had resulted in a massive failure — and that it might lead to failing to create a hugely successful company. But as I reflected on what had happened, I realized so much more.

As exciting as it would be to have a unicorn-bound start-up, what it would take to get there did not appear to align with my values and priorities. First and foremost, I was Mom to three kids who needed me to be strong, healthy, and, most of all, present in their lives. They were what mattered more than anything. Everything else I did would have to take second place.

SPARK

Are you resilient? Think of two times you bounced back from mistakes or failure. Does friction, or fire, prevent you from trying? How can you flip that script?

I made peace with my situation. I chose to befriend that failure, allowing it to shine a light on which path not to choose. Resilience helped me bounce back from the disappointment I felt. The business might be different than I'd imagined, but it would work out fine. I would be agile, and the company (and I) would be OK.

Redefining Success Means Living in the Gray Space

Bootstrapping the company on my own, at my own pace, meant that success — as defined by typical business metrics — would not happen quickly. In fact, the only overnight successes were the long days and nights spent hard at work expanding the mission, platform, and reach to make a bigger impact.

I had to pivot and adjust my expectations for the business — and for myself. I had to give both of us the patience and grace we deserved. Success would not be black or white. I had to learn to live in the gray space. I had to redefine what success meant for 30Second Mom.

I decided that success meant growing the company at the pace my kids, my health, and my finances would allow. It meant serving our community with information and inspiration and connection that would make members' lives better. It meant trying new things, iterating, learning from mistakes, then trying again.

When I reached the point where I was ready to grow the business beyond 30Second Mom into 30Seconds.com, it required replacing the original technology platform. The new, custom-made 30Seconds tech platform would be built to scale, allowing us to host more and more contributors, users, and clients as we expanded our lifestyle content channel offerings.

To help finance the relaunch, I was ready to take on outside capital — but it had to be the right investor. I wanted someone who aligned with and believed in our mission. Most importantly, I wanted someone I could trust.

Mary Dillon had always been a role model for me. As the fourth of six children from a working-class family, Mary is a self-made success story. She put herself through school, then rose through the executive ranks at Quaker, PepsiCo, and McDonald's, eventually landing the CEO job at UScellular. Then, as CEO of Ulta Beauty, she transformed the business and more than tripled the company's market capitalization — all while building an inclusive culture of respect, growth, and diversity. As the mother of four children herself, Mary's grit, drive, and visionary leadership served as constant inspiration to me along my journey.

When I told Mary about my vision for 30Seconds, she seemed impressed and intrigued enough to say yes when I asked her if she would invest in the business. With her support as an angel investor, I moved forward with the rebuilding and relaunching and rebranding of 30Seconds.com.

Over time, it was clear the relaunched site was making an impact. More and more users told us that something we published really resonated with them, that it made their life better in some way. We worked even harder, and we tried more new things. We launched additional content channels: Food, Health, Dad, Pregnancy, Beauty, Travel. We continued to iterate because we saw the effect we were having. And still, we wondered if all that hard work and all those overnights would result in a breakthrough.

Then more people noticed what we were doing. We started to get feedback not only from readers but also from amazing organizations that wanted to partner with or promote our brand. The business community was paying attention, and things started to happen that helped propel our efforts. For example, we were invited to become featured publishers with top news aggregator sites like Google News and Flipboard. That meant those companies believed we were producing high-quality content, and they wanted to share it with their users.

As we doubled down on our commitment and effort, we started hitting even more significant milestones, hosting millions of unique users every month. Our growth was nearly all organic, meaning we spent next to nothing on paid marketing, customer acquisition, and building an audience. We grew our community member by member, article by article, recipe by recipe, tip by tip, interaction by interaction, comment by comment, email by email, try by try.

We grew because we viewed each failure as a lesson, teaching us what *not* to do. We prioritized analytics, followed the data, and grew by doing more of what worked and less of what didn't.

By viewing success not as black or white (such as unicorn or bust) but as something to be found in the gray space, I was able to redefine what success meant for 30Seconds and for me as its founder. Although I failed to realize my vision of a "TikTok for moms," I succeeded at not aligning myself with investors or partners who harassed me. I succeeded at creating a mission-driven, profitable business that was built on my own timetable, on my own dime, and was backed by someone I admired. I succeeded at growing a platform that truly makes life better for the community. This is something I was — and am — very proud of. And that equals success in any color.

SPARK

When have you pivoted in a new direction? Think of a situation in which you failed, then tried again in a different way. What does success mean to you? Come up with your own definition of success.

The Virtuous Loop of Becoming Friends with Failure

To become the fire, you first need to fail. By failing, you grow your resilience, ignite your curiosity to find another way, learning and course correcting along the path to success. With resilience, you can be agile in response to life's fires and pivot in new directions. When you redefine success so it's not always black or white, and reframe failure as an opportunity to learn and grow, each lesson teaches you something you need to know — even if it's in the gray space — leading you closer to success.

This pattern played out for me again and again. Resilience enabled me to bounce back from bumps and detours on my path. It helped me learn from each mistake, iterating as I went along. Resilience helped me stay agile and pivot as needed, flexing as each situation required. The more I became friends with failure, learning to live in the gray space, the more success I achieved.

Let's break down that formula with what was going on for me when I was in the early stages of building 30Seconds.

Being friends with failure means seeing failure as a lesson, strengthening your resilience. Each time I failed, I looked at it as an opportunity to learn and grow. I thought of failure as an iterative process, helping me understand what wasn't working and be open to new ways of thinking and doing.

Resilience enables you to be agile and pivot in new directions. Being resilient allowed me to flex as needed and to reframe my thinking. By pivoting in new directions when I hit a bump in the road, I created new pathways and definitions of success I didn't initially see.

The more you become friends with failure, the more success you achieve. Viewing failure as a lesson meant success wouldn't be black or white. I created new definitions of success in the gray space. The more I learned from what wasn't working, and did more of what *was* working, the more success I achieved.

This basic formula applies no matter where you are in your journey to become the fire. Use it when you've made a mistake, when something doesn't go your way, when you're trying to define success, or when you feel that you've failed. Remember that the more resilient you are, the more agile you'll become, and the more you'll learn and grow!

FLAME • Paula Boggs

First Jobs: Guitar teacher, candy striper in a psychiatric hospital
Education: BA (international studies), Johns Hopkins University; JD, University of California, Berkeley
Personal Life: Married, parent of one
Board/Civic Roles: Board member, Avid; board member, Seattle Symphony Orchestra; governor, Pacific Northwest Chapter, Recording Academy
Key Takeaway: "We all fail. What separates successful people is how we respond to that failure."

Paula Boggs was just twenty-one years old the first time she jumped out of a perfectly good airplane. If you had told her even a few months before that she'd be leaping from a military C-130 the summer between her junior and senior years of college, she would have laughed. "I think you have me confused with someone who isn't afraid of heights," she told US Army captain Larry Satterwhite, her ROTC military science professor, with her usual broad grin.

That's when Captain Satterwhite grabbed the smiling army cadet by her shoulders and uttered the words that helped shape who Paula would become: "You are not serious. You're about to enter this man's army, and you are not ready. You need an edge. You need to go to Airborne School."

Paula stopped smiling. She looked at Captain Satterwhite as if he had told her she was about to go to Mars, but he continued: "All you have to remember is that no matter how awful they make you feel — and they will — it's all designed so when they say 'Jump,' you'll jump — and you'll land safely."

Paula reluctantly accepted the opportunity to earn her wings as an elite Army Airborne paratrooper. That life-changing experience taught her lessons in courage, resilience, and overcoming failure that serve her to this day. "Fear is human. Fear is rational," Paula says. "The trick of it is how to manage one's fears in order to achieve a successful outcome."

Joining the program at a time when Airborne School had just opened to women is only one of the many challenges Paula embraced on her way to achieving huge success in the corporate world. "There was a lot of hostility toward women" in Airborne School, she says. And despite Captain Satterwhite's reassurances repeating like a mantra in her mind, Paula injured herself on her first jump — a failure that nearly led to her being removed from the elite military program. Not to be deterred, she pretended she wasn't hurt so she could continue the program, and resilience enabled her to bounce back. "I had four more qualifying jumps to do in four days, and I did it — I earned my wings!"

"Becoming Airborne" became a metaphor for overcoming the failures, and fires, that would follow. "When I failed the bar exam, I said, 'I can do this. I am Airborne.' As a federal prosecutor, I would say, 'I can do this. I am Airborne.'"

Paula wasn't the only one in her family to blaze a new trail. Her great-grandmother was the first in her family to be born free in the United States, and the lessons Paula learned from her set the stage for Paula's life. "She was a woman of grit and determination, and she was an inspiration to me."

Paula's father, Nathaniel Boggs Jr., earned Howard University's first PhD in zoology when Paula was four years old. The family then moved to Chesterfield, Virginia, where Paula's father worked as a science professor and eventually a dean at Virginia State, a historically Black college, and later at Florida A&M. The oldest of four children, Paula got used to standing out and being the *first*, or the *only*, no matter where she was. "We were Roman Catholic, and I was the only Black girl in a class of fifty students in the only integrated school."

Paula learned to navigate her multicultural world, excelling within the diversity of people, religions, views, and cultures she was exposed to. She credits her mother, Janice Barber, a social worker, teacher, and principal, for showing her what courage looks like and for teaching her and her siblings to be resilient in the face of challenges. Paula points to her early role models — her parents and grandparents — as crucial to her confidence. "I had the good fortune of adults infusing me with 'You can do this.' That was particularly important while living in the segregated South, where people were telling you 'You're not good enough.'"

Paula had a passion for music and learned to play the piano and then the clarinet. By the time she moved on to the guitar, she was ten and her parents were wary of investing in yet another musical instrument. They struck a deal with young Paula: they would rent a guitar for her lessons but would not buy one unless she paid for half of it. "I started teaching kids in the neighborhood to play guitar for a nickel a lesson. I would take my own lesson and then go teach them to play what I'd just learned," Paula says with a laugh. "Before I knew it, I had earned twenty dollars, then told my parents I was ready to buy a forty-dollar guitar."

After Paula's parents divorced, her mother accepted a position teaching military children in Europe through the US Department of Defense. That's how, when Paula was just thirteen, she and her siblings moved with their mother to a military base in Germany. And that's when Paula learned that being resilient would be crucial to her success. "I learned not only to exist within the diversity of people, views, religions — but to excel."

By age sixteen, Paula realized that her mother would not be able to afford to send her four kids to college. As an exceptional student athlete, Paula decided to enter the Reserve Officers' Training Corps (ROTC) so she could attend Johns Hopkins University.

Fast-forward to earning her wings in Airborne, and Paula's life was forever changed as courage and becoming friends with failure became part of her identity. "People sometimes assume I am fearless because I have mastered the ability to manage my fear. But I think it's important for people to be fearful, for there to be a sense of fear, urgency, and uncertainty in life. That's what makes it interesting."

After graduating first in her ROTC class, Paula decided to delay active military duty by going to law school. Continuing her education fueled her love of learning. "Find joy in being a lifelong learner," she advises. "Be excited by something you didn't know yesterday. Be genuinely curious."

It was resilience that helped Paula during one of the darkest moments of her life: she was working at her first legal job, in the Pentagon, but had failed the bar exam — twice. "There I was, working in the Army General Counsel's office, and I had not passed the bar. Here I am, faced with the thing that would launch my career, and I can't get it done."

As part of the ROTC program, Paula had a four-year commitment to the military. Unless she passed the bar, she was concerned that the army would ship her off to a far-flung duty assignment. "It was a dark time for me. I didn't understand why I couldn't succeed."

Depressed as she was, Paula knew she had to continue showing up and giving it her best. By being resilient in the face of her fires, she connected with the person who would provide her next opportunity: Amoretta Hoeber, who oversaw the army's Strategic Defense Initiative ("Star Wars"). Through Hoeber, Paula learned that the army was being sued by the city of Cambridge, Massachusetts, regarding chemical and biological warfare. Paula wrote a compelling brief on behalf of the army, and the argument she put forth "won the day."

Paula knew this was her opportunity to get out of the situation she was in — that painful waiting to be sent away from the Pentagon and Washington, DC — and to "redeem" herself. One night, while working late at the Pentagon, she followed Hoeber into the ladies' room to make her request. "I asked Amie if I could work for her directly on her team. A week later, she rescued me by saying yes."

Though Paula passed the bar on her third try, she credits those early failures with her eventual successes. "Had I not failed the bar exam — twice — I would not have become general counsel of Starbucks." She explains: "Had I not worked for Amie, I would not have met Bill Lytton [one of her mentors]. Had I not met Bill Lytton, I would not have become a federal prosecutor. There's a direct line between failing the bar and becoming Starbucks GC."

Paula stresses that failure is part of every person's story, and we shouldn't shy away from it. "We all fail. What separates successful people is how we respond to that failure."

Those experiences taught Paula to not be afraid of making a mistake, even if at the time it feels catastrophic. "Having started my career with failure, the gift was to know you can overcome it. Recognize it and give yourself the space to not freak out when it happens, because it will happen."

For Paula, failure was a reminder to keep a smile on her face, no matter what. "Don't take yourself, or any situation, too seriously. You can always find the humor in any situation if you look hard enough."

Paula's first job as a licensed lawyer involved working in the White House as a member of the Iran-Contra Legal Task Force. As a new lawyer, she was tasked with helping prepare Vice President George H. W. Bush for his deposition. Seriously. "It was a high-pressure, 24-7 situation that people were reading about in the papers. I think about that now, and I shudder when I think of the opportunities given to me with very little experience. But it gave me the confidence to take risks and set the stage for everything that followed."

Paula served eight years in the army and was honorably discharged. She became an assistant US attorney in Washington State, where she prosecuted a variety of federal crimes, from fraud to illegal immigration. There were times when Paula was the only Black female federal prosecutor across ten states, and every environment she was in was male dominated. She notes that being Airborne gave her a way to disarm the men who would automatically underestimate her based on her gender.

"Men could be dismissive, either overtly or covertly," she says. "Guys would come into my office with swagger, then they would see my Airborne certificate and their body language would change. 'You're Airborne?!' they would ask. 'Yeah, I'm Airborne.' And everything would change. The vibe I would put out was that I was as good as them or better."

Paula became part of the team investigating the Tailhook sexual assault and harassment scandal through the Department of Defense in Washington, DC. She served as the first African American female partner at the law firm of Preston, Gates & Ellis (now K&L Gates). But Paula's world truly changed when she moved across the country to join the executive team at Austin-based Dell.

Her time at Dell was a turning point for Paula in many ways. While she was a senior executive there, Dell quadrupled in size. But even more impactful was how the Dell job affected her personally. "Have you ever had a secret you held so tight inside you that it made you ill? For me, it took a job offer, from Texas no less, to come out of the closet. I did not honor my authentic self for the first fourteen years of my career. I was a closeted gay person. It made a difference in how I moved through the world. My decision to come out was motivated by self-interest."

As the first openly gay executive and the first African American female executive at Dell, Paula was a catalyst for change. Dell instituted domestic partnership health insurance while she was there, and everyone from Michael Dell on down treated Paula and her spouse, the artist Randee Fox, as a couple from day one.

By the time she was offered the chief legal officer role at Starbucks in 2002, the closet was in Paula's rearview mirror. The new position enabled Paula and Randee to move back to Seattle as an openly gay couple. Paula led the law department for a decade, building a world-class legal team to match Starbucks's growing global footprint.

Paula's resilience was more important than ever when tragedy struck. Her sister-in-law Julie Boggs, wife of her brother Dallas, was killed in a car crash. The couple's daughter, Jada, was only two years old at the time. Paula and Randee eventually became Jada's legal guardians, though Dallas remains an active father from his home base in Oregon.

The grief over her sister-in-law's death drove Paula to pick up her guitar once again and use music as a creative outlet. She wrote songs, which led to performing at open mic nights once a month. By 2007, she had formed the Paula Boggs Band.

Paula left Starbucks in 2012 to continue following her "true north." She was appointed by President Barack Obama to the White House Council for Community Solutions, and later to the President's Committee on the Arts and Humanities. It turned out that the timing of Paula's departure from Starbucks coincided with President Obama's reelection campaign. "The campaign was inspiring, and I wanted to be a part of it."

Paula keeps her business and legal mind engaged by serving on the boards of the Seattle Symphony Orchestra and Avid Technology, a $400 million public digital media tech company. "As 'the first' anything, there is nowhere to hide, and my example will impact those who follow me. I've always taken that responsibility seriously."

Finally allowing her passion for music to take center stage, as the full-time front for the Paula Boggs Band, she's redefining success every step of the way. "In this role as an emerging artist, conventional wisdom would suggest this is a losing proposition, but that's never stopped me before." Once described as the Joan Baez of this generation, Paula says she is living authentically by growing as a musician. "Artistic journeys are my fuel. Find ways to stay in touch with your passion. Being true to yourself is incredibly important to being the whole you."

With resilience as a foundation, Paula sees her life as a series of chapters. From jumping out of planes to working in the White House, from prosecuting criminals to leading the global law team of one of the world's greatest companies — being friends with failure has been a theme throughout her story.

"And now, here I am in this chapter. It feels very vibrant and urgent. It is what it's supposed to be right now, until it's not. I don't have a crystal ball, but I trust my gut to know when it's time for the next chapter."

BLAZE

When I fail, I learn. Failure is a teacher.

I don't let mistakes or failures hold me back.

I am resilient, and I bounce back from setbacks.

I am agile, and I pivot in new directions.

Success is not black or white. It's often found in the gray space.

The more I see failure as a friend, the more success I achieve.

6

Be a Maker

To become the fire, you need to make things happen. Looking at the world through the eyes of a maker, you use the skill of *creativity* to envision ways to add to or improve upon it. Seeing possibilities, you use your imagination to picture an outcome or a solution, then move from dreaming to doing. By transforming your idea into a reality, you become a maker. The more you make happen, or the more you improve upon what already exists, the more success you'll achieve.

Growing up, many of us learned to use our imaginations to make life better. When you face fire frequently, you get creative and adaptable — and find ways to thrive. Even after childhood, when you didn't have the right tools, structure, or resources, you got good at dreaming of better times and better ways to do things. And ultimately, that's how you become a maker.

When you think of the word *maker*, you may picture a crafter, a woodworker, a metalworker, a designer, a DIYer, a hacker, a tinkerer. When I think of a maker, I see someone who uses their imagination to picture an outcome or a solution — a design, product, service, business, or charity the world needs. But a maker is someone who does more than just imagine. A maker moves from dreaming to doing. A maker actually *makes* things happen.

Coming up with a viable idea is not just about brainstorming on a whiteboard in a conference room or laboring over a vision board at a desk. To ideate, no planning sessions, flowcharts, or blueprints are necessarily needed. But ideating does require "white space" of all kinds, found in many different, often unexpected, places.

White space means giving yourself room to think, to ideate, wherever you find yourself. It's about looking at the world around you and finding creative inspiration in the everyday, often mundane or chaotic, things that surround you. No matter what form or color it takes, white space is about giving yourself a blank canvas in your mind so you can explore the possibilities.

Once you've come up with a solid idea, it takes even more to make it a reality. Having a maker mindset is key. The mindset of a maker is innovative and entrepreneurial, with an underlying core of creativity. That creativity is what fuels makers to succeed.

Makers are resilient and resourceful, and what they don't know, they figure out. They are curious problem solvers who don't fear failure. On the contrary, makers know that trial and error is part of the process of creating. They accept failure and iteration as part of the journey, and they learn from their mistakes. Makers believe that failure is a catalyst for success, so mistakes and setbacks are not only par for the course but also needed for the course. Makers are willing to take a risk and put themselves out there to create something new or better.

Makers know dreams are just that — a work in progress — until they become reality. Though makers may live with their heads in the clouds, they always keep their feet on the ground. Their roots keep them firmly planted while they reach toward the sun. Makers try. Makers learn. Makers grow.

When I think about being a maker, I remember the makers in my family. My father's parents settled their immigrant family in a small farm town in downstate Illinois. Using their woodworking skills, my grandparents started a custom cabinet shop that turned into a thriving business. Their three sons worked alongside them, and the youngest eventually took over the shop. (My dad and his middle brother both became architects.)

Growing up, I spent a lot of time downstate with my grandparents and my uncle's family, who also lived there. The cabinet shop was a magical place filled with fascinating tools and machines that could cut the perfect piece, drill the perfect hole, sand the perfect edge. The smell of fresh sawdust filled the air with possibility. One of my favorite pastimes was drawing doodles with my finger in the many sawdust-created "canvases" covering the machinery and floor. Like magnets, my fingers were drawn to any untouched patch of sawdust I could use as a white space to create.

Watching my grandfather, my uncle, and their employees work in the shop, I absorbed early lessons in becoming a maker. Seeing those master craftsmen transform pieces of wood into something both functional and beautiful took my breath away. Strolling through the showroom, which displayed sample cabinet styles and even full custom kitchens to inspire customers, made me believe in endless possibilities. There seemed to be nothing those makers could not create out of the white space that was wood.

I felt the same way watching my grandmother in her kitchen. She was always busy preparing Old World dishes that were often made from the fish or wild game that she and my grandfather had hunted on their trips out west: *sarma, burek, krumpirusa, janjetina, strudel* — recipes handed down from generation to generation that took her hours (sometimes days) to lovingly prepare.

When she wasn't cooking, you could find Grandma in her

favorite chair next to the custom wood and glass gun cabinet filled with their rifles and shotguns. Surrounded by her hunting and fishing trophies, she sat there sewing, knitting, crocheting, or embroidering; there seemed to be no needlework she couldn't expertly do. Every room was filled with her creations: embroidered pillowcases on the beds, crocheted doilies on the tables, knitted afghans on the couch.

But I think Grandma's favorite place was in her garden. From my perch high up in my favorite climbing trees in her yard, I watched Grandma grow everything from tomatoes and beans to peaches and strawberries. She canned her own pickles, sauces, jams, and jellies. She would call me down when she needed help with her harvest or with whatever was on the menu that night.

When I was at Grandma's, there wasn't much I'd eat that she hadn't caught, shot, grown, or made from scratch. And I was expected to help however I could, learning by doing. Mistakes were OK; I'd just have to keep trying until I got it right. When I was with Grandma, white space looked like flour, fabric, and fertilizer.

Mi madre's parents (*mis abuelos*) were makers, too. They owned a farm (*la finca*), high up in a remote mountain range in southwestern Puerto Rico, where they grew coffee beans, plantains, bananas, and oranges. The crops they didn't sell, they would use to feed their growing family: *pasteles, tostones, guineos, surullitos, platanos* — recipes handed down from generation to generation, many made from ingredients they harvested themselves.

When she wasn't farming or cooking, *mi abuela* was busy making clothes for people in their *pequeño pueblo* to earn extra money to feed her children. She made something out of every little thing she had.

Out in the Puerto Rican countryside, life was very different than in suburban Chicago. Instead of an alarm clock, I was awakened each morning by the colorful roosters. Every single dawn, the roosters would strut from their nests and let out their piercing cock-a-doodle-doos, which made me literally jump out of bed in the morning. Because I had no choice but to get used to it, eventually I lost the urge to clamp their little beaks shut. I even started to grow fond of them (though I didn't miss the startling rooster wake-up calls when I was back home).

On *la finca* and in the nearby *pequeño pueblo*, side-stepping past clucking chickens, stray cats, and scaly lizards, and dodging the many crawling and flying insects that were often as big as hummingbirds, was part of everyday life. *Mis abuelos* owned a tiny three-bedroom, one-bathroom house in town — one bedroom for the boys, and one for the girls. It was always *so hot*, and there was no air-conditioning.

I learned to crack open the hurricane shutters and turn on the creaky fans to at least move the humid air around. Sleeping under a mosquito net to ward off the ubiquitous mosquitoes (and many other island critters), I had to be careful to not allow any creatures access when getting in and out of bed. Too often, I woke up drenched in sweat with plenty of bugbites all over me anyway.

Rubbing the sleep and sweat from my eyes, I'd walk into town on my own to explore what the other early risers were up to. My favorite thing was to visit the local bakery (*la panadería*) and watch the bakers (the makers!) at work. At *la panadería*, I would buy a loaf of fresh-baked Puerto Rican water bread (*pan de agua*) in a paper sleeve, still warm from the oven; a block of fresh white cheese (*queso del país*); and a can of pineapple juice (*jugo de piña*). Sometimes, the owner would hand me a cup of hot island coffee with milk, too — just because. The smell of that potent *café con leche*, combined with the *pan*, *queso*, and *jugo*, was a little slice of heaven, and that meal would fuel me all day long.

In Puerto Rico, success meant making the most of what *was* there — not lamenting what *wasn't* there. With a lack of luxuries, and even without many basics, I learned to be in the moment and to use what I had to make something out of nothing.

For example, when rain showers suddenly appeared out of the clear, blue, sunny skies, I discovered that giant banana leaves made excellent on-the-go umbrellas. To beat back the heat, I learned that feathery palm fronds made easy take-with-you fans.

Often left to my own devices, I would make my own fun, creating games and toys from natural resources. I could be found chasing green geckos up tree trunks, searching for the elusive *coquí* (tiny tree frogs native to Puerto Rico) in the brush, and making maracas from coffee bean pods. I was always finding white space in which to create, no matter what shape or color the white space was. And in Puerto Rico, white space looked like crops, critters, and coffee.

Those experiences delivered important lessons in becoming a maker. But even if you weren't raised around makers, you have likely learned many of these lessons, too. That's because when life is chaotic and you don't have the right tools, structure, or resources, you get good at dreaming of better times and better ways to do things. I'll bet you have ideas about how to make life better, either for yourself or others, by creating something new or improving something that already exists. I'll bet you dream of the possibilities.

But dreaming is only the start. When becoming a maker, the key is creativity. Being creative means you observe the world around you, envision opportunities to create something, then actually *make it happen*. It means being an ideator, a big-picture thinker, who uses the imagination to picture an outcome or a solution — something that someone in the world wants or needs — then moves from dreaming to doing.

It's when you decide to take your ideas — those doodles you create in the white space of your life — and make them a reality that you become a maker. The more creative you are, the more possibilities you will see. The more possibilities you see, the more you can make happen. And the more you make happen, the more likely you are to succeed.

In this chapter, I will show you what it means to be a maker, then help you become more creative — using the white space in your own life — so you can make more things happen and achieve more success.

Creativity Is Key to Becoming a Maker

To become a maker, you have to be creative, which means two things: (1) envisioning original ideas to create something new or improve upon something that already exists, and (2) making those ideas into realities in some way, shape, or form. Being creative enables you not only to observe the world around you and see the possibilities but also to make something happen from those possibilities.

We enhance our creativity by being curious and trying to solve problems. Always learning, we strive to come up with new or better ways to do things. We iterate, knowing that trial and error is part of the process of creating, and we learn from our mistakes.

Creativity means we envision our ideas, then we try to make them realities. We fail. We learn from the failure. We try again. Rinse and repeat. Every step we take informs the next step in the journey. Creativity fuels us to innovate and drives us to become more entrepreneurial. It is the path through which we evolve. The creative process is how we grow ourselves into makers. And when we become makers, we are more likely to succeed.

Growing up around makers, I caught the maker bug early. I was always finding white space, whether for drawing, building, or writing. I used my imagination to escape the chaos around me, giving myself a blank canvas in my mind to create.

As a child who was frequently bullied for not fitting in, I dreamed of all the fancy clothes I wished I had. I would draw picture after picture of girls wearing dresses, skirts and stylish tops, and long draping coats paired with fabulous heels and handbags. I drew my doodles on any white space I could find: an old spiral notebook, the inside cover of my latest Nancy Drew novel, even the blank sides of my homework assignments. But it wasn't until high school that I took my first real art classes, finally getting access to formal creative spaces and tools.

It was in my jewelry design class that I really *felt* like a maker. The space looked like a cross between an artist's studio and an auto-body shop with workbenches, metalsmith tools, wax molds, blowtorches, and exhaust fans. It was a place for ideation and execution. If ever there was a creative space for makers, that was it.

One of my most memorable assignments was to make a box out of silver. The first step was ideation. I spent a lot of time drawing ideas for the box in my sketchbook. As much as I wanted to stay true to the assignment of making a box, I also wanted to make something I could wear — not just set down somewhere. A box I could wear? Hmm.

I ideated, and I drew the possibilities I saw. Box earrings? Too small. Box ring? Too big. Box pendant? I wouldn't be able to see it easily. Many iterations later, I decided on a box bracelet. After researching how metal boxes could be constructed, I envisioned how mine would come together. I pictured the top of my bracelet as a box that could be opened and closed — with a hinge on one side and a clasp on the other. Almost like a locket, where you could tuck away a photo or memento. On top of the lid, there would be an oval stone of black onyx.

I ended up with a vision for a black onyx and silver locket box and presented a series of drawings to my teacher for approval. He liked the novel approach. He offered his feedback on how to improve the design and suggested specific materials and tools that would work best to make my vision a reality.

After refining my sketches, the next step was to buy the needed materials at the local rock shop. Who knew you could buy raw silver, silver solder, and exactly the right stone to suit any design at a store specializing in rocks? The shop was enough to make me giddy with metals and stones of every variety, size, shape, and color lining its shelves and display cases. As I put the raw materials I'd purchased into my toolbox — alongside my pliers, wire cutters, fine files, and saw blades — my excitement only grew.

The process of taking the idea I had labored over on a piece of paper and transforming it into a usable, wearable reality was not as easy as I would have liked. My first mistake was mismeasuring the amount of silver I would need for the box, so I had to return to the rock shop for more. Next, as I cut the pieces for each side of the box, I broke the fine saw blade I was using — more than once.

I moved on to the soldering stage, where I'd fuse together the silver pieces to form the box. I applied flux; I snipped and placed solder; I lit my torch and melted the solder, fusing the silver. When it was time to create the setting for the black onyx, it took several tries to cut the perfect-size bezel to fit the stone, then solder the bezel to the top of the box. I tried. I failed. I tried again. I succeeded. Finally, I burnished and polished the whole piece until it shone.

Placing the finished bracelet on my wrist, I couldn't help but smile. The bracelet fit my wrist just right. The box opened and clasped shut, as designed. The black onyx glistened against its shiny silver base. I had taken my idea from imagination to reality.

SPARK

Do you consider yourself creative? Why or why not? Have you ever looked at the world and wished there was a better way to do something — imagining something totally new or improving on something that already exists? What did you do about it, or what could you do about it?

I had gone from dreaming to doing. I had become a maker.

Toiling over that box, I realized that the creative process would not necessarily be easy. Ideas need refinement. Research is vital. Mistakes are made. Tools often break. Materials need adjustment. You may need to start over. But every step along the way is important because it teaches you something — even if it's what *not* to do. Every iteration helps you learn and grow, gets you closer to realizing your vision, and moves you from dreaming to doing. And as a maker, that's how you achieve more success.

Creativity Means Being Mindful, Giving Yourself Space to Create

One important thing I noticed about being creative was that it kept me in the present moment. Focused on what I was making, I could more easily tune out the stressors around me: being bullied, being left behind, being around my parents' fighting. Absorbed in a project, I was "miles away" from the fire — even if still nearby.

It's not a coincidence that many creative activities are also mindfulness activities. It turns out that mindfulness is an important part of the creative process. That's because mindfulness offers us the ability to be fully present, aware of our thoughts and feelings, but without judgment. It's about freeing your mind from stressors of the past and worries for the future, so you can concentrate on the here and now, even if only for brief moments.

I think of mindfulness as giving you space in your mind, allowing you to focus. It helps you find that blank canvas you need, to express yourself in your own unique way. Mindfulness helps you look at the world through the eyes of a maker, using a lens of creativity. When you give yourself that space to create, you enhance your ability to see the possibilities. When you pair mindfulness with the creative process, you amplify your ability to become a maker.

In my life, mindfulness has manifested in various ways, such as drawing, painting, designing, building, renovating, writing, cooking, and baking. But there's nothing like the emergence of life and nurturing it along. Maybe that's why I love gardening; it means growth.

I've found that in both career and life in general, a maker mindset is very similar to a growth mindset. In her book *Mindset*, Stanford professor Dr. Carol Dweck explains that with a growth mindset, people believe that their natural abilities can be developed through dedication and hard work; innate talent is just the starting point. This way of thinking creates a love of learning and an ability to be resilient, which are necessary for success.

As a maker, cultivating a growth mindset has been a vital part of my journey. Creativity and curiosity are the core; passion and problem-solving are the fuel. It's about constantly striving to create and build, to do better and be better, to inspire and be inspired.

That's why you'll always find me growing stuff — vegetables and flowers, family and friends, business and community — always learning and evolving in the garden that is life, because the most satisfying thing to grow is yourself.

I think of gardening as a "moving meditation" that not only allows you to focus on an activity that keeps you in the present moment, but also provides a rewarding result — whether you see the bloom of flowers that you planted or you eat vegetables that you grew yourself.

As a maker, my father gardened to detach from work and lose

himself in an activity that brought him joy. He was practicing mindfulness. Today, my dad's bountiful garden has taken over his backyard — and most of his free time. His garden helps keep him healthy and happy. It helps him continue to be a maker, even as an octogenarian, and that inspires me (and many others who know him).

Hoping to pass on the growth mindset to my children, I taught my kids to grow herbs in pots in our kitchen, fill planters with flowers outside, and grow fruits and vegetables in our backyard. Indoors, we grow orchids, avocado plants from pits, and, most recently, lemon trees.

SPARK

Where do you find the white space? Do you practice mindfulness or engage in any mindful activities? How can you incorporate more mindful moments into your life?

I notice that after I spend time gardening or doing other mindful activities — such as baking, which is like therapy — that's when I have the most ideas and creative energy. My mind, refreshed after being fully present in a moment of making, seems turbocharged.

Those are the times when I find the most inspiration to write or to solve a problem or challenge I've been trying to work through. By taking time to be mindful, I've given myself the gift of a blank canvas in my mind. The white space that is my garden helps me be a better maker.

Being a Maker Means Seeing Possibilities — Then Making Them Happen

You know how I came up with the vision for iParenting during my first pregnancy, inspired by a need I experienced in my own life? Yeah, that happened again when I started 30Seconds.

I was working at Disney when I started to realize the magnitude of what was happening with the evolution and proliferation of mobile phones. As a busy mom of three and an executive for one of the world's largest media companies, I found myself constantly reaching for my phone to multitask and get things done. With a company-issued BlackBerry (the standard business phone provided to executives at the time), I was not only able to take calls and schedule meetings but also check my emails and send texts, making communication so much easier.

But when Apple debuted its first iPhone, in 2007, I couldn't wait to get my hands on one. As an avid technology user (and tech company founder), it was easy to see why I'd be an early adopter of a device that was being hyped as an all-in-one iPod, phone, camera, internet communicator, and web browser.

I bought that very first iPhone while on a work trip to Los Angeles, and I remember showing it to skeptical business colleagues who couldn't imagine giving up their trusty BlackBerry for that odd touch-screen device.

But that novel device, created by the visionary Steve Jobs and his team at Apple, changed my life — and life as we knew it. The iPhone was a game changer in every sense of the word. I could now not only take calls, schedule meetings, check emails, and send texts — as I did on my BlackBerry — but also surf the web, watch videos, clip coupons, access GPS, search reviews, share good-quality photos to social media, and so much more. All from the compact computer in the palm of my hand.

Those smartphone features may seem like no big deal now (and many of us take them for granted), but then, those things were transformative long before the word *app* became part of our daily lexicon. I found myself using my BlackBerry less and less and my iPhone more and more.

Whether I was queued up in the school carpool line, standing in a store checkout, or running my business, my phone had become the most important tool in my utility belt. And it was clear I was not alone. Waiting with all the other moms for our kids to get out of school, I noticed that every single one of those moms was glued to their smartphone.

I saw the same thing while at the supermarket: moms pushing babies in grocery carts, tending to toddlers, searching for products on shelves — all the while scrolling through shopping lists on their phone, searching for coupons, looking up recipes, checking product reviews. It was almost as if they were consulting their personal assistant.

It was becoming clear to me how important mobile was for on-the-go moms. Whether we needed expert advice, a parenting hack, a quick recipe for dinner that night, or even just a game to play, moms were using those little bits of time we had, snatched here and there, to find information and inspiration before life interrupted us again. Trying to balance it all, in little windows of time, we needed all the help we could get. Smartphones had become not only our mobile command center but also the place we found "me time" to take a break throughout the course of our hectic days.

The growing research data about moms' mobile phone usage backed me up. There was a sea change in how moms were consuming information and media; connecting with their family, friends, and community; and learning about brands and products.

The business implications were massive: women account for the majority of all consumer purchases, yet many women believe that brands don't understand them. I knew moms needed expert advice, helpful tips, easy recipes, inspirational stories, and community connection — delivered straight to their phone. It was also clear to me that brands needed a way to reach busy moms on their mobile device, in those little bits of time they had here and there.

I started to imagine the possibilities. What if I could create a way, using technology, for brands to connect and engage with those on-the-go moms in a format that helped moms? There had to be a way to make life better for them, and if I could make it happen, it would be a huge win for moms and brands alike.

When I left Disney in 2009, it was bittersweet to bid farewell to my colleagues (especially my boss, Emily Smith, whose story I share in chapter 7). But I was excited about this spark of an idea that was burning in my mind: to provide information and inspiration to moms on mobile. I knew it would be my next big business challenge as an entrepreneur and my next big creative endeavor as a maker.

Going through a difficult divorce, then adjusting to life as a single mom, I thought about ways to make life better — for myself and for other mothers (and, by extension, for our children). I envisioned a transformative tech platform that would succinctly deliver helpful and engaging content to support, empower, and connect busy moms.

The credible, to-the-point content would be created by experts, journalists, and *passionistas* (this was a term I coined for people who were knowledgeable and passionate about a certain topic but not necessarily credentialed "experts"). The site would be sponsored by respected brands I felt good about, whose products or services aligned with moms' needs.

Realizing that a mother's time is precious, I focused on the length of time each piece of content would take a mom to process. I considered the "noise" and clutter that assail mobile users.

With so many sites and apps vying for your attention, it's hard to focus on something for very long before external forces (a tugging toddler, an impatient boss, an oven timer) or distractions from the phone itself (social media notifications, calendar reminders, text messages) pull you away. In an increasingly on-demand mobile world, I knew time was the most precious commodity — and cutting through the clutter was key.

I thought about how we'd been trained by television to absorb an advertisement and call to action in a thirty-second TV commercial. Timing out how long it took to read articles and watch videos on my phone before I got pulled away by one thing or another, I concluded that thirty seconds would be ideal.

That's how I landed on thirty seconds as the right amount of time each piece of content should take to read or view. And that's when I decided to launch 30Second Mom with the mission to provide mobile moms with quick and helpful tips from experts and passionistas, delivered straight to their phone, in the same amount of time it takes to watch an ad on TV.

Starting with a blank canvas in my mind, I envisioned 30Second Mom as an engaging website with a tip stream that users could customize to suit their needs. I primed my canvas with formal research data about moms' mobile usage, their preferences, their likes and dislikes, their wants and needs. I painted my canvas with my own observations, discovered in the white space of my life, and started to doodle.

Coffee with a friend became a fact-finding mission. Doctor visits and grocery shopping yielded content ideas. Social media provided instant feedback. The possibilities were crystallizing and starting to come into focus.

The next step was hiring designers and developers (more makers!) to take my visions and translate them onto the screen. I had poured my whole self into this concept, and it became a mission from my heart. That's why watching my sketches come to life, in full color, was like watching flowers bloom or vegetables grow in my garden.

30Second Mom was a seed that had been planted, but it required care so it could come to life. Each day, I made sure it got enough water and sunshine. Mistakes and failures sprung up like weeds, which, like chaos or fire, is to be expected. When you're out there growing stuff — a garden, a business, a life — you're going to encounter weeds.

In the garden, they can show up as crabgrass, clover, or dandelions. In a career, they can show up as market fluctuations, a bad boss or employee, or naysayers trying to bring you down. In your personal life, they can appear as health challenges, relationship issues, or parenting or financial struggles. And as I was building 30Second Mom, I encountered myriad weeds.

However they manifest, weeds are challenges to be overcome on the way to achieving a healthy garden, a successful career, or a happy life. As gardeners, it's tempting to focus just on the flowers or the vegetables: the aspects of our gardens that are pretty or enjoyable.

But as gardeners, as makers, we also need to be vigilant about tending to the weeds. If we let them take hold, they will grow until they threaten the life of our plants. And before we know it, our garden could be overrun, affecting the growth we're trying to achieve, the reality we're trying to create, and the difference we're trying to make.

Watch the weeds, my fellow gardener. Get to the roots, and don't feel bad about pulling them from your garden, one by one.

SPARK

How can you be more creative? Come up with two ways to enhance your growth mindset. How can the concept of moving from dreaming to doing manifest in your own life?

Then watch your garden thrive. That's exactly what I did to build 30Second Mom, growing it into the broader platform of 30Seconds.com. By pulling the weeds I encountered along the way, I created an empowering resource and an engaging community — a garden that is thriving.

Starting with a blank canvas, I had dreamed of the possibilities. As a maker, I had shaped my vision and made it a reality. The result: a successful business that is true to its mission to make the world a happier, healthier, and more delicious place, thirty seconds at a time.

The Virtuous Loop of Becoming a Maker

To become the fire, you need to make things happen. Looking at the world around you, you envision creative ideas to make life better in some way, shape, or form. You use your imagination to see the possibilities. You picture an outcome or a solution, then move from dreaming to doing. Creativity fuels you to make your idea into a reality. By ideating — and then actually creating — your vision, you become a maker. The more possibilities you see, the more you can make happen. The more you make happen, the more success you'll achieve.

This pattern played out for me throughout the course of my life. Creativity enabled me to look at the world through the eyes of a maker. I used my imagination to escape the chaos around me and create a blank canvas in my mind. I envisioned ways to make life better, for myself and others, based on my authentic self and the skills I knew I had.

I pictured solutions for moms like me — first during pregnancy, then later as a parent — but I didn't just dream about them. I ideated, then I created my visions. By transforming my ideas into realities, I became a maker. The more I made happen, using the white space in my life, the more success I achieved.

Let's break down that formula with what was going on for me when I was coming up with the concept for and creating 30Second Mom.

Being a maker means using your imagination to see the possibilities, which fuels your creativity. I noticed what was happening with the evolution of mobile phones and how that was impacting moms' information and media usage. I realized there had to be a way of cutting through the clutter to provide moms with helpful information while respecting their precious time. I saw possibilities, which ignited my creativity.

Creativity enables you to move from dreaming to doing, so you can transform your vision into a reality. I looked at the challenge (and opportunity) of moms and mobile through the eyes of a maker. Starting with a blank canvas in my mind, I aligned my research on moms and mobile with my own observations. I envisioned new ways to share content, succinctly, with on-the-go moms. Then I took the idea from concept to reality and brought 30Second Mom to life.

The more realities you can make happen, the more success you can achieve. By guiding and growing 30Second Mom from idea to execution, I had made something new in the world that was transformative for the moms I was serving and for the brand clients who wanted to reach them. I succeeded in building an inspiring media platform that is a thriving business.

This basic formula applies no matter where you are in your journey to become the fire. Use it when you seek creative inspiration, when you need a blank canvas, or when you want to enhance your maker mindset. What can you make happen? The world can't wait to find out!

FLAME • Kim Oster-Holstein

First Jobs: Lifeguard, camp counselor
Education: BBA (marketing), University of Texas at Austin;
      MSA (advertising), Northwestern University
Personal Life: Married, mother of three
Board/Civic Roles: Board member, Jewish Women International
Key Takeaway: "Be true to your creative spirit. Bring ideas to life
      with joy, enthusiasm, vision, and love."

Kim Oster was aimless and unconnected, working as an account manager for an ad agency when inspiration struck. "I was in a meeting about Sears Craftsmen tools, and all I could think about was making pretzels," she says. "The idea kept calling me, giving me hope in a place where I was miserable." Six months later, she met Scott Holstein — a fellow creative spirit who also felt trapped in the corporate world — and the idea for Kim & Scott's Gourmet Pretzels came to life.

Kim credits her authenticity and passion for helping her become an entrepreneur. But it was her underlying core of creativity that drove her to become a maker. Growing up Jewish in Texas, the middle child of three, Kim describes her upbringing as being "birthed within chaos," which meant she had to learn to be easygoing. "You have to ride the waves," she says.

In high school, Kim looked for part-time jobs that would help her discover who she was as a person. After working for a Houston city council member, Kim found herself with an internship at the White House. Yes, *that* White House.

Working in the Office of Private Sector Initiatives, Kim fell in love with the idea of business being able to help with social initiatives. "My

White House experience was the spark for my passion for companies having impact." In college, many of Kim's passions came together. "I started thinking about using business to make the world a better place."

But after graduation, she didn't know what to do. Feeling adrift, with no interest in the companies that came to the university to recruit new grads, Kim felt lost and alone. Her brother was living in Chicago, and Kim — eager to explore living in a new city — learned about Northwestern University's Integrated Marketing Communications program. She decided the postgrad program would be her next step, so she moved to Chicago to pursue her master's degree.

But after graduating, Kim found herself still unsure of what she wanted to do with her life. "It was an all-encompassing dilemma. I wanted to be an artist, to explore my art," she says. But at the same time, she needed to get a job. That's when Kim found herself in account management at Ogilvy & Mather, on a team that was marketing tools to women.

To find white space, Kim spent time reading and ideating — trying to figure out what she *really* wanted to do. That's when she read an article about a woman who was making pretzels at a farmers market. The idea stayed with her. "I became obsessed with the idea of making chocolate chip soft pretzels."

Wanting to move from dreaming to doing, Kim decided to take a step toward her idea. She went to the Women's Business Development Center and studied everything she could about starting a business. Not long after, she met Scott at a book signing. He would become not only her business partner but also her husband and the father of her three children. "We both had creative spirits that felt trapped by the work we were doing."

Fueling each other's creativity and maker mindsets, Kim and Scott first started a mural-painting company. Faced with the prospect of painting murals outside in the Chicago snow, the couple — who had been dating for just six months — decided to instead pursue Kim's passion for pretzels. The first step was finding other makers to help. After a handful of rough starts, they found a chef to help them with their recipes and a facility in which to make them. With Kim still working at the advertising agency, the company secured a line of credit to finance the burgeoning business.

Meanwhile, Kim and Scott's relationship progressed. They got engaged, then married — all the while working together on the pretzel company. Although being married to her cofounder made for a sometimes-complicated dynamic, Kim's main concern was quitting her steady job at the agency. But trusting her intuition, Kim seized the opportunity to leave the corporate world for good. "I jumped off a ledge and into something that fulfills me. I had utter joy. It felt like angels were cheering."

With Kim on board full-time as CEO and CIO (chief inspiration officer), Kim & Scott's Gourmet Pretzels took off. "I left the known and unhappy path I was on — the outwardly secure and paved path with health insurance and benefits — to pave my own path, one with its own twists and turns, but one that I created and navigated. That freedom in creativity, expression, and building something with purpose changed the course of my life," she says.

Being an entrepreneur wasn't always easy, though. "Like a pretzel, there are lots of twists and turns on the journey." But Kim's highlight reel from that time in her life includes many "pinch-me" moments: building a profitable business from the ground up; selling her pretzels on QVC to 90 million households; having the pretzels sold in national grocery chains, from Costco to Walmart, Kroger to Whole Foods; and experiencing the joy of kids, especially those with nut allergies, loving their pretzels. "To create a product that nourishes the spirits, souls, and stomachs of our world community is a huge highlight of my career."

Kim grew her family as she grew her business, and like a pretzel, everything was intertwined. "I would nurse my babies in my office, or I would work from home," she says. "I loved having the flexibility and making my own schedule. Business and family — it was all tied together."

Kim stayed true to her vision of business making the world a better place. To make an impact, the company donated pretzels, time, and a portion of proceeds to not-for-profits that make a positive difference in the world. Kim and Scott used their business experience to inspire students to become entrepreneurs, giving speeches and writing entrepreneurship lessons to help the next generation of business leaders.

But as the company grew into a bigger and more complex enterprise, generating millions of dollars in sales, the challenges of staying profitable also grew. "It costs a lot of money to stay on store shelves. We needed to raise investment capital or sell the business." The problem was that Kim didn't want to take on investors or sell her business. "Bringing in money meant working for other people. I wanted to maintain control of my schedule."

Kim was so in love with her pretzel company that she couldn't imagine selling it. "A simple idea can come to you, and you fill it with the hope, creativity, love, aspirations, and all you dream of. That idea will become much more than a pretzel or a widget, or whatever you come up with. It's a catalyst to build your life centered around the essence of you and all you desire to manifest."

Letting go of the catalyst on which she'd built her life became a lengthy process and one of the most difficult things she has ever done. "I did it kicking and screaming. One of our top competitors was always after us to buy the company because we took a lot of business from them. Scott and our other advisers felt we had to seize the opportunity."

The couple ended up selling Kim & Scott's Gourmet Pretzels to J&J Snack Foods, a $1 billion food company. Though Kim felt some relief when the sale was completed, there was mostly grief. "People don't realize the emotional hardship of selling a company. I grieved for the loss of our amazing team, the trade shows, the suppliers, and all the things I loved about building such a magical company. I felt good that the pretzels were still out there, but I had to mourn the loss of the spirit of Kim & Scott's."

Kim dove into the practice of yoga, Pilates, and meditation and enhanced her maker mindset through mindfulness activities like feng shui, Chinese medicine, and functional foods. Over time, Kim opened her heart again to the possibilities. Working on boards and chairing an organization that empowers women and girls, she looked for opportunities to help her continue to grow as a person. "Creating a daily spiritual practice, including meditation, prayer, walking in nature, and setting intentions for the life you want to manifest — this practice provides a calm center that helps you make grounded decisions for business and life," she explains.

These actions helped Kim create a blank canvas in her mind, and her creativity came alive. "Scott and I had invested in a juice business because Scott always wanted fresh-squeezed lime juice for craft margaritas at our Mexican-themed birthday parties [Kim and Scott's birthdays are two days apart in May]. At the same time, restaurants and bars wanted fresh-squeezed juices on their premises." The result was Industry Juice, a company devoted to bringing fresh juice to the hospitality industry.

When Kim was ready to take the leap back into full-time entrepreneurship, the couple bought out the other partner and got to work on rebranding the business. Working with the marketing team that had created the packaging for the popular energy bar RXBAR, Kim and Scott rebranded the company in half an hour. The new name, Twisted Alchemy, was a nod to their "twisted" pretzel company, as well as the "seemingly magical process of transformation, creation, or combination" that is alchemy.

Twisted Alchemy handcrafts fresh-squeezed juices that provide the hospitality industry with a convenient alternative to squeezing on premises — and Kim is back in her entrepreneurial element. "There's nothing more exciting than building something out of nothing," she says. "Building our business is a labor of love."

But as with the pretzel business, the juice business also has been filled with twists and turns — especially during the pandemic, when the company had to make lemonade from lemons. "With the quarantine time, and the need to transform our cold-pressed juice business to home experiences, I thought a lot about pivots and how we can all make tweaks and plant new seeds," she says. "When all the bars and restaurants closed around the country, in a matter of days, our business tanked to zero in revenues. We had to reinvent ourselves. And I've been energized and inspired in that reinvention."

That reinvention meant a shift from their mission to "elevate spirits in bars and restaurants" to that of "elevating the spirits of people." The new mission is in line with Kim's personal mission of inspiring with love. "With inspiration to motivate and engage your team in the vision, you provide the team with hope and support to make the vision a reality. I feel that's an innate part of who I am, and when I live my mission, I'm being my authentic self. I'm filled with hope and excitement over this shift, and there are great possibilities."

As someone who seeks to inspire not only her team but also women in business, Kim advises others to create from a place of authenticity. "Bring all of *you* forward in your business. The more you are yourself, and create from that place, the more fulfilling the journey will be. If you build your business with purpose and intention, it will have more fuel to grow. Start this intention to make a difference at the beginning, so it's a critical core of your foundation."

As a maker and entrepreneur, Kim reflects on her success. "Success lies at being true to your creative spirit, bringing ideas to life with joy, enthusiasm, vision, and love. I have been most fortunate to experience this in my life, and it gives me the ultimate feeling of fulfillment."

And yet Kim notes there's much more to look forward to. "My dad always said, 'Success is a journey, not a destination.' I love this quote, and it fits. Yes, there have been some remarkable moments along the way. But it's really in the journey that we experience the most about life and ourselves. There is so much ahead for me to learn and experience."

BLAZE

I see possibilities everywhere, and the possibilities are endless.

I am creative. I am an ideator. I am a big-picture thinker.

I move from dreaming to doing. I bring ideas to life.

I am a maker who makes a difference in the world.

The more creative I am, the more I can make happen.

The more I make happen, the more success I achieve.

7

Be Viable

To become the fire, you need to be viable. Being viable means you've enhanced the skill of *capability*: you know how to acquire the knowledge, qualities, and abilities needed to be successful at a task or in a role or in a business. Knowing you are equipped, and having others recognize that you have what it takes, means you can accomplish more goals. The more capable you are, the more viable you will be. And the more viable you are, the more success you can achieve.

At its most basic, *viability* means "capable of living." But viability translates into being capable of so much more than just living.

When you think of viability in a career, you may think of knowing the rules or being capable of performing a job's required tasks. When you think of viability in business, you may think of paying the bills or being capable of achieving a profit. But there's more to capability than just what *you* think.

Although it's important that *you* feel capable, when it comes to viability, it's also crucial that *other people* see you as being capable. Whether they are hiring you, promoting you, buying from you, partnering with you, or investing in you, people want to know that you are capable of being successful in a role, within a company, or as an entrepreneur before they will back you.

That's why, when it comes to success, your mission is to become capable so you can prove your viability. Things like staying up to speed on technology; learning new tools, programs, and regulations; and keeping abreast of changes in your industry all prove your relevance and help you grow your capability. By staying curious and finding new ways to learn and advance your knowledge, you become more viable.

But there's even more to viability. Sometimes, becoming or staying viable means being on the giving or receiving end of very tough decisions. To get out of the red or to stay in the black — to pay down debt, afford your bills, make payroll, turn a profit, and even bank savings or make investments — often means overcoming significant challenges.

As an employee, for example, you may endure layoffs. As an employer, you may be the one doing the layoffs. Cost cutting, downsizing, rightsizing, outsourcing, offshoring — these are all practices used by people and organizations looking to become more viable. That's why it's important to remember that a job or a business could end at any time, so you are better prepared for financial insecurity.

To be viable as a person, you first need to live, to survive. And if there's one thing outsiders have, it's a strong survival instinct. Facing all that fire has made you smarter and more resilient. It has made you capable. Once you unleash your instinct to survive, you can channel it toward becoming viable. Viability means not only surviving but also thriving.

When you are truly viable, other people view you as being qualified to get the job done. In their eyes, being capable means you have the knowledge, qualities, and abilities to be successful in a role or within an organization. They feel comfortable working with you because your competence makes them believe you will be viable. And when you demonstrate your viability, your chances of success increase exponentially.

To assess your viability, it's helpful to recognize when other people see you as effective. When you are viewed as capable, you'll notice that other people want to work with you or for you; they want to promote you or buy from you; they want to invest in you or even acquire your business. People have to work with other people, after all, and wanting to ensure their own viability and success, they choose to work with people who are capable. Let's make sure that's you!

Those who are capable are more likely to build viable careers and businesses. That's why it's important to do more of what you're good at, constantly advancing your proficiency, and to continually improve your knowledge, abilities, and even your attitude.

On your journey to becoming capable, you may find yourself jumping from college major to major, or from job to job, or from career to career until you find the right fit that enables you to grow and advance through the ranks. Your business idea also may need time to find its legs. It may require testing different concepts, business models, and ways to do things.

So how do you know if you (or your career or your business) are viable? A viable employee is recognized and promoted through the ranks of leadership. A viable career is one that evolves and advances. A viable business is one that grows and flourishes. Whether as an organization or as an individual, viability means you provide value to others — which keeps them paying your invoices or paychecks and coming back for more of your products or services.

When I think about becoming viable, I remember how my family influenced me along my journey. My grandparents' cabinet business started out as a small woodworking shop next door to their house on a quiet residential street. As their business became viable, the shop expanded in size to take up several lots. My father, the architect, and *mi madre*, the teacher, both modeled what getting an education and building a solid career looked like — despite their immigrant challenges.

But as an independent, creative spirit, I often wanted to do things *my* way, and sometimes that meant learning about viability the hard way. Watching my grandparents and parents manage their careers and lives, I clearly saw the value of a strong work ethic. That meant that, from a young age, I was capable. But it took me a while to understand and achieve true viability.

Take the decision I made to go to the University of Wisconsin–Madison, for example. I opted to go to UW because it was my dream to study fashion design there. It was where I wanted to go and what I wanted to do. And because I was capable of working, I was happy to take on part-time jobs and student loans to pay for the significant portion of that hefty out-of-state tuition that my parents didn't cover (as I shared in chapter 2).

Following my dream was a fine decision made by the seventeen-year-old me. But had I gone to the University of Illinois, as my dad had strongly preferred, I likely would have ended up with a similar liberal arts education at a fraction of the cost — and would have graduated debt-free. That means I could have been more financially viable (and a lot less stressed) had I taken my parents' advice.

Looking back, would I have changed my mind about attending UW? No. I view the fulfilling of that dream as a critical part of my journey. I owned the decision and every moment of the experience. I loved Madison, and all the financial, social, and academic adventures I had there helped make me into the person I am. Every single challenge I overcame at UW (and before and after being there) was foundational to my ability not only to be viable but also to be highly successful.

But my father wasn't done teaching me about viability. Not content to just try and change my mind about where to go to college, he also had a hand in swaying me to change my college majors, too. I'll never forget him telling me how impractical a fashion or art degree would be. "You'll never find a job; you won't be able to pay your bills," he would say. What he really meant was, "I'm afraid you won't be viable."

Because I seemed committed to some type of career in design, though, he wisely suggested I try to get a summer internship at his architecture firm, working with the graphics team. That way, I would see what at least one career in design could look like. I applied; I interviewed; I got the internship.

Based in a downtown high-rise along the Chicago River, that internship was valuable in several ways. I observed graphic designers in action and learned by doing. I understood the business use of graphics and its impact in marketing (and other) materials. And I interacted with professional designers and other business team members.

Most importantly, by working in the graphics department, I got to see up close and personal that I. Did. Not. Want. It. If that was the "business" side of art, I wasn't interested in doing graphic design for a living. That internship had a big influence on why I decided to change my major again.

Although at the time my dad seemed like a major buzzkill, I later understood what he was trying to do. To him, college was about becoming competent, building your skills, advancing your talents, proving your capabilities — with the ultimate goal of becoming viable. It was important to him that I get a good education, at an affordable price, in a major that would translate into career success. He wanted me to choose a field in which it would be easy to find a job at which I could be successful. He wanted me to be viable. I got there eventually — in my own time and in my own way — because I was capable.

It turns out that my identical twin daughters are also artists, both studying art in college. Like me, they grew up as makers, always designing, always creating. I've tried to strike a balance between supporting and encouraging their passion for art and teaching them about making it into a viable career. I've stressed the importance of learning about the business side of their art, and they're in the process of figuring it all out. I have confidence that, like me, they will get there in their own time and in their own way because they, too, are capable.

You may recognize what I'm talking about. That's because you, too, may have been told your dreams weren't practical or that your plans or ideas weren't viable. But no matter what *you* decide to do, being competent is key. The more capable you are, the more viable you will be. And the more viable you are, the more likely you are to succeed. Because I know you're capable, I have confidence that you will get there, too.

In this chapter, I will share what it means to be capable, then help you become more viable so you can show the world that you have the knowledge, qualities, and abilities needed to accomplish your goals and achieve more success.

Being Capable Is Key to Viability

To become viable, you have to be capable, which means two things: (1) *you* know you have the knowledge, qualities, and abilities to succeed at something, and (2) *other people* know you have the knowledge, qualities, and abilities to succeed at it.

Being capable means you have what it takes to accomplish your goals.

We enhance our capability in various ways: By becoming stronger — physically, intellectually, and emotionally. By staying relevant and curious and learning new things. By surrounding ourselves with positive people who support and inspire us. By starting with achievable goals, growing in competence and complexity as we go. By leveraging what we have, so we're not always recreating the wheel or starting from square one. By identifying what we're good at (and what we're not good at). By continually building our skills and advancing our talents.

Being capable fuels us to take on greater challenges, try new things, practice our craft, grow our proficiency. It's by knowing we have what it takes that we believe we are capable. It's when we demonstrate that competence that others see us as capable. And when we are capable, we can become viable.

Although I'd been working as a babysitter, I couldn't wait to get my first "real" job. To me, a real job meant going to a store, punching a clock, interacting with customers, having a boss and coworkers, and getting an actual paycheck.

That's why, when I was fifteen, I became a regular visitor to my local youth job center. My visits to the job center taught me a lot about the local economy, what types of jobs there were for teenagers, how to write a résumé, and how to prepare for a job interview.

After all that prep, applying for positions, and going on interviews, I finally got my first real job — working at an ice cream store. Scooping ice cream seemed like an ideal job. I mean, how hard could it be? And I'd get to eat all that ice cream!

It turned out that scooping ice cream is harder than it looks. Especially when you have a tough boss, and ice cream that was even tougher. As I was learning the ropes at the shop, the owner watched me like a hawk as I leaned into the freezing ice cream case, dug deep into the various flavors, and tried to craft perfectly sized scoops of ice cream or Italian ice into cones or sundae dishes.

As part of my training, my boss had me weigh each scoop to ensure it was exactly the size — four ounces — that he wanted each scoop to be. Any less, and the customer wouldn't feel they'd received value for their money. Any more, and my boss wouldn't turn a profit on the scoop. It was that precise. The business of ice cream is a business, after all. With a lease, freezers, blenders, inventory, employees, and other expenses, my boss always had his eye on the bottom line. Viability meant his business had to be profitable.

I'll never forget my struggles to scoop the lemon ice, which was literally as hard as ice. Trying to scoop it was more like chipping away at it. When I told my boss about this problem, he dismissively told me, "Go eat your Wheaties." Hmm.

It was clear he wanted me to figure it out on my own. Summoning all my strength, I tried and tried and tried, but that lemon ice just couldn't be scooped. Because I wasn't capable of perfectly scooping that popular flavor, I was beginning to doubt my ability to be successful at the job, and that did not feel good.

Then one day, I figured out how to do it. In the sink behind the ice cream case, I let the hot water run. Then, I put the metal scooper under the hot water for a minute. After heating the scooper, I was amazed — and relieved — to see it sink into that lemon ice like a hot knife through butter. When I excitedly told my boss about this discovery, he just shook his head and smiled. By the end of my training period, not only could I craft a perfect scoop of that stubborn lemon ice but I could also eyeball what four ounces of ice cream looked like — spot-on, nearly every time.

Although I didn't start eating additional bowls of Wheaties, scooping ice cream did help me become stronger, physically and emotionally. By trying again and again to succeed at a seemingly simple task that had stymied me, I expanded my capacity to handle challenges. By taking my boss's "Eat your Wheaties" comment as an opportunity to try a different approach, rather than an excuse to give up, I started to think outside (or beyond) the cereal box.

Instead of banging my head against the wall in frustration, I became intentional about responding to my failure. Determined to find a way to accomplish my goal of the perfect scoop, I tried something new to become more competent — and it worked.

SPARK

Think about a situation in which you worked on your skills and abilities and proved to yourself and to other people that you were capable. How did that experience impact you?

My discovery, and subsequent success, led me to strengthen my abilities. And when I demonstrated my proficiency, my boss also believed I had what it took. In his eyes, and in my own, I had become capable. I had shown that I was equipped to succeed at the ice cream shop, and I was on my way to becoming a viable employee.

Having a Capable Team Is Critical to Being Viable

Whether in your career or your life, whether as an employer or an employee, surrounding yourself with the right people is important. I've come to understand that having a capable team is critical to viability. Who you work with can make or break your career or your business. Whether you're working for a boss or you are the boss, choosing your coworkers wisely, and working with them productively, is key.

When you're in charge, it's tempting to think you can do it all on your own. After all, no one can run your department or your business as well as you can, right? The truth is, if you want to achieve success at scale, you really cannot do it alone. To get to where you want to be, it's essential to build a cohesive, mission-driven team. Very often, your team members are the lifeblood of the organization. As part of keeping my colleagues motivated and inspired, I build a personal connection, lead with empathy, and incentivize and reward their efforts.

I've been fortunate to work with some of the same amazing people across my two businesses. While growing iParenting, I built relationships with our many experts, writers, and editors — the team responsible for the content that led to us being recognized as a "Best of the Web" media platform. I'm happy that some of those experts, writers, and editors transitioned with me from iParenting to Disney and, later, from Disney to 30Seconds.

One relationship I'm particularly proud of is with a senior editorial team member. I'll call her *my colleague*. The year was 1999, and as with many of my editorial team members, we connected online. As a contributor to another popular lifestyle site, my colleague had identified iParenting as a site she would like to write for, so she emailed me to see if she could join our writing team.

When I reviewed my colleague's work and our email conversations, I felt like she was someone with a passion for the parenting, food, and other lifestyle topics we were covering. She seemed like someone I would enjoy working with — and iParenting was growing fast. For all those reasons, I thought she might make a good assistant editor.

When I approached her about the role, she hesitated, not because she wasn't interested but because she thought she might not be capable of doing the job. It entailed some coding, copyediting, and assignment editor duties — skills she did not yet have. Still, I believed I could teach her what she needed to know. I figured if it didn't work out, all I would have lost is some time. If it did work out, I would have gained a competent contributor who perhaps could become a viable team member.

With my assurances that I would train her and that I believed her to be capable of the role, my colleague accepted the assistant editor job. As I had hoped, she learned quickly and adapted to her new role. Over time, my colleague took on more and more responsibility, rising through the ranks to become senior editor and an integral part of our editorial team.

We got to know each other on a personal level, even though I worked in our corporate office and she worked from home in a different state. We'd meet up in person, and it would feel like we'd known each other forever. Through the years, we also raised our kids "together," virtually sharing the ups and downs of parenting along the way. By the time iParenting was sold to Disney, we had come to joke that, like an old married couple, my colleague could pretty much finish my sentences — and she sometimes knew what I wanted on the website at the same moment I did. I believed in her, and she believed in me.

When it came time to transition the iParenting team to Disney, some team members (including my colleague) weren't going to make the cut. That's because to keep the iParenting division viable, it had to continue to be profitable under its new Disney "mothership" structure, which carried a lot more overhead and expense than our much smaller but profitable business did on its own. So I advocated for my colleague. With my backing, Disney kept her on. She ended up working there for five years, surviving layoff after layoff that took out many other employees who had been at Disney even longer than she had.

When she finally was let go, in yet another round of Disney

layoffs intended to help keep the digital division of the media giant viable, we reconnected. She saw what I was building with 30Seconds, and she wanted to be part of it. Starting out as a contributor, my colleague again advanced into an integral role as a senior member of the team.

As our team grew the site from 30Second Mom to 30Seconds .com, my colleague was part of its evolution, flexing and pivoting with me as we navigated the business to viability. She never faltered in her belief that the company would succeed, and she did all she could to contribute to its success.

Therein lies the value of capable team members. When you find them, it's important to invest in them, trust them, and support them. Cultivating relationships with people who believe in you and your mission will help you become, or stay, viable. Surround yourself with talented people who fill in your gaps. If you're bootstrapping and finances are an issue, get creative. Consider using company equity, performance bonuses, and milestone incentives to compensate your team. Then as the business grows, be sure their income grows, too.

Although I've experienced the benefits of working with trustworthy team members (like my colleague), I've also experienced the setbacks of working with untrustworthy team members. I've learned, the hard way, the importance of removing toxic employees quickly, before they can infect others or permeate your entire organization. I've found it's true that a bad apple can spoil the entire bunch. If something feels off about a person you're working with, it's important to trust your instincts and get to the bottom of it. Figure out what's wrong, and either fix it or remove it. The viability of your organization just may depend on it.

Outside of our solid editorial team, there were other employees at iParenting who were not always as effective. From sales to accounting, and from IT to design (and beyond), we had many roles to fill, and we didn't always get it right. There was one person, I'll call them *the bad apple*, who spread rumors about other employees, sowed doubts about company viability, pretended to have greater authority than they had, and generally created chaos.

At first, we tried to give the bad apple the benefit of the doubt. We had discussions with them, trying to figure out what was happening and why. But the bad apple was a masterful con artist, showing one face to company management and quite another to various employees. It became clear that something was going terribly wrong. The situation worsened when other — formerly competent — employees also began acting differently, having been infected by the bad apple.

With the vibe in the office turning paranoid and ugly, what was once a happy place to work became a place I dreaded going. A once highly effective team was no longer fully viable, and it was starting to impact the business.

That's when we knew it was time to clean house. It's never comfortable to fire someone, but it's a bit easier when they give you a very good reason for it. And when what you've worked so hard to achieve is at risk, taking this type of action is a necessary step toward ensuring company viability. We sat down with each of the affected team members and had a tough talk. Then we made the decisions we believed were in the best interests of the company.

The bad apple? Gone. The employees who had been infected by the bad apple? Also gone. Yes, cleaning house was painful and unsettling. But like removing the weeds to save the garden, it had to be done. Once the bad apple was removed, things improved. We had survived, and so had the part of our team that had not been infected.

Over time, the team was rebuilt, and the company was once again thriving. But that experience taught me much about choosing team members carefully. I became extra vigilant about the hiring process — multiple rounds of interviews, checking references — and always trusted my instincts.

I learned even more about company viability after Disney acquired iParenting and some of our employees had to be let go. That's because, at Disney, there was redundancy in some of the team members we had at iParenting. Redundancy meant added expense — and a less viable business. Because of that, we had to lay off the team members whose roles were already represented at Disney.

I didn't want to do it, so just as I went to bat for my colleague — enabling her to keep her job — I went to bat for other employees whom I felt were vital to the organization. But my new boss, Emily Smith, whose story I share in this chapter, let me know that the continued viability of iParenting was on my shoulders. She knew I was capable of keeping iParenting viable under the Disney umbrella, and I knew it was my responsibility. But being in charge meant I would be the one to deliver the layoff news to my team, one by one.

As much as it hurt, I did what I had to do: saying goodbye to several team members right away — and even more over time. I pruned my team to ensure the success of the business going forward, and that is a lesson in viability I will never forget.

SPARK

Do you consider yourself, or your business, viable? Come up with your own definition of *viability*. What is one area of your career, business, or life you can work on to ensure it becomes more viable?

A Side Hustle Can Grow into a Viable Business (and Other Lessons Learned)

If you have a business or creative idea but you're not sure it will be viable (at least not right away), a good way to test it out is by starting it as a side hustle. A side hustle is something you do in addition to your main job or full-time career. For example, some people side hustle as writers or artists, while others coach or consult. Then there are those who launch entire start-up companies as side hustles, using their main job's income to bootstrap the new business.

Side hustles can be especially helpful if you can't afford to leave your job to start a new business. A side hustle allows you to test-drive a concept in your free time, to see if it has legs, before quitting your job and diving into entrepreneurship headfirst.

A side hustle can be a permanent part-time gig. If you're not making ends meet with your main job, a side hustle can help you achieve viability in life by providing extra income. Or a side hustle can become viable on its own. If it takes off, you can leave your job to focus on it full-time.

When I started Pregnancy Today, I had no real concept of how big it could become. My dream was that it would be something I could do part-time from home as I raised my family. And it did start out that way. But after launching the second website, Babies Today, I knew the company would be viable and that my side hustle days were over. To scale the business, I had to move it from a side hustle to a full-time job.

With the help of my family and sitters, my kids were cared for. I was able to work and grow the company from the iParenting office, which was only a few minutes from home so I could go back and forth as needed. (I even went home to breastfeed.) That full-time job evolved into an entrepreneurial career that I could not be prouder of. Yet by starting small, I was able to be home with my babies, test the waters, see how it felt, and gauge the company's viability — all before taking the leap into full-time entrepreneurship.

When inspiration struck again with 30Seconds, I followed a similar path of easing back into full-time entrepreneurship. As a single mom, my kids were my priority. And this time, they were school-aged. I worked intently at night and while they were in school, so that when they were home, they got my full attention. If they were sick and stayed home from school, I would take a sick day, too.

Growing up, if I was too ill to go to school, I'd spend my sick days at home — alone. As a teacher, *mi madre* rarely took time off, aside from school holidays and breaks. Because we kids were used to letting ourselves into the house and being on our own for hours every day after school, we learned to fend for ourselves. My parents must have figured we'd be OK on our own, even when we were sick. And most of the time, we were.

But one day, I woke up feeling sicker than I could ever remember being. Before *mi madre* could leave for work, I went to tell her how sick I was. She felt my forehead, then gave me baby aspirin and a glass of 7UP to drink. *Mi madre* then sent me to bed, telling me she would call my grade school to let them know I wouldn't be there that day.

But as she prepared to leave for work, I started to cry. "Please, don't leave me here alone; stay home with me, please," I begged her. Surprised by my unexpected outburst, since I was usually fine on my own, *mi madre* paused. Feeling my forehead again, she decided she'd better stay home with me after all. As the day progressed and I became sicker, she decided it was time to take me to the doctor.

I was diagnosed with pneumonia. I was treated with medicines, humidifiers, Vicks VapoRub, and plenty of vitamins and bed rest. I remember the reassuring feeling of *mi madre* being there *with* me and *for* me. It gave me a sense of comfort, of being cared for, and the feeling that I was going to be OK.

That's the feeling I wanted my own children to have, whether they were sick or not. That's why it was so important to me that I be there for my kids, especially when they were sick. I didn't want them to have to beg me to stay home or to be there for them, as I did with *mi madre*.

But life often comes full circle. After their retirement, my parents became a constant and comforting presence in my life and in the lives of my children. Much of the time, it was *mi madre* — or *abuelita*, as my kids call her — who would help care for my kids. *Mi madre* took on the nurturing role as if she was made to be a grandmother. And somehow, her constant, loving presence in our lives healed a place in my heart I didn't even know needed healing.

Since her Alzheimer's disease diagnosis, *mi madre* has been speaking to me in our native tongue. As bits of my feisty *madre* slowly slip away, this has become a way to connect and remember one of the most important lessons she taught me — whether she realized it or not.

Remember that every day after *mi madre* got home from teaching, she would take a *siesta* to recharge before the family portion of her day began. Around 5:30 p.m., she would get up, go to the kitchen, and turn on the Spanish music. I lived for those times, not only because she would light up when she heard José Feliciano or Héctor Lavoe but also because she would sing and dance while she cooked dinner. I now know that was her mind-fulness activity time, and I reveled in her joy (and the aroma of Puerto Rican food).

I recently made the connection in my own life. Around 5:30 p.m. most days, I stop my work and head to the kitchen. The other day, my husband walked into the room, gave me a twirl, and said, "I love this time of day. You turn on the music, and you sing and dance." Surprised, I smiled in recognition, even though I hadn't made the conscious connection.

All those years, *mi madre* had been showing me her way to find happiness in the everyday, and her joy gave me joy. Then I effortlessly picked up that baton and danced with it. It turns out that joy is contagious. It's always there to be found; you just have to pick a station and turn up the volume.

So with my parents helping out if I needed to work, 30Seconds grew similarly to iParenting: day by day, article by article, email by email — but also Facebook post by post, Pinterest pin by pin, and Twitter tweet by tweet. Starting 30Seconds as a side hustle enabled me to be there for my kids and determine the company's viability before again taking the leap into full-time entrepreneurship.

I'm very fortunate to have been able to structure my work life around my kids and to have had the support of my family. Parents are pulled in so many different directions, having to literally do it all, and childcare is often a (costly) necessity. That's why, if you want to be an entrepreneur of any kind, starting your dream as a side hustle is something to seriously consider.

As you juggle the demands of work with the challenges of parenting, never be afraid to ask for

SPARK

If you could start a side hustle, what would it be? Do you have family, friends, or colleagues who support or inspire you? How can you cultivate positive relationships in your life — people who believe in you, and in whom you believe — to help get your side hustle started?

support from friends and family. You may be surprised by how much they want to help you become viable. Another option is connecting with neighbors or other fellow parents about creating a childcare co-op (or "pod"). You never know who else in your world could use some support, and taking turns watching each other's children, you'll discover valuable (and economical) work windows.

And if you're launching a side hustle or a start-up, many business incubators and coworking spaces often have access to lower-cost childcare options. For several years, 30Seconds was based at the 1871 tech incubator in downtown Chicago, providing us with economical shared office and meeting space, along with many other benefits (from networking to steaming lattes). See what you can discover, because finding even little chunks of time to devote to a side hustle can pay off big, allowing you to determine its viability.

Building a Leverageable Business Model
Leads to Viability

Whether you're working for an organization or running an organization, it's important to understand the impact of building a profitable, leverageable business model. A business built on a model that is leverageable means you've invested in your product or service offering as a fixed cost; then you can use that product or service offering over and over, and in different ways, without always starting from scratch. By leveraging what you've already spent money on, you don't need to reinvent the wheel. You're maximizing your return on investment, time, and energy. You're that much closer to being viable.

At iParenting, our main product was great content. We

invested in creating quality content and community features for our website, which then became a fixed cost. Because we owned the content and the platform, we could not only offer advertising opportunities to our brand clients but also repurpose the content for other uses. Almost everything we produced, from product reviews to my Editor's Letter, we could leverage into other areas of the business.

For example, we syndicated our created content to clients for use on their websites. We licensed the content to magazines that wanted to use it in print. The content often served as inspiration for my newspaper column and radio show. Much of the content we created fed into other content, supported it, or served as a base for helping something else in the business grow. That's what I mean by a leverageable business model.

30Seconds was built similarly, but as the market changed, the business model had to change, too. With the rise of mobile, the web got even noisier, with more and more companies, apps, and brands vying for attention. What started out as a site mostly focused on quick parenting tips grew into a digital lifestyle media company that publishes thousands of articles; recipes; cooking, travel, and beauty tips; health and wellness insights; and perspectives generated by a diverse and capable team.

Every day, when our editorial team logs into the 30Seconds content portal to see what's been submitted by our contributors and decide what to publish, it's like embarking on a treasure hunt. Although we follow an editorial calendar and offer great timely content, we also are delighted to find unique gems, and I personally learn something new every day. In that way, 30Seconds is like a box of chocolates: you may never know what you're going to get, but you know it's going to be good.

With an engaged and growing audience, the user traffic

clearly reflected a trajectory to success. But when you launch a start-up, the true test for success is finding a viable business model, which is often the hardest part. And a viable business needs recurring revenue.

To grow our revenue, we tested many models: content marketing, social media marketing, e-commerce affiliate marketing, content syndication, and, most significantly, direct advertising sales. But the lucrative ad sales model required building and managing relationships with advertisers, which takes a lot of time and tools. From creating the sales pipeline, pitching, implementing the ads, and running the campaign, to analyzing it to determine success and prove the ROI — it's a huge amount of work that requires a multi-person team. As a start-up, we didn't have the resources for that.

To find a solution for monetizing 30Seconds' available advertising space, or "inventory," I researched the market. I found many more options available to support high-quality digital publishers than had been there during the iParenting days, when we sold much of our ad inventory on our own. I discovered there was no longer any need to start from scratch.

By collaborating with complementary companies that believed in us, and that we believed in, we could leverage their digital tools, contacts, and communities. With partners like news aggregators (to help distribute our content and

SPARK

How can you build a leverageable model on the job or in your business? Think of two ways to repurpose some of what you do or have so you're not always beginning anew. How can you maximize your return on investment, time, and energy?

reach a wider audience) and ad sales companies (to help monetize our available ad inventory and generate more revenue), we were able to grow the business and enhance our viability.

By partnering with discerning distribution and monetization experts, we not only increased our profitability but also increased an even more precious resource: our available time. We were freed up to focus on what we do best: create amazing content, curate an inspiring community, and cultivate an engaged audience (in the millions every month and growing).

The more we dove into the analytics, followed the data, poured our passion into the website, and grew our audience, the more revenue we saw from our advertising business — making us even more viable. With more time to focus on creating inspiring content and building the 30Seconds community, we were able to succeed at our mission to make life better.

The Virtuous Loop of Being Viable

To become the fire, you need to be viable. Being viable means you're capable of acquiring the knowledge, qualities, and abilities needed to be successful at something. Knowing you are competent, and having other people back you because they recognize that you have what it takes, means you can accomplish more of what you set out to do. The more capable you are, the more viable you will be. And the more viable you are, the more success you can achieve.

This pattern played out for me time and time again. Demonstrating my proficiency helped me grow stronger, enhance my knowledge, develop positive relationships, leverage what I had, improve my skills, and be intentional about how I responded to my failures and fires. Whether working at an ice cream shop or building a business, being capable fueled me to take on challenges, try new things, and achieve more and more.

I believed I was capable when not only *I* knew I was proficient but *other people* knew I was — whether it was a boss, an employee, an investor, a customer, a partner, or a business acquirer. Once I was capable, I became more viable. The more viable I became, the more success I achieved.

Let's break down that formula with what was going on for me when I was navigating 30Seconds to viability.

Being viable means you need to be capable, knowing you are equipped to do something. As the market changed, the business had to change. I had the skills to make 30Seconds viable, so to find the path, I tested various business models to determine which would be most effective.

Secure in your skills and abilities, you work with others who recognize your competence — leading to viability. Because we had built a company with a good reputation, we partnered with complementary companies that viewed us as capable. The business became viable when not only *I* knew we had what it takes but when *other people* (from employees to suppliers, customers to partners) knew we were equipped for success.

The more viable you are, the more success you can achieve. By collaborating with a diverse and capable team and with discerning business partners who believed in us, we increased our profitability and viability. The more viable we became, the more we succeeded.

This basic formula applies no matter where you are in your journey to become the fire. Use it when you're doubting yourself, when you need reassurance that you're adept, or when you're trying to achieve viability in your job, business, or other areas of life. How will you continue to learn and grow? Being capable will allow you to shine!

FLAME • Emily Smith

First Jobs: Babysitter, ice cream store worker, hostess
Education: BA (English), University of California, Berkeley
Personal Life: Married, mother of three
Board/Civic Roles: Board member, Mamas Uncut
Key Takeaway: "Always be learning and making yourself better."

Emily Smith learned all she needed to know about career viability in one fell swoop. Ecstatic to have finally gotten her first post-college job in book publishing, Emily was taken aback when she arrived at work one day only to find that the entire art department of the company had been fired. To keep up with changing technologies, the art team had been given an opportunity to learn digital, but they hadn't taken the necessary coursework. Company management fired the entire team, telling them to go get training, then to reapply for their jobs when they were up to speed.

Emily was working as a proofreader, and her job was safe. But she learned one of the most impactful lessons of her career: be capable. "You need to always be learning and making yourself better," she says. "Staying up-to-date on tools and adapting quickly to change is so important." And those traits would serve her well throughout her career navigating the turbulent digital publishing industry.

As CEO of Wild Sky Media, a Comscore-ranked top-ten digital media platform, Emily commutes from San Francisco to New York City to run the company. She's a mother of three and a cancer survivor who continued to work as a senior executive while undergoing chemotherapy. And she's my former boss at Disney.

Emily's lessons in viability began long before her first career job. As the youngest of five children, born and raised in Southern California, Emily was schooled by her parents in being capable. "It was expected in our family that you got straight As and that you worked," she explains. "If you wanted to have a social life, you needed money, and my parents weren't in the habit of handing out money. You had to earn it."

For Emily, that translated into starting work as a babysitter by age eleven. By fourteen, she had moved on to her first "real" job — scooping ice cream at the local ice cream shop — because she could walk there from her house. "Caretaking and serving roles are a great way to learn humility and to develop a good work ethic," she says. "You learn skills that are foundational for being a good human."

In college, Emily continued to work in various roles — from bank teller to barista — and with her own children, she maintains the same philosophy as her parents. "I want them to learn to deal with a boss or to keep their cool when customers yell at them over unreasonable issues. If my daughter is babysitting, I'll ask her if she cleaned up the kids' dinner dishes. Employers notice a good work ethic, and they'll put you at the top of their list."

Emily's first career job taught her not only about viability but also about knowing the value of her skills. Excited to be promoted from proofreader to assistant editor, she asked her boss why the promotion came with a raise of only twenty-five cents per hour. When her boss told Emily "That's all we can do," Emily decided she was worth more than that.

After securing a new job in the nascent digital publishing industry that paid her 50 percent more than the current job, Emily again approached her boss, letting her know about the new job and pay. "When she said 'Let me see what I can do,' my brain opened up for the first time." Realizing that her boss had not been straight with her, Emily made up her mind about where she wanted to work. "She came back and matched my new pay, but I said no. I'd been trying to have an honest conversation with a woman I admired and trusted, but I learned that many bosses won't go to bat for you until they know you're willing to quit. It's a terrible game some employers play, where they mistreat you until you prove that you know your market rate."

Emily's new job thrust her into the forefront of the online publishing industry. Working at a digital start-up that had just been purchased by internet behemoth AOL, she was creating content and managing links for one of the web's first digital magazines. As an AOL employee, and as an early online adopter, Emily made sure to learn the code, tools, and technology she needed to know in order to be successful in her evolving role.

But the job ended when AOL abruptly shut down the website. That's when Emily took on her second job in the internet space — working at an online dating start-up — creating content to help inform matchmaking. A couple of years after that, Emily found herself moving to New York City to work for the fast-growing digital lifestyle platform iVillage.

That was during the "dot-com bubble," when it seemed like anyone with a promising digital start-up could potentially strike gold. But sensing that iVillage wasn't the right fit for her, Emily decided to take a job with Disney in New York City, working for the digital division. Primarily responsible for FamilyFun.com, Emily made her first move from the editorial side and grew into managing the business side.

With a focus on growing the site's user base and community, Emily learned more than she ever had about what it took to run a viable digital enterprise. Then, in 2000, the dot-com bubble burst. "Our ad business shrank in half overnight," she explains, "and Disney decided to shut down the New York office."

But that failure created another opportunity for Emily. Her boss, who had been running the New York office with fifty people, offered Emily the opportunity to move to Los Angeles and assume leadership of what would become the Disney Family division. There was only one catch: she would have to make it viable with only fourteen people. That meant thirty-six people would be laid off, and the business would have to at least break even without those roles in place. "I had to make the business work with only editors and developers," she remembers.

Becoming capable in unfamiliar territory, such as finance, pushed Emily outside her comfort zone. "It was scary — only two of us moved from New York to LA. But we made our numbers that first year, and we earned the right to survive."

As vice president of the Disney Family Group, Emily oversaw all creative and business aspects of the division. To grow reach, her team acquired and integrated three companies — including iParenting — adding content, community, and audience to its portfolio and raising its profile with advertisers and partners. Working under Emily after Disney's acquisition of iParenting, I learned much about grit, resilience, and viability, and Emily became a mentor to me.

Emily stresses the importance of staying on your toes, being nimble, and flexing with changes — no matter where you work. "That sense of security doesn't exist anymore," she explains. "You have to compartmentalize it. Even the most profitable companies let people go all the time. Look for ways to improve the business and focus on growth, putting personal fears and anxieties aside."

Emily's advice may sound something like "Feel the fear and do it anyway," but that's not how she sees it. It's more about effectiveness, being strategic, and ensuring your survival. "People whose careers, for a time, are moving up and to the right — their spending may become equivalent to their salaries, then they become trapped to maintain their lifestyles. But if you can build up some savings and hopefully have a cushion, then you'll have more flexibility in terms of your career choices."

A couple of years after I left Disney, Emily, too, made a move. Landing at the *Los Angeles Times*, she oversaw the newspaper's digital strategy — not an easy task for a legacy print-based publication trying to make it in the new world of online media. To make the new job even more challenging, Emily transitioned from managing a team of 150 employees to initially managing only two team members. "I learned that the number of people you manage does not equal success. Every career step you take does not necessarily mean you're managing more, getting paid more, securing a better title. Every opportunity must be weighed on its own merits. They're not all up and to the right."

Emily loved working for the *LA Times*, which she calls "a career high" for her, getting to work for the local paper she grew up reading. Because it was owned by the Chicago Tribune Company, she also got to head up the *Tribune*'s digital strategy and make frequent trips to

Chicago. "It was an important time for the company. I loved working with the CEO, trying to bring in people with technology expertise. We developed the team that built out the digital paywall. We made the case that digital journalism has value, that it's a product worth paying for."

That was right around the time when Emily was diagnosed with non-Hodgkin's lymphoma, a type of cancer that begins in the white blood cells. Emily was grateful to learn that the kind of cancer she had was typically curable through chemotherapy. "I was terrified, but I had such great support. Meals were being delivered by neighbors two or three times a week. The editor of the newspaper made me musical play-lists to listen to during chemo. Boyd [her husband] was so great. You don't know what your spouse is made of until you go through cancer."

As the primary breadwinner in her family, Emily continued to work throughout her cancer treatment, timing her business trips around her chemo sessions. "I didn't think about not working. I would only travel on the third week, after chemo, so my blood levels were better, and I could travel more safely. We're all entitled to our struggles and pain, but I comforted myself with the fact that what I was dealing with, other people were dealing with far worse."

After six rounds of chemo, Emily was declared cancer-free. "Cancer and chemo sucked. I was bald, terrified, and sick. But I was cured." After facing all that fire, Emily was ready for a change. She had spent fifteen years working for big companies, and she felt like she needed a smaller environment where she could make an even greater impact. "At big companies, you spend so much time convincing others to do what you think is right. At smaller companies, that happens a lot faster. I wanted to flex different muscles."

Emily and Boyd had met as students at the University of California, Berkeley, in the San Francisco Bay Area, so it felt like a good place to return with their family — especially when Emily was offered a leadership role at a fast-growing digital media and commerce company called Brit + Co. As president of media and chief growth officer for the start-up, which aimed to help people become more creative, Emily was excited to lead all product, marketing, and growth efforts.

After three years, Emily determined it was time for her to move on. "Know when to push for something, when to hold back, and when to make your move," she advises. "People hang on out of fear, but culture changes and power shifts. You have to be able to see when your effectiveness has run its course. If you start to be less effective, or less influential, you owe it to yourself and to the company to move on."

Yet Emily stresses the importance of giving your all to the job until the day you leave. "Don't quit before you quit. Don't start lowering your productivity, because it chips away at your self-confidence and reputation. You want to be the person other people call. You want to know that you've always brought your best self to work. When you're seen as a super-engaged employee, you build bridges with people."

Emily's instincts proved right when the next step in her journey eventually led her to the top spot: CEO. Drawn to a leadership role at the online gaming and publishing company RockYou Media, Emily experienced a bit of déjà vu. The company was building a portfolio of diverse, multicultural websites for millennial parents, which, to Emily, felt a bit like coming full circle, back to her Disney days — but at the warp speed of a start-up.

Two years in, however, a restructuring was implemented by the majority-owner private equity company. The gaming division was sold, media assets were spun off into a new company, and Emily's boss, the CEO, left.

Emily was promoted to president of this new media company, focusing on publishing useful content for women and parents. The private equity group installed an interim CEO to help get the new company on its feet. Feeling that she was the right person to lead the new company, now called Wild Sky Media, Emily met with the interim CEO to make her case to take over his temporary job. "He said, 'I didn't know you had that ambition.' I was shocked, like, 'Really? Why would you presume I wouldn't? I would love to make my case as to why I'm the best candidate.'"

That conversation opened the door to Emily being short-listed for the CEO job. Next, she met with the private equity group owners. "I stayed firm in my belief in myself. I was honest about my strengths and my gaps. I knew I needed a strong CFO to be my right-hand person.

It was a strength for me to tell them what I needed to be successful. Every CEO needs a good team."

After a nine-month-long process, Emily was finally named CEO of Wild Sky Media, overseeing its portfolio of women-focused digital media brands. "I never felt insecure that I'm not an expert at every aspect of the business. I would not want to work with someone who thinks that way."

Emily's journey has taught her many lessons that helped lead her to the top, the most important of which are to stay curious and always be humble. "I ask a lot of questions," she says. "It's OK if I get it wrong. I don't mind being corrected in front of people. Having an ego that needs to be protected is fatal."

Having not only survived, but thrived, during the volatile dot-com boom and bust years, Emily has learned to navigate — and even enjoy — the constantly choppy waters of her evolving industry. "I find digital publishing to be fascinating. Since age twenty-five, I've never had a year where I got bored. Change is so constant in this industry, and I've gotten addicted to it. I'm curious, and I always want to learn more. When you stop asking questions, you start exhibiting questionable leadership traits."

Reflecting on her career, Emily notes that success isn't about achieving and maintaining a title. "It's about, are my children happy and healthy? Were my ethics high? I want my children to go into the world and be confident, kind adults. If I can drive value and business success while doing those things, then I would consider it a success. Blending those things would pass the 'rocking chair test.'"

But because of the health battle she's already been through, Emily has already passed her rocking chair test. "Having gone through a major illness, I'm just so grateful to be here. I'm thankful to have another day and another tomorrow. I feel so lucky to have been able to do everything I've done and to have my family. The 'wants' don't consume me the way they once did. There's so much bounty in my life that it seems greedy. To ask for anything more seems ungrateful."

BLAZE

I am not only surviving; I am thriving.

I am capable. I constantly advance my skills and abilities.

Other people believe that I'm equipped for success.

I am continually learning and enhancing my effectiveness.

I grow more competent and become more viable each day.

The more viable I am, the more success I achieve.

8

Be Gritty

To become the fire, you need to be gritty. Being gritty means you use the skill of *perseverance* in pursuit of your goals despite any chaos, challenges, or fire that comes your way. Perseverance in the face of adversity enables you to overcome setbacks, stick with it, and try again and again until you succeed. The more you persevere, the grittier you will become. And the grittier you become, the more success you can achieve.

When you hear the word *grit*, you may picture cowboys and pioneers in old western movies, a rough surface, or even some dirt that needs to be swept from the floor. But when I consider grit, I think of determination, strength of character, an indomitable spirit, a force to be reckoned with: traits that translate into a powerful mindset enabling you to overcome challenges while staying focused on succeeding at what you want to do.

We've become an increasingly on-demand society. From the way we communicate to the way we arrange a ride or order food, we can get what we want at the touch of a button (or an app). As a result, when we try to accomplish our goals, we can become impatient and frustrated when things don't go smoothly. When success doesn't happen quickly, it's tempting to give up on our dreams.

That's when grit becomes important. And you can't become gritty unless you persevere. More than ever, perseverance stands out as a key quality for success. That's because to persevere, you need to be patient and determined and not expect everything to happen on demand. You have to be undaunted by mistakes, failures, and fires, knowing you can bounce back. You need to persist in pursuit of your goals, despite delays.

Perseverance means you have fortitude and are willing to stick with it, no matter what. You're determined to see it to conclusion, even in the face of adversity. And if there's a setback, you have the mental toughness to try again and again until you succeed.

In her book *Grit*, University of Pennsylvania professor Dr. Angela Duckworth defines *grit* as passion and perseverance for long-term goals. She explains that grit is about having a goal that is so important to you that it fuels almost everything you do. When you are gritty, you hold steadfast to your goal, even if you make mistakes or fail along the way.

People with a gritty mindset believe that perseverance is just as important as being gifted. For example, not everyone can be a talented artist, a standout athlete, or a rocket scientist. But everyone — including you — *can* be gritty. And when you are gritty, it helps level the playing field. Being gritty means that what you may lack in terms of natural ability, talents, and resources, you can make up for with perseverance, passion, and fortitude: grit.

That's why, when it comes to success, being gritty is just as valuable as having talent, skills, or even luck (and sometimes it's even more powerful). The gritty mindset drives persistence, commitment, and resilience, which are necessary for success.

Striving to achieve your goals, you need to persist so the obstacles you encounter along your journey won't faze you to the point where you give up. That perseverance will make you gritty.

You likely recognize what I mean by *grit*. That's because many of us who grew up with differences leveraged that feeling of being on the outside to fuel our desires and goals. We saw what we *didn't* have or *couldn't* do and decided to try to change it. We used what we *did* have and *could* do to try to achieve our goals.

You know when someone tells you something can't be done, but you show them it *can* be done anyway? That's grit, and it's what kept me going as I was building my businesses.

For example, as a young mom to three children, finding the sweet spot between work and parenting wasn't easy. I found "work-life balance" to be an oxymoron. When I focused on work, family life was affected. When I turned my attention to family, I tipped the scale in the other direction. Maintaining equilibrium was an ongoing struggle, and even though I loved it all, trying to keep the precarious balance took its toll on me. Long before "self-care" was sexy — or even really a thing — I was always putting myself last, like many moms.

Some well-meaning friends suggested I give up on the business. "Maybe you just can't get it all done," they said. The thinking was that, by not having a company to worry about, I would find more balance. But having birthed, nurtured, and grown my business, the thought of giving it up was unthinkable at the time. It had become part of my identity, and I just couldn't imagine not having it in my life.

Because I was so passionate about what I was doing, I stuck with it. Whether that meant taking an important call from a rocking chair in the nursery, jotting down ideas in line at the grocery store, or combining business trips with family vacations, I found creative ways to further my goals.

But a seed had been planted: maybe someday, I would be ready to transition my business (and that day would come sooner than I realized). In the meantime, grit helped me persist through the fires — even though that scale kept tipping. And I found it's often by persevering that I achieve the most success. Adjusting my mindset to "I can do it" often meant that I really could do it. With my goals always in mind, most of what I did helped advance my mission. That's grit. And the grittier I became, the more success I achieved.

This may sound familiar to you. That's because you have been persisting through fires, too. Perhaps your life's journey has been filled with potholes or you have often felt out of balance; this can test your ability to stick with your goal.

But those bumps in the road have also made you more adaptable, determined, and resilient — and that's all part of grit. Being gritty allows you to flex in response to the friction and fires of your life so you can persevere in pursuit of success.

You likely have goals and desires, and you're wondering how to make them happen. Because I know you can become gritty (if you're not already), I have confidence that you will keep trying until you achieve success.

But if perseverance doesn't come easily to you yet, don't worry. It takes patience and practice and the understanding that there may be a long road ahead. You may find that it takes effort to set both short- and long-term goals and to let them drive your actions.

All the time and effort you put into persistence will pay off, because as you persevere, your grit is amplified. And that grit will make you a force to be reckoned with. In this chapter, I will show you how to become gritty — to persevere despite life's challenges, chaos, and fire — so you can achieve more success.

Perseverance Is Key to Being Gritty

To become gritty, you have to persevere, which means two things: (1) with determination, you set a goal, then focus on it, and

(2) with an indomitable spirit, you stick to achieving that goal, confronting and resolving any challenges that come your way. Perseverance enables you to overcome setbacks and try again and again until you succeed.

We enhance our perseverance in various ways: By being patient, realizing that not everything will happen when we want it to happen. By flexing in response to life's friction, bouncing back from mistakes, failures, and fires. By allowing the inevitable bumps in the road to increase our fortitude, commitment, and mental toughness. By persisting in pursuit of short- and long-term goals, as well as smaller, and then increasingly bigger, goals. By not focusing on what we *don't* have or *can't* do and instead leveraging what we *do* have or *can* do.

When learning to be gritty, it's important to be proactive and just keep going. It's like what Dory, the bright blue fish in the Disney movie *Finding Nemo*, says to her friend Marlin, when encouraging him to not give up on finding his son Nemo: you have to "just keep swimming."

You can't sit back and just wait for things to happen. You must take action and actively look for opportunities in order to *make* things happen. If one door closes — meaning, you try a strategy that doesn't work or something derails your plans — it's not helpful to just lament and wait for another door to open. You have to get into the mindset of always moving forward, of opening another door yourself. Just as Dory encouraged Marlin, you have to look for other ways to accomplish your goals.

You don't have to be a CEO or an entrepreneur (or even a feisty fish) to open doors. Anyone can persevere and find ways to keep going, even if it takes more time and effort than you'd like. If you are passionate about something — if it really matters to you — then it will be worth the energy it takes to stick with it. One of the main drivers of proactivity, of opening doors, is passion. That fiery, intense love or desire you feel for your goals — that indefatigable spirit — is what fuels perseverance and, ultimately, grit.

I know this from experience because I'm passionate about what I do. Throughout my life, I've been driven by fierce and fiery love. That passion gave me the energy to stick with it, to keep opening doors, even when things were hard or went sideways.

When building iParenting, we didn't always have the answers, and we ran into many roadblocks. Fires flared frequently, and we had to fight them on the fly. Learning to run a business required trial and error: from securing IP to building awareness; from managing finances to hiring a team. But every time my perseverance solved a problem (we got the domain name we wanted), generated exposure for the company (we were featured by another publication), achieved a revenue milestone (we landed a new client), or improved our team (we hired a key employee), I was fulfilled. Then that growing grit would drive me to do even more.

I loved what I was doing so much that it never felt like "work." It was my mission, so I didn't give up. Through that process, I found that when you pursue your passion with unwavering determination, chances are very good that you will stick with it to conclusion. And the more you persevere, the better the chances that you will succeed.

We succeeded in building a transformative media platform, and we succeeded again later when we sold it to Disney. As director and executive editor for the Disney Interactive Media Group, I was working with a team based in Los Angeles while managing my office, team, and family in Chicagoland (and traveling back and forth between the two). Although it didn't seem possible, my work-life challenges intensified.

Despite the hectic schedule, time zone differences, deadlines, and two offices of people to coordinate and collaborate with, I was enjoying every moment of the roller-coaster ride and finding ways to open doors whenever I encountered a bump in the road.

That transition, from growing a fast-paced entrepreneurial business to working for one of the biggest media companies in the world, required patience — and keeping an open mind to new ways of doing things. I had a lot to learn about navigating multiple layers of a global business. For example, if I wanted to make a change to the website or launch a new idea, it was no longer just a matter of making a decision and getting my team to execute it. Like most big businesses, Disney required new ideas to go through several departments (marketing, finance, legal, etc.) before getting approved (or not). That meant I had to learn who to talk to about what, making my rounds through the company organizational chart.

I discovered that to be effective in my new role, I would have to be proactive and constantly knock on doors. I had to make my case by writing report after report, specific to each department; get buy-in from multiple stakeholders; be patient with their review process; and above all, stick with it, even if I was at the same time caring for a sick kid, dealing with a staffing issue, meeting a client deadline, or catching a late-night flight. If I wanted to get something done, I had to persevere.

One of my favorite memories of that time was creating and hosting a series of professionally produced videos for the Disney Family Group. I'd realized that informative online video was becoming more important and would only grow in demand with the rise of mobile. My passion had found new purpose, and I was inspired to produce food, health, and exercise videos for moms.

My Disney team thought it was a good idea, but that initial reaction only meant I could move it from a concept to a possible plan. The next step was fleshing out the proposal, then presenting it to stakeholders in various departments. From establishing a budget to gathering editorial, graphics, and other creative input to clearing legal hurdles — opening doors meant going through layer after layer of review and approvals. After one door was successfully opened, I moved on to the next.

But that perseverance paid off when everything finally lined up and the video series was green-lighted for production. Every team member — from creative, marketing, business, legal, finance, and production areas — had a role to play, and I had to coordinate it all. Even though it was a lot to manage, I loved what I was doing so much that I never tired of it. When at last the videos went live on the website, I was elated (and exhausted). But the time, effort, and energy were all worth it.

SPARK

What are you most passionate about? Think of an example of passion in your life. Then think about a time when you believed you could succeed, despite challenges, chaos, or fire that stood in your way. What was the result?

When building 30Seconds, I was again driven by passion. The fire in my heart continues to fuel me, despite similar work-life challenges. I find that 30Seconds requires the same time, energy, and resources as my roles at iParenting and Disney did. Yet because it's my passion, the relentless demands of running a business are simply woven into my life. When the results of my efforts are positive, I'm driven to work harder to make an even greater impact.

That's why one of the best answers I can give to those who ask me "How can I achieve success, too?" is this: do what you love, work harder than anyone else, be relentless, and stick with it, and success will follow. When you love what you do, you'll be good at it. When you love what you do, you'll open door after door for it. When you love what you do, you'll be recognized for it. When you love what you do, it's contagious. When you love what you do, you'll be passionate about it. And that passion you feel means you'll never "work" a day in your life.

Being Gritty Means Focusing on What You *Can* Do

Being gritty is about not fixating on what you *don't* have or *can't* do. It's about throwing your energy behind what you *do* have or *can* do. When you grow up with a lack of resources, connections, abilities, or possessions, it's often easier to see limitations instead of opportunities and fall into a scarcity mindset.

In his 1989 bestselling book, *The 7 Habits of Highly Effective People*, author Stephen Covey describes the scarcity mindset as a way of thinking that implies when one person wins, another has to lose; if one person succeeds, another has to fail; if one person has something, another does not. In essence, it's the belief that there aren't enough successes, resources, or things to go around.

The opposite view is the abundance mindset, a way of thinking that implies there is enough of everything for everyone. The abundance mindset aligns with being gritty. They're both just a matter of adjusting the lens through which you view the world.

The scarcity mindset begins with the feeling that you are lacking in something, such as opportunities, money, time, abilities, experiences, or possessions. And because you feel those things are scarce or in limited supply, you feel frustrated and deprived.

That feeling of deprivation may manifest as negativity or a lack of motivation. For example, some people may think, "Since I don't have X, I can't do Y." But this is not a helpful way of looking at life. It can make you feel defeated before you even start the game, and this way of thinking can be a ticket to nowhere.

Whether I was living in a war zone, dealing with bullies,

coping with being left behind, or enduring my parents' fighting, it would have been easy to fall into a scarcity mindset — that feeling of being deprived. Deprived of a safe or stable environment. Deprived of the "right" clothes or possessions. Deprived of enough friends or of being included. Deprived of my parents' time or resources.

There may have been stuff I didn't have. But when I spent time with family and friends who lived in actual poverty or from paycheck to paycheck, barely making ends meet, I realized there was a bunch of stuff I *did* have: family, food, clothing, shelter, and more. My situational awareness told me I was privileged to have abundance all around, and for that, I was grateful.

Perhaps most importantly, I discovered I had the ability to work. That meant that if ever there was something material I felt was lacking, I could work toward getting it myself. Adjusting my lens to focus on what I *could* do, instead of what I *couldn't* do, made me feel positive and productive — traits that align with an abundance mindset and are foundational to grit.

No matter what I was doing, looking at life through the lens of "I can do this" helped me persevere through challenges that often felt insurmountable, reminding me to focus on what I do have, instead of what I don't. That gritty mindset carried me from grade school to high school and college and propelled me in my career, through my health issues, and even throughout pregnancy and parenting.

I built 30Seconds with single-minded intensity. But many times, my life felt overwhelming. The challenges of single motherhood, running a household, and managing a company — all while dealing with serious health challenges — sometimes felt like too much to handle. And that was if everything was going smoothly.

Everyone experiences times when life throws you a curveball.

Although I try not to be surprised by surprises (since they happen so often), they can upset the precarious applecart of life. Just when you think you have it all balanced, something happens to throw everything off.

In my attempts to "do it all," I often felt I was burning the candle at both ends — and most days, my hair was on fire as well. So many things were falling through the cracks. I couldn't do this project on time or solve that problem perfectly. The laundry wasn't getting done, or the dog made a mess in the kitchen (or ate the kids' homework) again. It seemed like there was just so much I couldn't do.

I saw my life as a series of waves: surges that just kept coming. Some were big and some were small, but they were relentless, like fire. And if I let the waves overtake me, I would surely drown. To rise above that feeling, it had to be OK that I couldn't get it all done. I didn't have to do every last thing. I had to shift my focus from what I *couldn't* do to what I *could* do.

I started to think about how waves can be unsettling, or they can be soothing. Just as fire can be unsettling, but a fireplace can be soothing. The way that waves, and fires, present themselves in life is all a matter of how you look at them.

I reframed my thinking so I wasn't as worried about the waves. Since I knew they would keep coming, I decided to let them come. Instead of fighting them or resisting them, I would ride them — one at a time. I told myself I was not going to drown in those waves, even if it sometimes felt as if I were.

As my cousins taught me to say in Croatian when I visited them in my father's homeland: *lako ćemo*, meaning "Stress less. Take it easy. It'll be OK." (In Croatia, we often accompanied this phrase with a shot of slivovitz, a "medicinal" homemade plum brandy, which seemed to help, too!) Using *lako ćemo* as a mantra, I rode those waves as best I could. Inhaling peace, exhaling stress,

I kept breathing — and that helped calm the waters. I took each wave one by one, catching my breath in between while preparing for the next one, which was surely coming.

I told myself "You can do this," even when the challenges of single motherhood overwhelmed me, and many times I couldn't work as much as I wanted to. Even when my health battles side-lined me, and I (literally) couldn't catch my breath, I pictured those waves. I breathed in and out. Even while in the hospital, and many times with an IV in my arm, I focused on what I could do: take a breath, comfort a child, call someone, send an email, share an article, tweet some inspiration.

But it was during one of my hospital stays, before I had been diagnosed, that things got particularly dire. My heart rate had been swinging from too low (bradycardia) to too high (tachycardia) for hours. After several episodes of near fainting, combined with per-sistent chest pain, I was back in an ambulance, being rushed to the emergency room. Though appearing, on the outside, to be a healthy forty-something-year-old (the blessing and the curse of having an "invisible illness"), I underwent all the "did you have a heart attack?" tests. Then I was admitted to the hospital.

In my hospital room, I breathed through the pain and tried to get some rest. But my heart was still struggling to find an even beat. As the numbers on the heart rate monitor went higher, and my already low blood pressure numbers went lower, my nurse looked concerned. She stayed with me, watching the numbers bounce around. When I told her the chest pain was getting worse and that I was light-headed, and the numbers showed my heart beating about two hundred beats per minute, she called a code blue.

Although I didn't know this at the time, *code blue* is the term used in some hospitals to quickly alert staff that there's a medical emergency happening. By calling a code blue, nurses and doctors can quickly mobilize and access the specialists and tools needed to save someone's life. Within moments of my nurse calling the code, a team pushing a crash cart, loaded with life-saving equipment, burst through my hospital room door.

I remember faces above me, and then nothing. I don't know how long I was out, but when I woke up, a new nurse was on duty. She asked me how I was feeling (dazed, confused, out of it) and let me know the doctor would be there soon.

My conversation with the doctor was frightening. He explained that he suspected I had an "electrical" problem with my heart, an arrhythmia that was causing the heart to beat abnormally, and that I might need a pacemaker. Hmm. I could barely comprehend what he was telling me, but that feeling of having been near death stayed with me. I knew I would do whatever it would take to get better, to keep going, to never say die. Fast-forward to my trips to the Mayo Clinic, where I was diagnosed, and the ensuing treatments, which helped stabilize my condition.

SPARK
When have you persisted in achieving a goal, despite bumps in the road? What made you keep going? Are there any words (mantras) you use to help you persevere? How would you define *perseverance* in your own life?

When I think back on those scary experiences, I realize it was grit that got me through. My intense love and desire to be there for my children, my fiery passion for my work, my drive to make a difference — those feelings fueled me not only to survive but also to do what it would take to thrive.

Being Gritty Means Persevering toward Possibilities

That "never say die" attitude carried over to 30Seconds. As hard as things got in my personal and professional lives, I refused to quit. Giving up was simply not an option. Even when potential investors and business partners sexually harassed me. Even when I couldn't safely raise the capital I needed to grow the business bigger, faster. Even when I couldn't lease the best office or hire all the people I needed. All those things I couldn't do were balanced by seeing the possibilities of what I *could* do.

I may not have gotten funded by venture capitalists, but that didn't stop me from raising capital with an angel investor, Mary Dillon, whom I was so proud to have backing me. I may not have been able to hire every employee I needed, but that didn't stop me from working with mission-driven people, like the ones I worked with across my two companies, who were almost as passionate about the business as I was. And it couldn't stop us from building a diverse community of contributors who believed in and supported our mission to inspire and be inspired.

Although I couldn't sign a long-term lease for a fancy office, that didn't stop me from creating a vibrant workspace in one of the first, and best, tech incubators in the world: the 1871 tech center in downtown Chicago. The 1871 incubator is a lively coworking space that's home to Chicago's leading entrepreneurs. What was once just an idea dreamed up by visionary J. B. Pritzker (who later became governor of Illinois) has become a force behind growth, jobs, and success. "We wanted to build a place where start-ups could get off the ground, grow, and mature," explains Pritzker, a billionaire, entrepreneur, venture capitalist, politician, and dad.

When I heard about 1871, I applied for membership right away. For just a few hundred dollars a month, I had my own desk in the "reserved" space, with access to conference rooms, event space, a kitchen, a reception area, and much more. I'm proud to say that 30Seconds became one of 1871's first start-up members.

And there, I continued to open doors and focus on what I *could* do. Because I was considered a high-potential member of 1871, I was nominated for an intensive accelerator program through Google for Startups and Blackbox Connect.

Google and Blackbox identified the most promising founders and start-ups from hundreds of nominations submitted by partner organizations around the world, including 1871. After making it through multiple interviews and the selection process, I was invited to participate in the program. As excited as I was, I had no idea how much of an impact it would have on me, especially in terms of persevering toward possibilities.

Spending two weeks in Silicon Valley, with nineteen other female founders from around the world, I was immersed in what's been described as an elite "boot camp" for the most promising global start-ups. Five of us were from the United States. The other fifteen hailed from as far away as Australia, Dubai, France, Germany, India, Ireland, and Uganda. The companies all had launched a successful product with consumer or client traction.

Living and working together, and sharing meals, outings, seminars, workshops, and even late-night conversations by the firepit, created invaluable camaraderie. Connections were made; collaborations were formed; inspiration was shared.

Through Blackbox, I connected with the amazing tech guru who would become our chief technology officer (CTO) — the team member who was instrumental in building out the new and improved 30Seconds tech platform. Not only did he become a trusted and respected colleague, but our families have also become friends.

Because Google was founded in a garage more than two decades ago, its team values what it takes to start small — but dream big. Spending a day as "Googlers" on the company's Silicon Valley campus, each founder was paired with a Google employee mentor who gave us constructive feedback on our businesses (it's incredibly cool to talk user experience with a Google product manager!). We ate in the employee cafeteria, took a break in a nap pod, interacted with team leaders, and, above all, were inspired by the "moonshot" mindset that makes Google, well, Google. (Ever heard of self-driving cars?)

We refined our business pitches until we could share our message as a handshake pitch, an elevator pitch, a napkin pitch, and the initial investor pitch that we delivered at our end-of-program showcase dinner. It was an iterative process that resulted in clear messaging.

The culmination of those two intense weeks was a *Shark Tank*–style presentation on an outdoor stage in front of an audience including venture capitalists, angel investors, executives, and entrepreneurs. Each founder had three minutes to present, then another couple of minutes for Q and A. It was nerve-racking and exhilarating all at once.

Sometimes you're so busy dealing with the minutiae of all that must get done on any given day that you miss the bigger opportunity — all the possibilities. Those two weeks allowed me to focus on my mission and enhance the plan to make it happen. I "graduated" with a road map for my business, pairing my passion with my strategic business goals. I saw the opportunities, and my abundance mindset was in overdrive.

That's why the word buzzing in my mind after the program was *possibilities*. Having just been immersed in Silicon Valley, the word *unicorn* was also floating around. The unicorn concept opens a world of possibilities — possibilities that expand the mind to inhabit a universe in which mere mortals can achieve magical things.

Although becoming a unicorn (a start-up valued at more than $1 billion) is rare, there's more potential for start-ups today than ever before. We're seeing more and more female-founded companies become unicorns. While that's very motivating, there's much more work ahead to ensure women from all walks of life can achieve life-changing success. As more diverse women realize their dreams, more of us can see ourselves doing the same, creating our own paths to success.

But billion-dollar valuation or not, the "shoot for the moon" mentality is what every one of us should feel when building our careers and businesses, because even nonunicorns can be the best of their kind and change the world for the better, in their own unique ways. And when you focus on what you can do, instead of what you can't, the possibilities truly are endless.

At 30Seconds, we define what it means to be a unicorn in our own way. We persevere. We keep dreaming. We keep doing. We keep imagining. We keep creating. We keep trying. We keep inspiring. We keep sharing our unique energy, and we reach more and more people. We put good into the world, people pass it on, our audience grows, and our business thrives. Being gritty is in our DNA, and that is why we succeed.

SPARK
How can you enhance your grit? Come up with your own definition of being gritty. How can the gritty mindset manifest in your own life so you can see more possibilities?

The Virtuous Loop of Being Gritty

To become the fire, you need to be gritty. Being gritty means you're determined and you know you can accomplish whatever you set out to do. With indomitable spirit, you persevere in pursuit of your goals — despite any challenge, chaos, or fire that comes your way. Perseverance in the face of adversity means you overcome setbacks and stick with it, trying again and again until you succeed. The more you persevere, the grittier you will become. And the grittier you become, the more success you will achieve.

This pattern played out for me repeatedly. Perseverance helped me set goals and stick with them; overcome adversity, even when things got hard; and achieve what mattered most, no matter what. Whether I was building a business while raising my family or advancing my career while battling health issues, perseverance fueled me to stick with it, trying and trying again until I achieved my goals. The more I accomplished, the grittier I became. And the grittier I became, the more success I achieved.

Let's break down that formula with what was going on for me when I was finding the path forward for 30Seconds.

Being gritty means you set goals and are determined to stick to them. When big success didn't happen right away and some doors closed, I found ways to open other doors. Determined to achieve my goals, I looked for creative ways to make that happen.

With indomitable spirit, you persevere despite adversity, which increases your grit. Instead of focusing on what I didn't have or couldn't do, I let passion fuel my perseverance. Commitment helped me overcome obstacles and leverage what I did have and what I could do.

The grittier you are, the more success you can achieve. The more I persevered through my challenges, working through them wave by wave, the more my grit grew. And the grittier I became, the more success I achieved.

This basic formula applies no matter where you are in your journey to become the fire. Use it when you're not sure you can do it, when you need inspiration to stick with it, or when you need to intensify your persistence. Remember to "just keep swimming" so you can make your own big splash!

FLAME • Winnie Park

First Job: Developed motivational programs for students in Los Angeles during the LA riots

Education: BA (public and international affairs), Princeton University; MBA (corporate finance and marketing), Northwestern University

Personal Life: Divorced, mother of one

Board/Civic Roles: Board member, Express; board member, Dollar Tree Stores

Key Takeaway: "Be willing to roll up your sleeves and do the work."

Winnie Park never dreamed of becoming a CEO. In fact, her goal in life was almost the opposite: to follow her passion, come what may. Early on, she decided that by being passionate about whatever she was doing, she'd figure out how to clothe, feed, and care for herself. She purposely never worried about making money.

Winnie believed that by doing what she loved, the money and success would follow — despite any hardships along the way. "You have to figure out what makes your heart beat fast," Winnie says. And by being gritty, that's exactly what she did.

As the new CEO of fashion retailer Forever 21, a Los Angeles–based fast-fashion industry leader with about 450 locations in the United States and online, Winnie is focused on a fresh start — for the brand and for herself. Founded by Korean American immigrants in Los Angeles more than thirty years ago and having recently been purchased out of bankruptcy by strategic investors, Forever 21 is poised for the next step in its evolution. And so is its CEO — herself a Korean American immigrant who most recently led her former company, Paper Source, through bankruptcy to a successful sale.

The road Winnie took wasn't easy — especially since she wasn't even born in the United States. But perseverance and grit have served Winnie her entire life. At age two and a half, she emigrated from Korea to the United States with her parents, who had only $500 in their pockets. The immigrant family first landed in Chicago, where Winnie's father, a doctor, had to take five buses in order to get to work. Winnie and her parents eventually moved to rural Tennessee, just outside Chattanooga, where her father established his medical practice.

Growing up as a petite Korean girl in rural Tennessee wasn't easy. Winnie was mercilessly bullied because of her race, her gender, her size — and just about everything else — so becoming mentally tough was key. "People had preconceived notions of me based on my appearance," she explains. "I had to work hard to define who I was and what I was capable of, so I became very self-aware from an early age."

Winnie channeled her adversity into her education. As the child of immigrants, she knew her parents wanted her to learn as much as she could so she, too, could have her shot at the American dream. "My parents wanted me to think critically and aspire to do something I loved. But also to go beyond that, by giving back to the community and contributing to society."

Winnie's parents and her maternal grandmother were her biggest role models. Like many immigrant families, Winnie's parents had to make tough decisions — one of which was leaving Winnie's infant sister, Susie, behind in Korea while they immigrated to the United States. When the family went back for Susie a year and a half later, Winnie, then age four, was thrilled to reunite with her baby sister. "I met my best friend, and a soul mate," she remembers.

Winnie's grandmother, who came to live with the family in the United States when Winnie was ten, also had a profound impact on her. When her grandmother, as a young woman, found herself widowed with a child, she worked as a maid to make money to feed, clothe, and educate her daughter. "She loved fashion, like my mother. She was always working, but she was always happy in the moment with what she had. She knew she would succeed."

Winnie adopted that gritty mindset and aimed it straight at her studies. Her passion for learning helped her navigate the friction and fires of her life. Because she was so passionate about school, she excelled — despite the bullies that made life difficult.

After Winnie graduated from Princeton, her first career job was working as executive director of Princeton's Project 55, a nonprofit focused on social change that was started by consumer rights advocate (and fellow Princeton alum) Ralph Nader and the Princeton class of 1955. Because Winnie was passionate about giving back to the community, she loved the job. But since it paid her only $18,000 a year, to make ends meet, she found herself also working as an aerobics instructor at Gold's Gym and on the sales floor at fashion retailer Banana Republic.

Winnie learned a lot from those side jobs — even if they weren't exactly where she thought she might be after graduating. At Gold's Gym, "I got paid to work out. I learned how to be in front of an audience of fifty people. I learned stage presence, improvisation, and to be on time."

Winnie got her job at Banana Republic simply because she loved shopping there. "My mother was a pharmacist, but her true passion was fashion, and she instilled that in me." Winnie shopped often at a particular Banana Republic store, and the manager noticed her. "She invited me to work there. I learned about building relationships with customers. I learned that you have to ask for the sale, the importance of starting a dialogue to connect with the customer, and that customer experience in retail is about people — not just product."

Winnie also studied in Paris, London, and Japan. She spent a year at Kyoto University studying Japanese while also teaching English. During that time, Winnie traveled to Bali, Hong Kong, and Thailand as a backpacker. "I am inspired by being a student of new cultures. My wanderlust is something that has always given me a broader perspective on life."

After a year abroad, she returned to Chicago to pursue her MBA. After graduating from Northwestern, Winnie realized she had a lot more to learn about business. She decided to continue her journey at the strategy consulting firm McKinsey & Company.

After working on the company's retail, marketing, and consumer digital practices, Winnie was eventually recruited by clothing company Levi Strauss. There she found her passion for merchandising. "I was excited to have the opportunity to work in the fashion industry — even though people were taking a risk on me because I didn't have the experience."

Winnie succeeded at Levi Strauss, despite not having industry experience, for one simple reason: she had grit. At that company, she took on tough projects that no one else wanted. Working on the Dockers brand, "I was not afraid to do the grunt work. I found myself doing everything from pinning fabric on boards for marketing meetings to developing a new fit strategy for the plus-customer. I learned the business from the ground up."

Winnie was eventually asked to run the entire Dockers women's business. By going above and beyond her role, she had earned the respect of company management, which led to increasing recognition and opportunities.

Running a wholesale business at Levi's led Winnie to want to learn more about retail stores and e-commerce, owning the last mile with the end customer. So she jumped at the opportunity to join Hong Kong–based DFS Group Limited, the world's leading luxury travel retailer. DFS Group, majority-owned by Louis Vuitton Moët Hennessy (LVMH), offers a curated selection of products from some of the world's most prestigious brands, via duty-free stores located in airports and downtown and resort locations on four continents.

As global vice president of fashion, and later as executive vice president of marketing, Winnie traded her sprawling five-thousand-square-foot house in the San Francisco Bay Area for a tiny Hong Kong apartment — and she loved it. "You realize you don't need all that 'stuff.' A simplified life is so nice."

Winnie traveled the world, growing luxury fashion on an international scale for DFS. "I did everything from sitting in the front row at fashion shows for Gucci and Chloé, to building the DFS website and launching e-commerce, to growing the business in places as far away as Abu Dhabi and India."

Winnie again credits her success at LVMH to grit. "In that role, I was stretched. I was given opportunities because of my work ethic and sweat equity, because I'm comfortable solving tough problems and building teams from the ground up."

Winnie notes that being open to learning and staying humble helped her grow as a leader. "The humility to work with world-class talent who can teach you about everything from how to do business in India to building an e-commerce platform is amazing. You don't have to be the expert, or always be right. Be willing to roll up your sleeves and do the work."

Winnie views her career in terms of perseverance, of taking steps — each one leading to something greater. "I take risks. I know I'm going to be uncomfortable. When you are willing to learn with humility, empower amazing teams, and you deliver results, you're given opportunities to do more."

That's exactly what happened before Winnie was offered the CEO job at Paper Source. "Philippe Schaus [then CEO of DFS Group, now CEO of Moët Hennessy Wines and Spirits Division] told me I could be a CEO. He empowered me to dream of running a company as a CEO, and he pushed me out of my comfort zone with this goal in mind."

Winnie may not originally have had the goal of becoming a CEO, but a CEO job found her anyway. A private equity fund behind Paper Source — a national retailer with about 155 stores offering a range of unique paper products, crafting workshops, and gifts — reached out to her about taking the top job at the Chicago-based company. At the time, Winnie had recently gotten divorced and was raising her preteen daughter, Anabelle, on her own in Hong Kong. Moving back to Chicago appealed to her. "I decided to jump into the deep end of the pool," she recalls.

Winnie dove right in and found the water was fine. Heading up Paper Source allowed her to bring creativity to life. "We had so much fun combining humor, whimsy, handmade beauty that speaks to our customers, celebrating small life moments or momentous occasions."

Key to her success as CEO was deciding that she was not the most important person. "I decided to build a team, a culture. I hired people who are so much better than I am. Our CFO ran circles around me; our CMO was so much better than me."

Today, Winnie still surrounds herself with people who have a variety of talents to create a well-rounded team. "I always ask, 'Can I learn something from this person?' I get all the geniuses in one room and unify them. You don't have to be the smartest person in the room. When the boss says 'I don't know. What do you think?' it's very empowering for her people."

Winnie believes women should support each other, so that's part of the culture she fosters. "In every meaningful job I've had, I've been lucky enough to have a female boss or mentor push me to do more, be better, and to stand up for me. This has been critical in my career progression, and something I take seriously in my role."

Paper Source had been expanding before the pandemic, transforming from just a retailer into an omnichannel lifestyle brand. But the global health crisis had a severe impact on its business. Winnie's grit would become more important than ever as she led the company through filing for Chapter 11 bankruptcy protection, then the sale to a strategic investor.

What she is perhaps most proud of is how her team navigated the choppy waters. "We retained our team and talent. It was a real exercise in leading from the top, to keep everyone super energized and excited." After transitioning the company to new ownership, Winnie decided it was time to shift gears. "I had to let go. I needed to exhale. Businesses and brands need to evolve. I needed to reconnect with my daughter. It was time for me to move on."

When Winnie was offered the CEO job at Forever 21, everything came full circle: her love for fashion, her retail experience, her leadership abilities, even her ethnic heritage. "Our stores and website have the potential to be places where our customers can find community and content, not just great products. It's exciting, like that feeling when you go on a first date — that anxious anticipation of great things to come."

You might think taking the next step in her career could be daunting, especially since Winnie is commuting to work in Los Angeles from her home in Chicago so Anabelle can finish high school. But Winnie is undaunted. "Because of what we went through at Paper Source, there's very little left to fear. My journey has taught me every humbling lesson. My ego has become a nonissue. It's about the belief of people and teams: what's held in their minds and hearts. Leaders set the tone, but it's their job to unleash the power of the people they work with, because when people are operating in their zone of genius, there is no stopping them."

But what Winnie considers the most important part of her story is that she's Mama to Anabelle, who was instrumental in Winnie's decision to take the Forever 21 job. "It's one of her favorite brands. She said the brand and I both deserve a fresh start; that's why it's the perfect fit for me."

Raising Anabelle to be gritty has been a key component of her parenting. "I tell her that life is a journey with no map; it's not a destination. I teach her how to stand up for herself, that there will always be naysayers and negative feedback. Sometimes, the biggest naysayer is the voice in each of us that doubts we can achieve our potential."

As a single mother, navigating the world of parenting has been challenging. "I wish that being a parent came with an instruction manual, but what it does come with is guilt, as you think of everything you could do better."

That work-life roller coaster requires enormous grit to keep it all going smoothly. "I've never had work-life balance, and that's OK. I believe that truly successful people see their work and life as a continuum, not hard stops. If you don't, you will always resent work. As a CEO, I can spend more time with my employees than with my family. Always feeling like you are owed, or that things don't measure up, is a formula for unhappiness."

So how do you not build up resentment? "Stop doing the equation; stop keeping score. To find some balance, for example, take an hour before work to get in some exercise," she suggests. "It's a continuum. Release yourself from the bonds of money. Don't think of money and accolades as success."

Winnie never dreads returning to work after the weekend. "I never get the Sunday blues," she says. "I wake up happy, knowing I can make a difference. I'm comfortable in the moment. That is success to me. But what motivates me the most is that I can tell my daughter respects the work I do. Making her proud is my greatest accomplishment of all."

BLAZE

I am gritty. I know I can do it.

I stick with it, no matter what.

I am patient. I am passionate. I am determined.

I am undaunted by mistakes, failures, and fires.

I am mentally tough, and I persevere to achieve my goals.

If one door closes, I open another door.

The grittier I am, the more success I achieve.

9

Be the Inspiration

To become the fire, you need to inspire and be inspired. Being the inspiration means you use the skill of *leadership* to motivate yourself and others to make the world a better place. Using positivity to fuel your purpose, you generate sparks that can turn into a mission to serve the greater good. Showing leadership enables you to bring out the best in yourself and in others so you can effect positive change. The more you lead with empathy, the more inspiring you will be. And as you become the inspiration, you'll achieve more success.

You know how powerful it is for someone to provide inspiration, shine a light, or spark positivity. But you can't just sit back and wait for that to happen to you. You have to be the inspiration for yourself. When you look at the world through a lens of making it better, you will see possibilities all around you. Whether it's within your family, neighborhood, community, school, work — or an even broader scale — using empathy to notice what is needed, or what can be improved, can trigger ideas to make that corner of the world a better place.

By identifying what you or others need, what upsets you, or what you would like to change, you can spark the inspiration it takes to solve problems or find solutions. Then you can come up with a plan for making positive change. This gives you a mission and empowers you. Moving forward with positivity inspires you to bring helpful ideas to life. As you make progress, you will inspire others to join you or to create their own ideas (or both).

Starting small, transforming manageable goals into realities, you will be inspired to come up with bigger and bigger visions that make an even greater impact on the world, and your inner light will shine for all to see.

Projecting a ray of light to others while retaining a strong inner resolve, you will be seen as a leader. This is a superpower many of us develop without even knowing we are honing this skill. That's because we have gone through fire and have come out on the other side of it — stronger than before. And that inner strength radiates like a beacon.

But leadership is not just about inspiring others. Leadership starts within, by inspiring *yourself*. Leaders are open to new experiences and different ways of doing things. They are optimistic about their abilities, and they know they can make a difference, no matter how big or small. Despite how bleak things may seem, leaders create positive change in themselves first. That positive energy is contagious, spreading to those around them like wildfire.

Leaders are self-starters with inner strength, which enables them to find, and fuel, their motivation. Driven by a mission or purpose that is authentic to them, they not only find inspiration — often in the mundane or chaotic everyday moments of life — but also act on that inspiration. Leaders manifest their inspiration, transforming their ideas into real-world change.

When you are inspired, you not only motivate yourself to

create but also motivate others to develop creative ideas. As a leader, you inspire yourself and other people to achieve. And you are open to receiving inspiration from them in return.

Those who inspire others dedicate themselves to their missions for the betterment of a community, not just themselves. By taking action — by walking the walk, not just talking the talk — they become a positive force that guides others to achieve a mission, too (whether they join the leader's mission, create their own, or both). Leaders are forward thinkers, with clarity and focus, who motivate others to work with them toward a goal that serves the greater good.

Right about now you may be thinking, "But I'm not a leader (at least not yet anyway)." That's OK, because developing leadership skill takes time, effort, and trial and error. But the good news is that anyone can be a leader — including you. Leaders aren't just born; they are made. And often, it's the challenges we overcome, the chaos we work through, and the fires we battle that forge the inner strength it takes to lead and inspire.

As I was growing up, I wasn't thinking much about inspiration, but it was happening anyway. Often surrounded by stuff that seemed to go wrong, I spent a lot of time figuring out how to make things better. And frequently, it's the most traumatic events that motivate you to make a difference.

Mi madre had a friend, *la amiga,* who lived in a two-flat apartment building right across the street from our massive public high school. Like *mi madre,* she was from Puerto Rico. *La amiga* lived in a rough-and-tumble neighborhood, with gang members who hung out on street corners and sold drugs in plain sight. *Mi madre* would take me on visits to *la amiga,* and the two would spend hours speaking rapid-fire *Español* and laughing like schoolgirls.

I mostly enjoyed going on these visits because *la amiga* had cats everywhere. And one of those cats was usually having kittens, which meant there were always kittens everywhere. So going to visit *la amiga* meant I was going to spend time with the kittens, and it didn't matter that I was largely ignored by *mi madre* and *la amiga*.

But it turned out the cats were largely ignored, too. It made me sad that there was usually no food or water and that the litter box was always horribly full (and hopelessly gross). To improve the situation, I spent part of my visits cleaning the litter box, wiping up messes, searching for food, filling water bowls, and caring for the neglected kittens. Seeing problems, feeling empathy, finding solutions, making life better — I was taking leadership in my own little ways.

The adult cats were skittish and scared, not used to getting attention. They would hiss or raise a paw full of claws in aggression if I approached them. So I mostly left them alone. But the kittens had not yet been affected by the lack of care or love in their environment.

To effect positive change, I tried my best to make up for that apathy. I would hold them, sing to them, and give those scrawny kittens a bath in the sink, one by one. As I ran an old wire brush through their freshly cleaned fur, the kittens would purr and fall asleep in my arms. The time I spent with them was likely some of the only care they got, and I was sad knowing they would grow up and become scared and aggressive — if they survived at all.

Inevitably, I would fall in love with one of the kittens and, when it was time to go home, I would beg and plead with *mi madre* to let me take one with us. I figured if I could "save" one of the kittens, I would be making at least a little bit of a difference. I wanted to interrupt the cycle of "uncared-for kitten turns into aggressive cat," rescuing a little life in my own tiny way. But *mi madre* always said no. As a mom of three who worked outside the home, I'm sure she felt she had enough on her plate.

But on one of those visits, that changed after a neighbor of *la amiga* had a mental breakdown and was nearly killed. I was tending to the kittens when I heard screaming from outside the apartment building. I ran to the open, screened window to see what the crisis was.

The downstairs neighbor was on the front lawn, completely naked, shouting at no one *en Español*. I knew somebody had to do something to help, and I decided that person was me. I ran to find *mi madre* and *la amiga*, telling them about the screaming woman. By the time *mi madre* and *la amiga* made it to the window, the neighbor was running into the busy street, catching the speeding drivers by surprise.

As *la amiga* called 911, I yelled out the window, damp kitten in hand, for the cars to stop so they wouldn't hit the neighbor — hoping my voice would carry and somehow save her from being struck by two lanes of oncoming traffic. But then it got worse. The neighbor stopped in the middle of the street and dropped to the ground. She stretched herself out, prepared to be run over.

Horrified and desperate to be heard, I raised my voice even louder. I watched and yelled as some cars swerved, narrowly missing her. Some cars pulled over, and some just kept going. Then I heard sirens and saw flashing lights. Police cars, ambulances, fire trucks — all the first responders were arriving and jostling for position on an already chaotic street.

With traffic now stopped, police and paramedics rushed to the neighbor and tried to get her off the ground. She resisted mightily, coffee-colored limbs flailing, cursing *en Español*. I'm not sure they understood what she was saying, but somehow, they picked her up and strapped her securely onto a stretcher. Then they moved her, still cursing loudly, into an ambulance and drove away.

Once the street was cleared, *mi madre* pulled me — gasping

for breath, still clutching the kitten — away from the window. "*Vamos, Elisita*. Let's go home," *mi madre* said. "And you can bring the kitten with you."

Feeling like I was outside my body, I looked down and saw the kitten — somehow still asleep, despite the ruckus — in my arms. It was an orange tabby with rust-colored stripes, almost like a tiger cub. In the car on our way home, as my breathing calmed and the kitten slept, I tried to process what had just happened.

Although I would never know if anyone on the street had heard me yelling in my attempt to help save the neighbor's life, I did know that I'd been the catalyst for that lifesaving 911 call. I also knew I had saved that kitten. Born in chaos, adopted through fire, the burnt-orange tiger cub kitten was a reminder that by being inspired to help, I could make a difference.

I saw that my actions, no matter how big or small, had an impact. Realizing that I had a voice and two hands to effect change, I discovered I could make life better in my own ways. I felt motivated and empowered by the experience, and that's how leadership begins.

Maybe you've lived through some intense experiences like this one. I know you have overcome many challenges, worked through plenty of chaos, and battled your share of fires. And I'm pretty sure that's given you more empathy and inner strength than you may realize. That strength can shine through you like a beam of light, serving as motivation for yourself and other people. The more you use your positive energy to lead, the more you will inspire. And as you become the inspiration, you will achieve more success.

In this chapter, I will show you how to become the inspiration — to develop your leadership skill, motivating yourself and others — so you can achieve more success.

Leadership Is Key to Being the Inspiration

To become the inspiration, you have to show leadership, which means two things: (1) with empathy, you identify what is important to you or others, what you'd like to help with, make better, or fix, and (2) with positivity, you create and execute ideas that make a difference, motivating others to join you, to come up with their own ideas, or both. The more positively you lead, the more inspiring you will become.

Leadership can sound like such an elite concept — one that's reserved for top executives, high-ranking politicians, or successful entrepreneurs. But leadership happens in everyday moments, by everyday people, doing everyday things.

Children show leadership every day, whether by rescuing a neglected kitten or intervening when a bully attacks a classmate at school.

Teenagers show leadership every day, whether by volunteering with the student council or tutoring classmates after school.

Moms show leadership every day, whether by spearheading a fundraiser or serving as a scout leader.

Dads show leadership every day, whether by coaching their kids' baseball team or joining the PTA.

Employees show leadership every day, whether by doing undesirable tasks without being asked or mentoring a new hire.

Entrepreneurs show leadership every day, whether by building a team to execute an idea or developing a better solution to serve their customers.

Although leadership looks different from person to person, leaders of all kinds are united by a certain set of traits. Chief among them is that they're purpose-driven people who want to make a difference. Through the positive energy they direct toward their goals, they motivate themselves and others, inspiring action.

Leaders are clear and focused and know how to effectively communicate their ideas. By igniting in themselves a desire to make change, they can also spark others to help transform ideas into realities. By bringing out the best in themselves and other people, leaders serve a community and work toward the greater good. Their purpose guides and fuels them to make life better.

Leaders can engage in a give-and-take of inspiration with talented people, building a team that works together to achieve a shared mission. Not intimidated by working with people who are smarter or better than them in some way, effective leaders take pride in helping others become their best selves.

When you're able to inspire and be inspired and can unite your team around a shared vision, that's when the magic happens. And by empowering others to shine, you inspire them to become leaders, too. The more we empower positive leaders, the more the world benefits — a win-win for everyone.

We develop our leadership skill by using empathy to notice that which moves us, upsets us, affects us, or makes us feel passionate. Once we are motivated, feeling that urge to do something about it, we start with small accomplishments, then work toward bigger goals.

Taking action, no matter how big or small, keeps the fire burning within us and ignites a spark in others. When we share the positive energy we feel about our mission with other people, they also can feel motivated to create and achieve. Leaders can transform apathy to empathy by the sheer force of their passion. The more leaders motivate themselves and others, the more they become the inspiration.

When I think about developing leadership, I remember an important class project I spearheaded in college. The project meant a lot to me because it was one of the first times I felt that my leadership made a positive impact within the community.

Each student had to come up with a proposal about a company or organization we wanted to work with (the client) to generate awareness for it through a pro bono (no fee) promotional campaign. We had to pitch what the organization was, why we wanted to promote it, what the campaign would entail, and how we would measure success. Then the class would choose four proposals to execute.

This was after my experience of being sexually assaulted at the fraternity house (see chapter 2). Since that time, I had become aware of the growing (but hidden) problem of date rape on campus, so I was focused on how to make life better for women who had been through an experience similar to — or even worse than — mine. I decided to throw my energy behind an organization that was making a difference in the lives of young women who had been sexually assaulted or raped.

I researched local organizations working to help these survivors and found one that seemed just right. The organization provided support services to survivors of all forms of sexual violence. I reached out, and grateful for the interest and potential awareness on campus, they enthusiastically agreed to be my client.

Preparing my proposal, I thought about how wrong it was that I'd had no idea this organization even existed before I did the research. In my view, every girl in every dorm should have been made aware of this resource as soon as she arrived on campus. Perhaps by knowing what date rape was, and how to avoid it, students could help prevent it.

I included that background as part of my "why," then moved on to building the campaign. The first step would be a phone survey to determine how much awareness of the organization there was among my target population of female students in four of the high-rise dorms on campus.

Next, my group and I would create flyers with tear-off

informational tabs at the bottom and hang them in the common areas on every floor where female students lived. The plan was to later go back and visually assess how many of the tabs had been pulled off the flyers. Then we would do a follow-up phone survey to determine how much awareness of the organization there was after our campaign. The results would be compiled, and a summary would be delivered to the client.

Each student pitched their proposal to the class and professor, then the class voted. I was surprised and grateful when my proposal made the cut and work could begin to raise awareness of my client — ultimately benefiting young women.

As team leader, I coordinated executing the phone surveys, distributing the flyers, ascertaining how many tabs had been pulled, compiling the data, and presenting our results. Prior to our campaign, the majority of our target audience had never heard of the organization. But after the campaign, the majority of our target audience *had* heard of it. When asked how they'd heard of it, they answered "Flyer in my dorm."

The realization that our campaign was responsible for the significant increase in awareness for our client meant so much more than a successful class project. It meant we had raised awareness of date rape and had potentially helped prevent it from happening. And if it did occur, survivors would know where to go for support. That was very inspiring to me.

SPARK

Think of a situation in which you were motivated to solve a problem or make positive change. What was the outcome? Next, think of a situation that upset you but you felt you couldn't do anything about it. What could you have done differently to create a better outcome?

As my leadership skill grew, I continued to motivate myself. By doing so, I motivated others, too. The more I identified problems, came up with solutions, shared what I was passionate about, and put positive energy into the world (and got positive energy back), the more I could inspire and be inspired.

Leadership Means Being Like the Sun: Light on the Outside with a Strong Inner Core

As you grow toward being a leader, remember there are many different leadership styles. From democratic to authoritarian, from coaching to transactional, from visionary to transformational, there are a variety of ways to lead. What's key is finding the leadership style that's authentic to you because that's the one that will bring you the most joy, and the most success.

As I continued to grow as a leader, I started to notice what was working and what was not. Even more helpful was getting feedback from employees and colleagues, business partners and friends. (This was before formal performance reviews became standard.) When I paired my internal knowledge with external feedback, along with other success metrics like company growth and employee satisfaction, I landed on my own authentic leadership style.

The way I lead may best be explained by sharing how some of my colleagues have described me: "She's like sunshine — with a stealth bomber inside" and "Don't let the fact that she's so nice surprise you — Boss Lady is tough." What this means is that, like the sun, I project light on the outside by relying on a strong core. That firm inner resolve helps me navigate life's challenges, while that light helps me inspire and be inspired. Knowing how I'm viewed as a leader is helpful as I focus the lens through which I view the world.

At iParenting, the company became my mission. I felt so much inspiration that I often wondered if something greater was at work within me. Whether I was writing an Editor's Letter or a newspaper column, scripting a radio show or a video, I felt an incredibly strong connection not only to the community I was serving but also to the universe — the source that was helping to guide me on that journey.

With my mind ablaze with all the potential I saw — all the possibilities — my body and soul were filled with positive energy. With passion, I channeled that energy toward my purpose. It was rewarding to hear from others that they could see my "inner light shining."

I was so inspired, I was able to work without distraction in the same room as people who were talking or watching TV. With focus and clarity, I could work in the early morning, throughout the day, or in the evening. I'd sometimes wake in the middle of the night and write down ideas I'd thought of while sleeping. I was *that* excited about what I was doing and the difference I was making. That's because what inspires you, fuels you. You become driven by your mission, especially when the light you shine effects positive change.

By acting on my inspiration, I made good things happen — and that inspired others to act, too. As people responded to that light, they wanted to be part of it; they wanted to shine their own light. Whether that meant writing, designing, coding, marketing, or doing some other creative or business function, people joined the team because they, too, wanted to make a difference in the lives of parents.

One of my favorite leadership moments at iParenting happened after the Disney acquisition. As a member of several nonprofit boards, I had been busy planning a board meeting to be held at the iParenting-Disney office, in our large conference room, after work hours. My team was knocking off for the day, and they saw me going back and forth between the kitchen and conference room, setting up for the meeting.

"Hey, Boss Lady, let us help you with that," one of my employees said. Before I knew it, several team members had started clearing the conference room, wiping down the whiteboards, setting out flowers, pouring pitchers of water, moving chairs, and placing glasses, napkins, plates, and food across the long table. What would have required so much time and effort to do by myself was done by my team in a matter of minutes.

Not only did they help me set up but they also stayed to help welcome board members, hang coats, and give office tours — all without being asked to do a thing. It was only after the board members were settled into the conference room, ready to begin the meeting, that my colleagues left for the day. "Call if you need anything," they said as they walked out the door.

After my team left, some of the board members remarked on how amazing the employees were: considerate, helpful, welcoming — that's how they described the iParenting-Disney staffers, who made hosting look effortless.

The culture of kind camaraderie in our office, going the extra mile for each other, was the result of reciprocal inspiration. With empathy, I got to know my employees and their families, and they got to know mine. We put ourselves in each other's shoes, so we could view our jobs — and the world — from the other's perspective. We cared about each other.

With that give-and-take of inspiration, we worked together with respect and understanding. I shined the warm light of kindness on my colleagues, and they shined it back on me. We brought our best selves to work every day, and that led to more success for all of us.

Radiating light and leading with empathy are powerful

SPARK

What inspires you, moves you, or makes you feel empathy? Think of a way to do something about it. How would you define *leadership* in your own life?

emotional intelligence skills. But equally necessary are inner strength and the ability to manage the not-so-nice stuff. There were plenty of times when mistakes or attitudes needed to be dealt with or when difficult work dilemmas had to be handled. And I was often who they called when something needed to be negotiated or someone required a firm response.

Although certain business challenges could be quite uncomfortable (for example, when someone wouldn't hold up their end of an agreement), I learned to flip a switch inside of me — from "sunshine" mode to "stealth bomber" mode. When I was in stealth bomber mode, as long as the facts were on our side, chances were good that we'd resolve the issue we were facing.

That's when inner strength is needed most. Leaders need not only to inspire but also to overcome. They have to make the tough calls — and clean up the messes, too. Leaders must take the bad along with the good, and that's what the strong inner core is for.

These skills can make you indispensable at work and enable you to amass a community of loyal colleagues, customers, and collaborators. It's striking the balance between sunshine and strength that makes a good leader, the kind of leader who inspires everyone to bring out their best selves every day.

Leadership Means Fueling Your Ability to Inspire and Be Inspired

Being a consistent leader requires the constant ability to inspire and be inspired. That means you need to be refreshing and nourishing yourself every day so your well never runs dry. To maintain the positive energy required to lead, you must keep your batteries charged so you can continue to motivate yourself. And if someone else's motivation needs a jump start, you'll have plenty of sparks in reserve to help.

Being inspired opens your eyes and your mind to possibilities. Inspiration is creative fuel, and as I shared in chapter 6, creativity is necessary to achieve success. To keep the inspiration flowing, you can't expect it to magically appear; you have to actively cultivate it. But it's not always easy.

We all have our personal "stuff" that we deal with, that challenges us, that makes it tough on some days to put on our brave face for the world. The thing is, though, that the very act of putting on our brave face often makes the difference: In whether we show up. In whether we accomplish our goals. In whether we succeed in our missions. In whether we touch those around us. In whether we make a difference, in our own lives and in those of others. That's what drives me more than anything.

So, each day, I get up, put on my brave face, and show up in the world because I want to make a difference for my family, friends, colleagues, community, and beyond. We all have that innate ability. We just have to reach inside and find it, even on those days when it may seem too deep to reach. And we all have those days — when our hopes, dreams, and goals can be overshadowed by the worries, concerns, and unknowns that go along with them.

On those tough days, it helps to remember that we're all putting on our brave faces as we deal with life in our own ways. That behind those faces are unique spirits working through their own challenges. That we're all doing the best we can. That kindness and empathy go a long way in a world that often hurts. That we all have the power to make a difference in many people's lives — or even just our own.

I think of this as fueling the ability to inspire and be inspired.

With a lot of trial and error, it's a practice I've honed over the years. I believe that inspiration is a form and byproduct of spirituality. Because of this, my spirituality and inspiration have become intertwined into one practice that works to balance, center, and motivate me. My practice keeps me connected to myself, my family and friends, my colleagues and community, my mission and purpose, God and the universe — the source that inspires me most of all.

Attending a Catholic grade school, I learned a lot about God, faith, and prayer. Those lessons and prayers have stayed with me, providing an anchor throughout the challenges, chaos, and fires of my life. And that religion will always serve as a base for my spirituality. But as I've approached life with an open mind and an open heart, my spirituality practice has grown far beyond my Catholic school days and far beyond the Catholic faith.

What I know now about spirituality is that it is unique to each person. That's why it's OK if I don't entirely agree with every tenet of the Catholic religion. Everyone has their own belief system and their own way of interpreting and living their spirituality. To me, it is about love, hope, belief, connection, empathy, faith, passion, positivity, purpose. Above all, spirituality is about how you can make the world a better place.

Because making life better has been my mission and purpose for so long, I've worked hard on my spirituality. Now it's integrated into my life in such a way that my spirituality not only helps keep me healthy but also helps fuel my inspiration. Here's what that looks like.

I pay attention to my intuition. Those physical manifestations of fear or excitement, those emotional reactions to external events or people, that feeling or knowing inside of me — I am highly attuned to what my body and mind are communicating. That's my intuition talking to me. And my intuition is usually spot-on.

I practice mindfulness. Whether I'm gardening, taking a walk, doing yoga, listening to music, dancing, cooking, or baking, the goal is to focus on an activity that keeps my mind fully in the present moment. By being intentional and taking time to be in the present, I give my brain a break — allowing it to refresh and recharge.

I focus on others. I'm blessed to be married to a wonderful husband, and together we have seven children and a large extended family. I'm grateful to have close friends, awesome colleagues, and an inspiring community, which means lots of people to connect with. Empathy helps take the focus off my own challenges so I can serve others and set my worries aside.

I pray and meditate. It's in prayer and meditation that I feel closest to God and the universe. Whether sitting by myself in a quiet place during the day or listening to guided meditations before drifting off to sleep, I find that these peaceful moments help me feel deeply rooted. It's often after meditation that I am filled with ideas or solutions to problems, even when I'm not actively trying to find them.

I use essential oils and do deep-breathing exercises. Diffusing essential oils — such as lavender or lemon, or special blends that help with immunity or stress relief — provides the science-backed benefits of aromatherapy. When I practice deep breathing, inhaling peace and exhaling stress, it boosts my clarity throughout the day or helps me wind down before sleep at night.

I write in a journal (or on the computer or even on my phone). Writing helps me get ideas onto a piece of paper (or onto a screen), where I can better process them. Writing things out helps me organize and crystallize my thinking. It serves not only as a creative outlet but also as a way to document thoughts and feelings. (Some of my journal entries have even found their way into this book.)

I stay grateful. No matter how difficult things may get, I remember that even though X may be going wrong, Y may be going right. And even though I don't have X, I do have Y and Z. The cup is always overflowing (with lemonade, not lemons). Gratitude centers me and brings me calm.

I share what I learn. You know how some people like to keep an amazing family recipe a secret? Or how they carefully guard what worked for them because they feel like if they share it, somehow another person's success may take something away from their own? That's the scarcity mindset at work. And that's not me. With an abundance mindset, I've spent most of my life sharing what works — not only for me but for others. That's the essence of iParenting and 30Seconds.

SPARK

How do you find inspiration? Think of activities that help you feel inspired. Do you have role models or a mentor? Have you ever mentored others? If not, think about how to make this happen.

And that's the goal of *Become the Fire*, too. I want you to know what I know, and what the other women who are featured in this book know, so you can learn from us and chart your own path to success. So your mind can come alive with possibilities. So you can achieve the life you dream of.

Because of that abundance mindset, I've been paying it forward for most of my life. I have served as a mentor, volunteer, fundraiser, adviser, scout leader, board member, and guest lecturer. Passing on what I've learned, within the give-and-take of all those roles, has been very rewarding. But mentoring has always held a special place in my heart, and this book is the best form of mentorship I can provide. After all, that's what leadership and inspiration are all about.

The Virtuous Loop of Being the Inspiration

To become the fire, you need to inspire and be inspired. Being the inspiration means you use your leadership skill to motivate yourself and others to make the world a better place. Leading with empathy, you pursue your purpose with positivity, serving the greater good and effecting change. The more you grow as a leader, the more inspiring you will become. As you become the inspiration, you will achieve more success.

This pattern repeated itself throughout my life. With empathy, I have been motivated to identify problems, find solutions, and make change. Empowered by passion and purpose, I have created and executed ideas that make life better for a community. Shining a light, I have inspired others to join me and to shine their own light. The more I have led with positive energy, the more I have inspired and been inspired. As I became the inspiration, I achieved more success.

Let's break down that formula with what was going on for me when I was building camaraderie with colleagues.

Being the inspiration means you use your leadership skill to motivate yourself and others to make the world a better place. Leading with empathy allowed me to bring out the best in myself and in my employees. With a give-and-take of inspiration, we worked together with understanding to effect positive change.

The more you lead with positivity and purpose, the more inspiring you will become. I shined light on my colleagues, and they shined light back on me. With purposeful passion to achieve my mission, I inspired others to join me and to shine their own light.

As you become the inspiration, you will achieve more success. By leading with positivity every day, I inspired my employees to do the same. The more we could inspire and be inspired, the more success we achieved.

This basic formula applies no matter where you are in your

journey to become the fire. Use it when you need motivation, when you're not sure how to lead, or when you want to fuel your inspiration. Remember that by shining strong like the sun, you'll grow as a leader and make life better!

FLAME • Talita Ramos Erickson

First Jobs: English teacher, customer service provider
Education: Bachelor (law), Universidade Federal do Paraná; LLM (law), Loyola University Chicago; European doctorate in law and economics; executive MBA, University of Chicago
Personal Life: Married, mother of one
Board/Civic Roles: Advisory council member, Hispanic Alliance for Career Enhancement
Key Takeaway: "The number one quality of leadership is empathy. It's very hard to lead when you don't care about people."

Talita Ramos Erickson's upbringing in Brazil served as the perfect backdrop for building a career in diversity and inclusion. Talita's neighborhood, near the Argentina and Paraguay borders, was "extra diverse," she says, exposing her to a wide variety of cultures and people.

With a grandmother who was half Black and half Indigenous Brazilian, and a godfather who was openly gay, Talita grew up with empathy for people of every shade of the rainbow. "Being connected to all kinds of people had a huge impact on how I see things," she explains.

This is why it makes perfect sense that Talita serves as chief diversity and inclusion (D & I) officer, as well as chief legal and compliance officer, for Barilla Group, a 140-year-old family-owned Italian food company. Barilla owns thirty production sites in ten countries, employs more than eight thousand people, and generates more than $4 billion in annual revenue.

And while you may be intimately familiar with the company's delicious pasta and other foods, you may not realize the importance it places on diversity as a key factor in its success. Barilla employees are encouraged to bring their authentic selves to work and to expect a culture of acceptance and understanding. As chief D & I officer, that's Talita's specialty. And Talita's job is as fascinating as the road she took to get there.

Talita is the youngest of three children born to a high school teacher mother and an environmental engineer father. Her parents have what Talita describes as a fairly "gender-equal relationship." Talita's mixed-race mom grew up "in extreme poverty," at times living on the streets. Still, she found a way to get an education and become a teacher, which made it very important that her children be educated, too. "She wanted to make sure we did well in school so we could take care of ourselves."

Talita's mother and grandmother were role models for her, showing her how to be a strong woman. Arguments about money with her mother led to Talita's early desire for independence. "I wanted to get tattoos or eyebrow piercings or to dye my hair blue," Talita says with a laugh. "My mom said she wouldn't be giving me money for that, so I needed to figure it out."

As a result, Talita got her first job, at age fourteen, teaching English at a language school. She learned skills that would help her succeed as her career unfolded. For example, when a student complained that Talita was explaining things in Portuguese instead of English, Talita learned to not take criticism personally. "I internalized the feedback, then I tried to do better."

In college, Talita undertook a five-year program geared toward practicing law. During school, she had an internship in the legal and compliance department of HSBC Bank Brazil, where she got the first opportunity to put her law education to practical use. Next, she secured a position with US-based Kraft Foods, where she started as an intern in the law department.

After five years, Talita graduated with the Brazilian equivalent of a JD degree. She continued working for Kraft as a lawyer, and eventually she was offered the opportunity to move from Brazil to the United States to work at Kraft headquarters in Northfield, Illinois. "The general counsel wanted to bring people from other countries to work with the team in the US, to make the legal department more international," she explains.

That's how Talita found herself as an Illinois-based attorney for a leading international food company. She rose through the ranks as senior assistant corporate secretary, then counsel for strategic transactions. While working at Kraft, Talita earned her master of laws (LLM) degree — a post-JD degree designed for attorneys who want to focus on a specific legal area — followed by her executive MBA. She later passed the bar exam in New York and registered as in-house counsel in Illinois.

Although it may sound like smooth sailing, there were plenty of choppy waters for Talita to navigate. She notes that it's the way you view challenges and failures that makes all the difference. "I failed — a lot," she recalls. "When you apply for something and don't get it, you can't let it bring you down. Experience that failure, then redirect yourself. By failing many times, you get better at it. You can't dwell on it or take it personally. It's not part of your identity."

As Talita took on more responsibility, managing more people, she realized she wanted more than just a job. She wanted a calling. "I had a belief that I am more than what I do. I wanted to impact people's lives. I started to think about how I could do that in a different way."

After Kraft went public in 2008, Talita felt the company shift from a stakeholder perspective to a shareholder perspective, which did not feel like a good fit for her. Sensing that it was time to move on, she decided to "break up" with the job. "I said to my boss, 'It's not you, it's me.'" Talita stayed to get the team through a hostile takeover and even helped train her replacement. When she left the company, she didn't have another job lined up, but she knew she would eventually figure out what was next. "Be self-aware, check in with how you're feeling," she advises. "Know when to pull the plug, even if you don't see the path clearly ahead."

A firm believer in the expression "Luck is when readiness meets opportunity," Talita worked on her readiness. That way, when opportunity arose, she could put her best foot forward. "In that equation, the only thing you can control is the readiness: study harder, get more degrees, do your best." She continued to expand her international experience, enrolling in the European doctorate program in law and economics, which was coordinated by three of Europe's leading universities.

After completing the two-year program, Talita was ready to take the next step in her career and to find a job that would be a calling. Yet a tough job market made it extra challenging. Realizing that companies were looking for specific people with specific backgrounds and skill sets, Talita went a step further to find the right fit. "Everyone was looking for a unicorn, so I needed to find a job for which I was the unicorn. I put an alert on LinkedIn so I would be notified if any company was looking for a lawyer in Chicago who spoke Portuguese."

Talita's extra effort paid off when she was notified by LinkedIn that Barilla was, indeed, looking for a lawyer with Talita's background to be its GC for the Americas. It turned out that Talita was Barilla's unicorn and that, at Barilla, Talita would find her calling. "It's an inspirational company and a much better fit for me. I got a number of opportunities to play a role outside of legal."

One of those opportunities would end up changing the course of Talita's career. Becoming global chief diversity officer, Talita led Barilla's Global Diversity and Inclusion Board. "Getting to do D & I opened up a world of opportunities to work on different projects and meet different people."

A few years later, the CEO called her with another opportunity. "He asked me if I wanted a second job — to lead our restaurant business. He wanted to give someone on the inside a chance, and that person was me." In addition to her GC role, Talita served as CEO of Casa Barilla, the company's restaurant division, until the pandemic effectively shut it down. "We went above and beyond to care for our people. The way we do business allows our managers to manage with compassion and empathy."

As her restaurant role wound down, the next opportunity was

waiting. Talita was named Barilla's chief legal and compliance officer and chief D & I officer, and the new job was based at the company's main headquarters in Parma, Italy. "When you do a good job, you earn trust. Having the credentials is the ticket to play, but the effort you put into relationships and being trustworthy — that's what gives you a shot at bigger opportunities," she says.

Today, Talita lives in Milan with her husband and son and commutes by train to the beautiful Barilla headquarters in quaint Parma. Talita and her family feel at home in Italy. "Culturally, Italy is more like Brazil. People are more social; they get closer to one another."

Talita also feels at home in her position at Barilla. "The most rewarding part of the job is creating an environment where people can succeed and feel that they're a better mom, friend, or father because they work for this company. Because of working for Barilla, I know things now that help me as I raise my son. I love the impact we have on people's lives."

Talita notes that mentorship has had a profound impact on her career — both being mentored and being a mentor. "Sometimes, mentorship just happens because you find someone you trust, and they trust you. You can ask for advice because you want to improve, or it can just happen spontaneously."

That is exactly what happened at her HSBC Bank Brazil internship, when the woman who would become her first mentor told her to lose the eyebrow piercing and her college backpack. "I wanted to be myself, but she warned me that I would be judged and, unfortunately, not taken seriously in that specific environment. She helped me in a lot of ways she may not even realize."

When looking for a mentor, Talita recommends actively seeking one out — but being careful about whom you approach. "You have to have a relationship with a person who wants to see you succeed. If you have that, then you can ask them for feedback or to meet more regularly."

Because Talita has benefited from mentors, to pay it forward, she regularly serves as a mentor — and an inspiration, especially for fellow outsiders. "I had students from both Loyola University and University of Chicago, in particular people in underrepresented groups, reach out to me because I was also a foreigner or different. I have always said yes."

Talita is part of a formal mentorship program at Barilla, and she takes on two or three mentees per year. She's proud to say she has mentored more than fifty people throughout her career. "I am intentional to engage with people from underrepresented groups, even for informal mentoring. I talk with them often, and I keep in touch with almost all my mentees."

Talita points to the need for inspiring role models, and the visibility of underrepresented groups in leadership, as key to more success for women from all walks of life. "You cannot be what you cannot see. When you see more underrepresented groups in leadership, it opens your mind to opportunities."

This is why, as a white-passing Latina, Talita is careful about how she is perceived. "Because I am Latina but light-skinned, I'm very aware of being put in places to talk about the Latinx experience. So I use my privilege to help improve things for others." For example, when Talita was recognized as a rising business leader of color, she would only accept the recognition if she could highlight a team member who's more visibly Latino, with darker skin.

Talita hopes to inspire the next generation of leaders and normalize a more diverse, inclusive, and compassionate definition of leadership. "The number one quality of leadership is empathy. It's very hard to lead when you don't care about people. As one of my colleagues said to me about the pandemic, 'We're all in the storm, but we're not all in the same boat.' If you're a leader, you need to acknowledge that everyone is in a different boat. That's empathy."

For Talita, success is "being happy with the situation you're in." And by that definition, she's nearly there. Missing her family in Brazil, there's a piece of the puzzle that's not quite in place. Yet she's happy with her choices and the impact she's making in the lives of so many. "I hope that when my path crosses other people's paths, they're better off because of it."

BLAZE

I inspire myself and other people.

I am motivated to make positive change.

I can make a difference, no matter how big or small.

I take leadership to bring out the best in myself and others.

I am positive, and I have a purpose.

I lead with empathy and understanding.

As I become the inspiration, I achieve more success.

10

Be the Best

To become the fire, you need to be the best at whatever you most love to do. Using the skill of *dedication* to bring your A game to whatever you choose to pursue, you measure success by the bar you set for yourself. When you set a high standard for performance and strive for excellence in what you care about most, you increase the chances that you will be very good at it and become recognized for it. Dedicating yourself to your best personal effort, you will shine and rise above the rest. And by becoming the best, you will achieve more success.

It's not easy to be the best — at anything. Whether you're in business, education, politics, healthcare, athletics, the arts, or some other field, competition is fierce. Today, more than ever, it takes a lot to rise to the top.

To give you an edge in life, maybe your parents (or others) pushed you to achieve more in academics, music, or athletics — as if playing piano, soccer, or basketball for hours every day would give you an easier path to playing that instrument or sport in college or even professionally. Or maybe, as a parent yourself, you're doing that for your own kids. If so, how is that working out for you or for your kids?

Perhaps, for a very small percentage of parents, that pushing paid off. It could be that their kids actually are (or will become) musical or athletic geniuses, like a mini Mozart, Mia Hamm, or Michael Jordan. Yet so many other parents become disappointed when their child either still doesn't make the cut, despite all that work, or decides to quit on their own because they are so burned out.

To be the best, you have to put your whole heart into it and dedicate yourself to giving it all you've got. You have to *want* to be the best — not for your parents or other people who may try to push you into it, but for yourself.

That's why you have to find what makes you light up inside. What puts a fire in your belly. What you feel so passionate about that you want to give it everything you've got. What makes you *want* to strive to be the best, because you care that much about it. No one can make you feel that way, no matter how early they expose you to it or make you practice it or push you to pursue it. No one can make that happen — except you.

It's often tempting to take the easy way out, to do just enough to get by. And most often, it's when you lack interest, inspiration, or motivation that you choose the path that requires the least amount of effort — the "average" path of checking the box but not ringing the bell. Yet taking the easy way out is not usually the path that leads to great achievement. Big success is rarely easy.

But when you find the thing that drives you, that you feel most passionate about, chances are good that your motivation to be the best you can be will kick in. And because you're dedicated to giving it your personal best, you are competing against no one but yourself.

As you start to measure success by how much you improve

at something, you'll find joy and satisfaction in seeing your progress. As your skills improve, as you become better and better, your
dedication to it will grow, and you will be motivated to try even
harder.

By giving it your best effort, putting forth your strongest self,
you will keep growing in your talent, and people will start to notice. Get into the mindset of being so good at it that others can't
overlook you. Be so good that you're the obvious choice for any
relevant opportunity. Be so good that they simply can't not notice.
As others recognize you for your talent, you'll become known for
it. And the more you become known for being the best, the more
you will succeed.

Striving to be the best becomes a virtuous cycle: the more you
love what you're doing, the more of it you will do; the more
you dedicate yourself to it — by practicing or working at it — the
better at it you will become. By giving it your all and holding
yourself to a high standard, you literally can become the best.

Because you're competing against yourself, measuring your
own progress and growth, there's no need to constantly look in
your side-view or rearview mirror. It really doesn't matter what
others are doing or how close behind you they might be. When
you dedicate yourself to improving on where you were yesterday,
your talent only grows — and your tomorrow looks that much
brighter.

With an abundance mindset, you know there's enough success to go around. That's why it doesn't matter if someone else
is also good at the same thing. You're measuring your success
against yourself, not others. As you improve, get better at it, and
ultimately become the best you can be, you will likely succeed at
it — no matter what anyone else is doing.

The key is to dedicate yourself to your personal best every
day — not to obsess about what others are doing every day. The

only things you can control are your own actions and efforts, so make them count. Don't waste your time comparing yourself to others. Compare yourself to yourself. If you are improving, you are succeeding.

Right about now you may be thinking, "But I'm not the best at anything, and I'm not sure I can be." That's because, when you were growing up, it may have felt hard to be your best self. The idea of becoming really good at anything might have seemed daunting to you as you worked through challenges and chaos. Or maybe you didn't feel passionate enough about something because you were too busy fighting fires. Or it may have been difficult to hold yourself to a high standard if there were not a lot of examples of integrity or excellence around you. Whatever the reason, being an outsider may have made it hard to feel like a standout in any given area.

But I'll bet you had an opinion about what (or who) the best was because you were always looking at it from the outside. That gave you valuable perspective and insight you can leverage as you pursue your own path to being the best.

Now it's your time to set high standards and dedicate yourself to excellence in whatever you wish to achieve. By being the best at what you choose to specialize in, you will shine, standing out from the crowd. Your commitment to excellence will pay off as you achieve greater success. I know you can do this because I did. And the other women in this book did. If we can do it, you can, too.

When I think about aspiring to be the best, I remember feeling "average" as a child.

I wasn't a straight A student. The classes I excelled in were the ones I was interested in. In other classes, I would often just do what it took to stay above the middle.

I wasn't a standout athlete. Although I played some sports pretty well (like baseball), in other sports, I warmed the bench.

I wasn't a talented musician. Although I took some piano lessons, I only learned to play a few songs by ear. "Heart and Soul" remains my strongest performance piece.

My childhood "averageness" in those areas was often a result of a lack of interest or passion for them. I didn't bring my A game because I wasn't motivated to be the best.

But one area I did feel passionate about was singing. I loved to sing — whether at home, belting out the songs on my vinyl records, or at church, singing in my school choir. For someone who couldn't read a note of sheet music, I had good pitch and a strong voice. And because I loved to sing, that passion came through in my performance.

I was given opportunities to perform solos — both during church masses and in school performances — which scared and delighted me all at once. As a child on the outside of the "in crowd," who lived in fear of being bullied, even the tiniest of spotlights was both a blessing and a curse. If I messed up or made a mistake, I felt that I would never live it down.

Yet the optimist in me saw the opposite perspective: if I did well, maybe I wouldn't get teased. Perhaps if I could do something better than they could, the bullies — even if they didn't have anything nice to say — wouldn't say anything at all. To me, that would equal success. The optimistic me turned out to be right: as I found more success in singing, life with the bullies got better. So I continued to sing and to find more opportunities — and success.

School plays provided another opportunity to perform. I grew in musical theater roles, from simple solos to character parts. Whether by rarely missing a practice or by rehearsing at home on my own, I dedicated myself to improving my singing. As an otherwise average kid, I had found a way to shine — and that lit a fire in my belly.

But surrounded by kids who loved to act, dance, and sing, I

found tryouts to be nerve-racking. And because I never took an acting class or a voice lesson, I was just figuring it out on my own. That's when I started to realize that all I had control of was my own effort. So instead of focusing on what other kids were doing to prepare or improve — external factors that were beyond my control — I turned the focus inward. I dedicated myself to becoming the best singer I could be, on my own. And when it was time to try out for a play, I would just give it my best effort and hope for a good result.

That's how, by my final year in grade school, I had worked my way up to auditioning for a lead role in our eighth-grade play, *Oliver!*, a musical based on the novel *Oliver Twist* by Charles Dickens. Surrounded by talented kids, I pushed the negative "You're not good enough" comparisons from my mind. Instead, as I walked onto the stage, I told myself "Just do your best." And that's what I did. I delivered the strongest performance I could, then I walked off that stage. The rest I had no control over.

I was thrilled to get one of the top supporting roles in the play — as Bet, the sidekick to Nancy, the female lead. Throughout that production, I worked hard at every practice and especially during our performances, which drew hundreds of friends, family, parishioners, faculty members, and community supporters. That dedication paid off in the form of building my self-respect as well as the respect of others (including the bullies).

I kept performing in high school, though I wasn't a "theater kid." My church youth group put on a musical each year. The youth group and play drew many kids from various schools, but it was a smaller and more familiar stage than at my massive high school. At a local community theater, the group put on productions of original plays that were written, musically scored, and produced entirely by parishioners and community members. It was a stage I felt better about trying to navigate.

Each year, I would practice and audition. And each year, I

would earn a better part. But I aspired to become the lead, so I dedicated myself to trying harder. It was in my senior year of high school that I finally got the female lead in the play. When I learned that I got the part of Lauren in our group's original production of *Winning Isn't Everything*, I was equal parts elated and terrified. After several years of playing supporting roles, it seemed like a pretty big deal to be the one who was literally front and center on stage.

For weeks, I rehearsed relentlessly — at play practice and on my own. I memorized all my lines until I could deliver them in my sleep. I practiced all my songs until I could sing them passionately by heart. By showtime, I was ready. All that dedication paid off as the play went smoothly. Stepping into the spotlight in front of an audience of hundreds, I had my moment to shine. And in high school, having a moment like that goes a long way.

But I think the most meaningful part of the experience was proving to myself that I could be the best by giving it my best. And that feeling — that knowing I could do it — empowered me. It set the stage for even more success, on bigger and bigger stages.

As you decide how to become the best in your chosen field, keep in mind that you don't necessarily have to be the best on the biggest stage. If a smaller or more familiar stage feels better to you, then success may be more achievable. *Best* is for you to define, and *you* get to pick the stage.

In this chapter, I will show you how to be the best — to set high standards and to dedicate yourself to being the best version of you (for whatever you choose to pursue) — so you can achieve more success.

Dedication Is Key to Being the Best

To become the best, you have to show dedication, which means two things: (1) you identify what you most love to do, and (2) you work at it relentlessly, giving it your best effort. The more passion you feel for what you're doing, the more time you will spend on it. And the more you dedicate yourself to it, the better at it you will become.

You know how, when you love something so much, you will decline other opportunities so you can spend more time doing it? Or how, when you feel so much passion for someone, you will stop seeing other people so you can devote yourself to that person? Or how, when a role, mission, or profession lights you up inside, you feel called to do it? That's dedication, and that's the fuel you need to propel you to become the best.

Dedication is a beautiful thing. It drives loyalty, fidelity, and commitment in relationships, activities, causes, career, and more. When you find the thing you want to dedicate yourself to, something very special happens. You get a clarity that helps you focus on that thing like a laser. Dedication drives you to pour your whole heart into that thing. You bring your A game because you want to be the best you can at it.

By being the best version of yourself, you keep improving at that thing. You set a high standard for yourself, and day after day, you start to excel at it. You measure your success by how much you improve. You find joy and satisfaction in seeing your progress. As you become better and better at that thing, your dedication to it grows — and your motivation to be the best kicks in.

Then others notice that you're really good at that thing, and they start to recognize you for it. When you're widely known for excelling at something, you often don't even need to proactively look for that recognition. Like a beacon, the flame within you is shining so brightly that others can see it for themselves. You have *become the fire.*

As you become known for being the best at something, more opportunities arise. That is precisely what happened with iParenting. As we built the company with passion and purpose, it became much more than a business. It became my calling. With dedication, I poured my whole heart into it. Because of that fire in my belly, I aspired to do better and better. As the website grew and improved, it drew more readers like a beacon.

We measured success by our progress on internal metrics like content, tools, audience, clients, and revenue. Although we did not obsess about what other websites were doing — looking in the side-view and rearview mirrors only served as a distraction — it was hard not to notice when a few of our more innovative ideas showed up on a competing website. We took that as another signal that we were on the right track and kept moving forward.

But the most important metric of all was how big of a difference we were making in the lives of our readers and community members. And by that metric, we were succeeding beyond measure.

Although at the time we weren't necessarily aspiring to build one of the best parenting websites in the world, because of our dedication to it, that's exactly what was happening. As we innovated, researched, created, connected, informed, and inspired, the word spread, and opportunities and recognition followed.

We earned "Best of the Web" accolades from leading news outlets such as *Newsweek*, *U.S. News & World Report*, and the *London Times*, among others.

Our team was asked to produce all the editorial content for five national newsstand magazines: *Pregnancy*, *Baby Years*, *Women's Health & Fitness*, *European Homes & Gardens*, and *The Buyer's Guide*, a product-review magazine that helped identify the best items for new parents. I became editor in chief of those publications.

Because of the editorial integrity and credibility we had built up through our various online and off-line publications, we were able to launch and scale the highly respected iParenting Awards, an intensive product-review and awards program that identified and promoted the best products for parents and parents-to-be.

I was asked to write a newspaper column for Pioneer Press newspapers (a division of Tribune Publishing). I was asked to cohost a radio show, *Points on Parenting*, on WTMX-FM in Chicago. And I was invited to become a member of the Council of One Hundred, a mentoring organization made up of Northwestern University's top alumnae.

SPARK

What lights a fire in your belly? What makes you feel motivated to bring out the best version of yourself? How can you dedicate yourself to it?

It was only by giving it everything we had that we were recognized in those ways. The more recognition we received, the more success we achieved. I tell you this to inspire you to become your own version of the best — whatever that looks like for you. And if I can do it, you can, too.

The key is to find the thing that you are most passionate about, that lights a fire in you. Once you find it, you'll want to dedicate yourself to it. That dedication will fuel your motivation to bring your best self to it every day. As you see progress, you will work even harder at it. Then one day you'll look up and notice that you can't even see anyone in your side-view or rearview mirror because you will have become the best. And you'll have found success.

Being the Best Means Shifting (and Keeping) the Power Dynamic in Your Favor

True dedication — whether to a cause, activity, relationship, business, career, or something else — means you're so passionate about something that you're all in on your commitment to it. You hold nothing back, you try every approach, and you look for opportunities to enhance it. Most of all, you're 100 percent committed to it and vested in its success.

That's where being the best becomes especially important. With dedication to giving it everything you've got, you strive to be at the top. You get so good that others can't overlook you. They can't discount you or ignore you. You become the obvious choice for opportunities that align with your expertise. You get so good that people simply can't not notice.

When you become known as being among the best in your field, an interesting thing happens: the power dynamic shifts. When you're recognized as a leader, or when you or your company are in demand, you generate awareness, opportunities, and access. Being the best opens doors that otherwise might have been closed (or nonexistent).

This is especially true for women and BIPOC, who often have to work much harder than their male or white counterparts for the same opportunities. (This is, of course, unacceptable, and we are working to change it.) The good news is that we can use the strengths and skills we have gained as outsiders to our advantage. We can learn to shift the power dynamic in our favor — and the best way I know how to do that is by being the best.

That's why you need to find what lights you up. Because when you're passionate about what you do, it doesn't feel like work (see chapter 8). Investing all that time and energy toward what you love makes it a joy to become better and better at it. And as you get so good that others can't help but notice, you'll achieve more success. Loving what you do and being really good at it go hand in hand, and they are a winning combination. Because of that, you will succeed — and much sooner than waiting for society to change.

Part of being the best is surrounding yourself with the best people, whether they're employees, suppliers, clients, advisers, mentors, or others in your orb. Setting a high bar for those you allow into your circle often makes a significant difference.

To ensure you have input and guidance from people you trust, consider building a personal board of directors — handpicked individuals to consult for advice or feedback. Ideally, they'll be diverse people skilled in areas that align with your goals, and they'll be genuinely interested in helping you succeed. Personal board members can serve as active mentors or coaches, occasional advisers or connectors, sporadic supporters or sounding boards. Whatever you decide, the goal is to surround yourself with the best so you can be your best.

When you're dedicated to what you do, you deserve to work with people who have a similar mindset — those you can bring out the best in, and who can bring out the best in you. Settling for anything less may mean you're not able to bring out your strongest self, which can affect your ability to succeed.

Just as being really good at what you do can make the right people notice you, for the right reasons, it also can make the wrong people notice you, for the wrong reasons.

When I was building 30Seconds, I battled my share of fires. But perhaps the most emotionally overwhelming challenges happened when some of the wrong people noticed me. Sexual harassment, in the form of unwelcome sexual advances, was the most disheartening. Through those (and other) experiences, I learned how important it is to surround myself with the best people so I can be my best self.

While creating the proof of concept for 30Second Mom, establishing a profitable business model was a key component of proving the website's viability. To be viable, the company would need clients that paid us to promote their brand via advertising.

I had a friend, a fellow single mom, who worked for a small but growing company that sold a product appealing to the mom market. As an ally, she sought to create a business collaboration between her company and mine, so she connected me with her boss, an entrepreneur who was looking to grow the reach of his brand.

Although his company was not a dream client (my initial thoughts were to work with the bigger consumer packaged goods and technology companies), after preliminary discussions and a meeting at their office, it seemed like they could become a paying customer. I viewed the company as a stepping-stone as I grew my roster of bigger clients.

When my ally's boss (I'll call him *the pervert*) suggested that the three of us plan our next business meeting to advance our discussions over dinner in downtown Chicago, it looked to be a positive step toward signing on a small client. And to a start-up founder trying to prove out a business model (and to pay mounting bills), it's often the client who has the power.

But a typical business dinner is not what the pervert had planned. First, he changed the restaurant venue several times. Next, he arranged for a car to pick up my ally and me, saying that, as single moms, we deserved a night off from driving. Then, over pre-dinner cocktails, he drank too much, too quickly, and told us inappropriate stories about his employees.

The drinking continued over dinner, with too much wine and too much sexual innuendo. By the end of the meal, I think the pervert assumed my ally and I were as drunk as he was, which may be why he had the audacity to ask us to accompany him to his room at the adjacent hotel so we could have a threesome. I. Am. Not. Joking.

The switch inside me had been teetering back and forth all

night, and it finally flipped — I went from sunshine mode to stealth bomber mode. The pervert needed a serious reality check, and I was just the one to give it to him. Feeling angry and betrayed, I let him know that his perverted fantasy would never happen, that he was a disgrace, and that there was no longer any chance for a potential business collaboration.

The look on the pervert's face was unforgettable. Stunned and speechless, it was clear he was taken aback by how I spoke to him. Seared by my fiery rebuke, he had just been torched by my strong inner core.

I think my ally was in shock. She had been watching the whole thing play out, paralyzed in disbelief. I grabbed her by the arm and we left him behind. On our way home, all I could think about was how he had tried to use us both to serve his perverted purpose — but that we were OK, and that's what mattered.

The experience drove home the importance of female allyship. My ally and I had been in the situation — and had gotten through it — together. And we had learned a valuable lesson in trust.

Most importantly, I had been reminded to never let down my guard, to never lower my standards, and to never relinquish my power. While the pervert, as a potential client, may have momentarily had the power, I reached out, grabbed it, and took it right back.

The pervert had the nerve to follow up with an apologetic voicemail, asking if we could please resume our business talks. Yeah, right. I responded with a curt email, reiterating the termination of any potential collaboration. And for me, that was that. For my ally, unfortunately, it wasn't over. As a single mom with a heavy financial burden, she couldn't just walk away from her job with his company. It was so unfair that she had to keep working for the pervert until she found another job, and as her ally, I did what I could to help her.

But that experience was an important one for me. As part of bringing my best self to 30Seconds, I resolved to never again let myself feel like I didn't have the power — even when it came to customers. Just as I set the bar high for the quality of our work, I would set the bar high for the quality of our clients. I wouldn't let the fact that they had revenue my company needed sway me to lower my standards. I would stick to what felt right and stay empowered.

Lest you think this type of situation only happens to single moms or at fancy dinners downtown, let me assure you that it can happen to any one of us at any time. In fact, it would happen to me again. But the next time, I was happily remarried — and it was at a meeting over coffee at my local Starbucks in the middle of the day.

Through mutual friends, I had connected with the former CEO of a successful company in the tech space (I'll call him *the former*). Intrigued when he heard about 30Seconds, the former offered to help with business strategy. Based on past experiences, my guard was up, but I thought it might be an opportunity to learn from a leader in my industry — someone who might be a good addition to my personal board of directors. Still, I proceeded with caution and met with him during the day at a busy coffee shop.

That meeting felt like the longest coffee of my life. The former proceeded to relentlessly drop sexist remarks, use offensive language, and make wildly inappropriate comments about the attractiveness of my team members and me — all the while stroking my arm up and down. It was like being subjected to Silicon Valley's infamous "bro culture" despite being thousands of miles away from it. Even after I asked him to stop, he did not. That's when I ended our meeting and our potential business relationship.

The former's behavior was in direct conflict with the culture of my team and my company. That meant that, even if I had tried to push past the irrelevant and uncomfortable nonsense to actually learn something from him, it would not have been worth it. He made me feel like I was lowering my standards. I was not being the best version of me, which meant it was not in the best interests of 30Seconds.

The journey to being the best is hard enough when you have the right people with you, so just imagine how much harder it is when you have the wrong people with you. It's just not worth it. Keep your guard up. Be aware and protect yourself. When people show you who they really are, believe them. And if who they are does not align with your values, lose them.

If something like this happens to you, don't let it derail you. Call upon your strong inner resolve. Stay in control and stay in your power. Remember that only you are in charge of you. You get to define *best*, and you get to pick the stage — and often even the players. Then put your head down and get back to work.

That's what I did. With dedication, I focused on bringing my strongest self to 30Seconds so it could become the best of its kind. Not unlike with iParenting, I was driven by passion and purpose. I set high standards of excellence. I surrounded myself with great people. I set a high bar for performance. But unlike with iParenting, at 30Seconds we intentionally aspired to build one of the best websites of its kind. And because of our dedication, it started to happen.

As we focused on making our own special kind of magic, more contributors signed on, more news media outlets featured us, more readers joined our community, and the word spread.

We started to be recognized for being among the best, and as the website inspired more people, recognition and opportunities followed. Here are a few examples of how the power dynamic shifted dramatically.

We were accepted into the third of three highly competitive accelerator programs we participated in for the highest-potential female entrepreneurs: WiSTEM (Women in STEM) at 1871 in Chicago.

We were selected from hundreds of applicants to be part of Mobile Futures, a program by snack food giant Mondelēz International to partner with the best tech start-ups creating mobile ventures. Of the twenty finalists, 30Seconds was the *only* female-founded company. Mondelēz flew the participants to its New Jersey headquarters, where we presented our ideas to iconic brands like Nabisco, Trident, Oreo, Halls, belVita, and Cadbury.

There I competed against better known companies, many of which had raised substantial venture capital funding. For example, the Waze app, which provides GPS tracking software to help you find the best routes, had already raised millions of dollars and would later be acquired by Google for $966 million. 30Seconds made the Mobile Futures list of "Top Companies to Watch in Mobile." The recognition led to more opportunities, all of which led to further recognition of 30Seconds as one of the best mobile tech start-ups.

I was invited to speak about courageousness in the workplace to hundreds of Procter & Gamble employees at their Cincinnati, Ohio, headquarters, as well as at other high-profile events.

Google highlighted us as one of its "Featured Publishers," then later selected us to represent the state of Illinois in its annual *Economic Impact Report*. Because Google is one of our favorite start-up success stories, this recognition really meant a lot to our team.

SPARK

Have you noticed that you have talent in a specific area? Think of two ways to work on being the best at it so you can shift the power dynamic in your favor. Do you have a personal board of directors? Who could you call on to help you along your journey?

Near and dear to my heart was learning I'd been selected as the recipient of the Entrepreneurial Achievement Award from UW–Madison. Surprised that my alma mater had been following my career and felt it was worthy of recognition, I was filled with pride. My three kids and I drove to Madison for the ceremony. I was presented with the award by UW chancellor Rebecca Blank, a renowned economist who's served three presidential administrations. Rebecca has since been appointed president of Northwestern University, my grad school alma mater, where decades ago she was one of the first tenured women in the economics department. In the new role, she was named the institution's first female president.

Perhaps the most powerful moment was seeing my children's smiling faces in the audience as I gave my acceptance speech. I hope they felt inspired and motivated to find their own passion, and to do their best someday, too.

The Virtuous Loop of Being the Best

To become the fire, you need to be the best at what you most love to do. With dedication, you bring your strongest self to it and measure success by the bar you set. When you maintain high standards for yourself and those in your orb, you increase the chances that you will be very good at it and become known for it. Dedicated to bringing your A game, you will shine and stand out from the crowd. And by becoming the best, you will achieve more success.

This cycle played itself out over the course of my life. The more I loved what I was doing, the more time I spent on it. And the more I dedicated myself to it — by working at it and surrounding myself with the best people — the better at it we became. By giving it everything we had and holding ourselves to a high standard, we were considered to be among the best in our space.

Let's break down that formula with what was going on when I was building 30Seconds.

Being the best means finding what you most love to do and dedicating yourself to it. When building 30Seconds, my team and I were driven by passion and purpose. We were dedicated to building one of the best websites of its kind so we could make a difference for our readers and community members.

The more you work at it, the better at it you will become. We set high standards of excellence — and set a high bar for performance — for everyone in our orb. By giving it our best effort, we became recognized as leaders.

As you become the best at it, you will achieve more success. Dedicated to our mission, we started to be recognized. As the website inspired more people, opportunities followed. The more we became known for being among the best, the more success we achieved.

This basic formula applies no matter where you are in your journey to become the fire. Use it when you want to figure out what matters most, when you need a reminder to give it your best, or when you seek to set a high bar for yourself and others. By pouring your heart into what you most love to do, you'll find yourself shining like never before!

FLAME • Angela Martinez Korompilas

First Jobs: Babysitter, yogurt store worker, sporting goods store associate

Education: BASc (pre-med), University of Illinois Chicago; Kellogg Management Institute Certificate, Northwestern University

Personal Life: Married, mother of one

Board/Civic Roles: Member, YPO; member, Economic Club of Chicago

Key Takeaway: "I set super high standards for myself and everyone around me. I always give it my best."

Angela Martinez Korompilas's Cuban father inspired her to believe that she could be the best at anything she wanted to be and that she could make just about anything happen. And Angela has been making things happen her whole life. Until recently, she was the CEO of American Hotel Register Company, a $1 billion business certified by Women's Business Enterprise with more than 150 years of history in the hospitality space.

Although Angela describes her upbringing in Chicago as lower middle class, her father would tell her and her three siblings that they could achieve whatever it was they set their minds to. She remembers that she had so much fun as a child that she didn't pay attention to her family's socioeconomic status.

But in a split second, nineteen-year-old Angela's world changed forever when her father, an electrician, suffered a severe spinal cord injury after a devastating fall on the job. "He was not wearing a harness. After he fell, he was so swollen and unrecognizable. I was at school, so they pulled me out of class, then took me to the hospital to see him."

As her father worked toward recovery, Angela recalls, "he wasn't able to grip a cup. He would always drag a leg behind him. His hearing and eyesight were affected. It scared me in a way I couldn't comprehend."

Her father retained his positive attitude, despite his disabilities. "He is my role model. He's so smart, curious, and loves to learn. That's where my love of learning comes from."

Angela's parents were high school sweethearts, and together they instilled in their daughter a foundation of resilience, a solid work ethic, and a sense that the sky was the limit. "I always felt empowered to be the very best me that I could be. There were no limits to what I could do."

By age fifteen, Angela had moved on from babysitting to a variety of part-time customer service jobs. At a bank, she became teller supervisor before she turned seventeen. "I learned well, and I did well in school. I liked to read, and I was always curious."

Angela set a high bar for her academic performance, so even though her parents couldn't afford to send her to college, not earning a degree was never an option. "My mindset was always, 'If you are capable, then you should. If you can, then do.'" She was capable, so she would find a way. And by setting high standards for herself, she did.

Angela put herself through college with academic scholarships and by working at a market research company, at a mailbox company, and by doing side jobs on weekends. "I had always wanted to make life-changing things happen." Before her father's accident, she wanted to become a doctor. "I was so interested in working at a hospital. I saw myself as a neurosurgeon, saving lives."

But after her dad's accident, Angela realized her life was going to be different than what she had previously planned. By the time she graduated with her pre-med degree, she'd decided she no longer wanted to be a doctor. "After going through all of that with my dad, I now could not imagine spending my whole life in a hospital surrounded by such sadness. So, I decided not to go to medical school."

As Angela contemplated what to do instead, she thought about her strengths — math and science — and the possibility of going into research or teaching. But her mom had a friend who worked for American Hotel, so Angela took a summer job in their medical supply and healthcare division. "They invited me to come work for their hotel side, where I could do more interesting things."

Although Angela had never considered a career in business, the American Hotel opportunity was too intriguing to pass up. And by diving into the hotel supply industry, she found a nice balance between her logical and creative sides. Starting out in sales, Angela worked her way up the American Hotel ladder to become vice president. Along the way, she met a fellow American Hotel employee named Jim, the man who would become her husband and the father to her son, Jimmy.

As her career grew, Angela became senior vice president and then, not even two years later, executive vice president and chief operating officer. As Angela's career skyrocketed, the couple decided that Jim should leave his job at American Hotel to be the stay-at-home parent.

The following year, she earned the title of president and CEO. "What I said to the board of directors when I became CEO was, 'Even on my very worst day, I will do my very best to take care of this company.'"

Angela attributes her success to always learning, always being authentic, and always bringing her strongest self. "I set super high standards for myself and everyone around me. I am not perfect, and I'm honest about who I am. But I always give it my best. When you dig a little deeper, that's where all the goodness is."

Part of bringing her A game includes being the most prepared person in the room and showing up in the way she wants to be seen. "On my worst day, it still may be someone's only opportunity to speak to me. A former manager told me once that we always want to be judged by our full body of work — not our best day and not our worst day. I always ask myself, 'Is that how you want to be remembered?'"

Angela follows an evening routine to ensure she shows up as her best self. Each night before she falls asleep, she says, "I lay in bed and, in my mind, I watch a movie of my day. As I review the movie, I reflect on what I could have done or said better. I'm a work in progress, but watching the movie of my day helps me to become a better leader and a better parent."

In 2021, American Hotel's core business was acquired by Consolidated Hospitality Supplies Holdings, a consolidation platform backed by HCI Equity Partners.

Since the acquisition and her departure from the company, Angela has finally been able to step off the rocket ship she's been on and exhale. She's having the time of her life spending more time with her family than ever before. "As I tell my son, we have gifts to the extent they can benefit others. So many people don't have the opportunities we have. It's a responsibility, and it's a privilege. We have to wake up every day and be grateful."

Reflecting on her career so far, Angela explains her definition of success. "It bothers me when someone tells me I'm lucky. The good fortune I've received is a result of good choices and hard work. You have to feel proud not only of your success but of how you achieved that success. Being successful means I can help my parents, my siblings. And because I could, I should."

At the end of the day, it's the legacy she leaves that matters most. "When people tell me that working with me has been one of the highlights of their career, there is nothing greater than that. The friendships I have made, the relationships that run so deep, the integrity I've maintained — that's a career well lived."

BLAZE

I am dedicated to being my best self.

I set and maintain high standards for myself and those around me.

I bring my A game to what I most love to do.

By doing my best, I stand out from the crowd.

The fire within me shines like a beacon.

As I become the best I can be, I achieve more success.

Conclusion

Along my winding health journey, a cardiologist told me I might be dealing with challenges related to my heart condition for the rest of my life. When I asked what I could do to make it better, he shared that one of the best ways for patients like me to achieve a better quality of life is with a holistic approach — in other words, treating not only the heart or autoimmune disease symptoms (which we'd be doing anyway) but also the whole person with an integrative approach. That's when he introduced me to the concept of integrative medicine.

Integrative medicine is designed to maximize wellness, especially for people like me with complex health conditions. It combines conventional and complementary medicine practices with personalized care to treat the whole person.

I was fortunate to connect with an amazing doctor who's the head of the integrative medicine practice at my local hospital. Over the years, she has helped to keep my health on solid footing as I navigate its ups and downs.

At one of our appointments not too long ago, I told her I was writing a book. Not surprised that I was taking on yet another challenge, she wondered if that was the best thing for me to be doing with all I had going on. Explaining why I felt compelled to do it, as part of my giving back and paying it forward, she smiled. "You are a fiery one," she said. "You never give up. You keep going, no matter what. There's so much fire in you."

Surprised, since I hadn't mentioned what the book was about, let alone the title, my eyebrows shot up. "The title of my book is *Become the Fire*," I said.

"Of course it is," she replied with that knowing smile.

When you have fire in you, people see it and feel it — especially when you use that energy to make a positive difference in the world. And just as there's fire in me, there's fire in you. After reading this book, you will be able to tap into that fire in a more intentional, actionable way. You, too, are now a fiery one.

Now that you know what I know, and what the other women in this book know, you can chart your own path to success. You can use all that fire in you to move forward and achieve the life you dream of.

You can use an integrative approach and incorporate all ten lessons, or you can cherry-pick the ones that seem most achievable to you. Decide which lessons resonate with you the most, and move ahead.

For example, maybe you'll be a visionary with courage; perhaps you'll be a maker with grit; or you may just focus on being the best at what you love most. You get to decide when and where to direct your fire and how to light up your corner of the world.

As I write this, 30Seconds continues to grow, which is humbling and gratifying. Our continued growth means we can shine brighter and inspire more people with our special kind of magic — and make life better for the community we serve. All the while, I'm able to make a positive difference for my family, friends, colleagues, charities, and communities. For someone who has continually measured herself by how much of an impact she can make in the world, that's success.

What will success mean to you? You get to decide what that looks like in your own life. And I simply can't wait to see what you achieve and how you make life better as you *become the fire*. I know that, because of your success, the world will be much better off. For that, I am grateful.

But please do me a favor. Once you achieve some success, look around and see who you can help along their journey. Find a fellow outsider and tell them how you did it. Share the lessons you learned from this book. Assure them that success is something they can make for themselves, and if you could do it, they can, too. Whether you choose to offer a word of encouragement, a connection, or even mentorship, you can help someone else get to where they want to be by paying it forward as an ally.

When you tell others what you know, hopefully they will realize that they can accomplish their goals. And maybe they will find the motivation and the inspiration to make it happen. Then, when they get to where they want to be, they can help someone else (maybe even you). That's how our success will spread like wildfire.

As you succeed, and as more women and BIPOC succeed, it paves the way for even more of us to succeed. And as more women from all walks of life manifest the lives they dream of, the world becomes a better place.

So, right now, I'd like you to set some final intentions with me:

> I am situationally aware, and I am visionary.
> I am self-aware, and I am my authentic self.
> I am self-confident, and I am comfortable with being uncomfortable.

I am motivated, and I am courageous.
I am resilient, and I am friends with failure.
I am creative, and I am a maker.
I am capable, and I am viable.
I persevere, and I am gritty.
I am a leader, and I am the inspiration.
I am dedicated, and I am the best at what I love most.

And say these out loud, over and over again:

I am the spark.
I am the flame.
I am the blaze.
I am *the fire*.

Now, go make life better with your fire!

Acknowledgments

My husband, Dieter, an exceptional ally and the best life partner I could hope for: thank you for your unending support and love. You have mine.

Our seven children, whom we love so much and who are the ultimate source of inspiration: our wish for each of you is to find your passion and to love what you do with your whole heart so you can make life better with your fire.

Mi madre and my father: *mil gracias* and *hvala* for your love and for the lessons you taught me, both intentional and unintentional. Without them, I never could have become the fire. I love you very much.

My loved sister and brother: we got through all that childhood chaos, individually and together. Thanks for being in the fire with me.

My father's family and *mi madre's familia* (and, most recently, my husband's family): you taught me so much. Each lesson helped shaped who I am. *Hvala, gracias, danke.*

Foreword author, angel investor, role model, and mentor

Mary Dillon: you are a blazing light in this world, and I am so grateful for you. Thank you for believing in me.

The ten inspiring women who shared their stories in this book — Jules Pieri, Sarah Hofstetter, Laura Desmond, Desirée Rogers, Paula Boggs, Kim Oster-Holstein, Emily Smith, Winnie Park, Talita Ramos Erickson, and Angela Martinez Korompilas: thank you for sharing your fire. You light up the world.

Georgia Hughes, who helped the fire burn more brightly: thank you for helping me expand my mission to make life better. I appreciate you, Kristen Cashman, and the rest of your talented team at New World Library.

Jacqueline Flynn at Joëlle Delbourgo Associates, who fanned the flames: you helped me be courageous, step outside my comfort zone, and truly tell my story. Thank you.

Jennie Nash, who helped me evolve from journalist to author: thanks, Coach, for helping to jump-start my book journey.

Heather Shumaker, first to read the overview for what would become this book: thanks for seeing the spark and helping me get started.

Donna John, who's been shining her light with me from iParenting to Disney to 30Seconds. It's because of you that I know teamwork makes the dream work. Thank you.

Kaspars, Jan, Terry, Susie, Jeff, Ann Marie, Amy, Melissa, Belinda, Mindy, Gigi, Fadi, Holly, Leslie, and countless other friends, allies, colleagues, and contributors at iParenting, Disney, and 30Seconds who believed, inspired, and supported me along my journey: you were there for me during some of the most chaotic — and life-changing — moments, and I am forever grateful.

All the women who asked me "How did you do it?" when what you *really* wanted to know was "How can *I* do it?": thank you for planting the seed for *Become the Fire*. I hope I answered the question so that now you can do it, too.

Resources

Here are some resources and organizations that could be helpful to you on your journey to *become the fire*.

For all the latest updates, interviews, information, and inspiration about *Become the Fire*, visit:

www.becomethefire.com

For all the latest updates on me as an author, visit:

www.elisaschmitz.com

To join the 30Seconds community, visit:

www.30Seconds.com

To learn more about the Springboard accelerator program, visit:

www.sb.co

To learn more about Google for Startups, visit:

www.startup.google.com

To learn more about the 1871 Chicago tech incubator, visit:

www.1871.com

To learn more about the WiSTEM accelerator program (now known as WMNtech Founders) at 1871 Chicago, visit:

www.1871.com/wmntech-founders

To learn more about the Women's Business Development Center, visit:

www.wbdc.org

To learn more about the Women's Business Enterprise National Council (WBENC) and its certification process, visit:

www.wbenc.org/about-wbenc

To learn more about the National Conference of Puerto Rican Women, visit:

www.nacoprw.org

Notes

Foreword

p. xi   *many women say the American dream can feel unattainable*: Mohamed Younis, "Most Americans See American Dream as Achievable," Gallup, July 17, 2019, https://news.gallup.com/poll/260741/americans -american-dream-achievable.aspx.

p. xiii   *With only 2 percent of venture capital funding*: Jordan Rubio and Priyamvada Mathur, "An Exceptional Year for Female Founders Still Means a Sliver of VC Funding," PitchBook, January 10, 2022, https://pitchbook.com/news/articles/female-founders-dashboard-2021 -vc-funding-wrap-up.

Introduction

p. 6   *"broken rung"*: Tiffany Burns et al., "Women in the Workplace 2021," McKinsey & Company, September 27, 2021, https://www.mckinsey .com/featured-insights/diversity-and-inclusion/women-in-the-work place.

Chapter 3: Be Comfortable with Being Uncomfortable

p. 74 *"impostor syndrome"*: Pauline Rose Clance, "Impostor Phenomenon (IP)," author website, accessed February 3, 2020, https://pauline roseclance.com/impostor_phenomenon.html.

Chapter 5: Be Friends with Failure

p. 127 *up to 81 percent of women*: Rhitu Chatterjee, "A New Survey Finds 81 Percent of Women Have Experienced Sexual Harassment," NPR, February 21, 2018, https://www.npr.org/sections/thetwo -way/2018/02/21/587671849/a-new-survey-finds-eighty-percent -of-women-have-experienced-sexual-harassment.

Chapter 6: Be a Maker

p. 151 *with a growth mindset, people believe*: Carol Dweck, *Mindset: The New Psychology of Success* (New York: Ballantine Books, 2007).

p. 154 *women account for the majority of all consumer purchases*: Michael J. Silverstein and Kate Sayre, "The Female Economy," *Harvard Business Review*, September 2009, https://hbr.org/2009/09/the-female-economy.

Chapter 8: Be Gritty

p. 200 *Dr. Angela Duckworth defines grit*: Angela Duckworth, *Grit: The Power of Passion and Perseverance* (New York: Scribner, 2016).

p. 207 *author Stephen Covey describes the scarcity mindset*: Stephen R. Covey, *The 7 Habits of Highly Effective People: 30th Anniversary Edition* (New York: Simon & Schuster, 2020).

p. 210 code blue *is the term used in some hospitals*: "What Is a Code Blue?" WebMD, April 19, 2021, https://www.webmd.com/a-to-z-guides /what-is-a-code-blue.

p. 212 *"We wanted to build a place"*: J.B. Pritzker, quoted in Elisa A. Schmitz, "Proud to Call 1871 Chicago Home," 30Seconds, accessed June 2, 2020, https://30seconds.com/mom/tip/14013/Proud-to-Call-1871 -Chicago-Home-Watch-This-Inspiring-Video-Celebrating-5-Years.

Chapter 10: Be the Best

p. 267 *acquired by Google for $966 million*: Dara Kerr, "Google Reveals It
Spent $966 Million in Waze Acquisition," CNET, July 25, 2013,
https://www.cnet.com/tech/services-and-software/google-reveals-it
-spent-966-million-in-waze-acquisition.

Conclusion

p. 275 *It combines conventional and complementary medicine practices*: "Integrative Medicine," Mayo Clinic, June 19, 2020, https://www.mayoclinic
.org/tests-procedures/complementary-alternative-medicine/about
/pac-20393581.

Index

About the Author

Elisa A. Schmitz is an award-winning entrepreneur and professional journalist. She's the Latina founder and CEO of 30Seconds.com, an inspiring digital media platform that makes the world a happier, healthier, and more delicious place — 30 seconds at a time. She's also the founder of iParenting, a "Best of the Web" digital media company that was acquired by the Walt Disney Company. After the sale, Elisa worked for Disney as director and executive editor of the Disney Interactive Media Group. She has been a newspaper columnist, magazine editor, radio and video host, and creator of content and marketing programs for various Fortune 500 companies.

Elisa earned her bachelor's degree in communication arts from the University of Wisconsin–Madison, where she serves on the Communication Arts board. She earned her master's degree in journalism from the Medill School of Journalism at Northwestern University, where she's a member of the Council of One Hundred, a mentoring organization made up of Northwestern's leading alumnae.

Elisa is no stranger to life's fire. The daughter of a Puerto Rican mother and a Yugoslavian immigrant father, Elisa learned to use her "differentness" to make a difference as she grew up in Puerto Rico, war-torn Lebanon, and suburban Chicago. All along, she created what she needed to survive and thrive.

Connect with Elisa online at **www.elisaschmitz.com**.

NEW WORLD LIBRARY is dedicated to publishing books and other media that inspire and challenge us to improve the quality of our lives and the world.

We are a socially and environmentally aware company. We recognize that we have an ethical responsibility to our readers, our authors, our staff members, and our planet.

We serve our readers by creating the finest publications possible on personal growth, creativity, spirituality, wellness, and other areas of emerging importance. We serve our authors by working with them to produce and promote quality books that reach a wide audience. We serve New World Library employees with generous benefits, significant profit sharing, and constant encouragement to pursue their most expansive dreams.

Whenever possible, we print our books with soy-based ink on 100 percent postconsumer-waste recycled paper. We power our offices with solar energy and contribute to nonprofit organizations working to make the world a better place for us all.

Our products are available wherever books are sold. Visit our website to download our catalog, subscribe to our e-newsletter, read our blog, and link to authors' websites, videos, and podcasts.

customerservice@newworldlibrary.com
Phone: 415-884-2100 or 800-972-6657
Orders: Ext. 110 • Catalog requests: Ext. 110
Fax: 415-884-2199

www.newworldlibrary.com

Personal Growth / Business

$19.95 U.S

TURN OBSTACLES INTO FUEL FOR
FULFILLMENT AND **SUCCESS**

What does it mean to *become the fire*? It means not allowing yourself to be *in the* fire of life's challenges, getting burned, but instead *using* the fire to ignite your motivation and drive, passion and grit. It means not focusing on what you *don't* have or *can't* do, but instead leveraging what you *do* have and *can* do. It means using your differences to your advantage and seeing life's chaos as fuel to prope your success. Using her own story of entrepreneurial success as well as interviews with ten diverse and successful women, Elisa Schmitz presents ten actionable lessons for putting your personal power to work, with unstoppable results.

"Elisa Schmitz knows what it takes not only to overcome life's fire but also to let it forge the inner strength, vision, authenticity, and resilience needed to turn challenges into success.... An engaging read that will inspire you to make, or expand, your own mark in the world!"
— **KAIRA ROUDA,** *USA TODAY* bestselling author of *Real You Incorporated*

"Takes you deep into the thought processes and decision-making of elite, proven, and highly relatable women....This exceptional book, fueled by Elisa's enthusiasm, is among the best I have read."
— **DANIEL JOSHUA RUBIN,** author of *27 Essential Principles of Story*

"Takes you on inspirational journeys of women who seized the fire within them to achieve remarkable success."
— **KAY KOPLOVITZ,** founder and former CEO of USA Networks

"*Anyone* looking to have a successful and, more importantly, *fulfilling* career should read *Become the Fire!*"
— **JANAE BAKKEN,** Emmy-nominated executive producer and TV writer of *Scrubs, Anger Management,* and other shows

Scott Thompson

ELISA A. SCHMITZ is an award-winning Latina entrepreneur and journalist. She is the founder and CEO of 30Seconds.com, with millions of unique users every month. She is also the founder of iParenting, a "Best of the Web" digital media company that was acquired by the Walt Disney Company. She lives in the Chicago area.
www.elisaschmitz.com   www.becomethefire.com

Cover design by Howie Severson • Cover illustration © Shutterstock.com
Printed on 100% postconsumer-waste recycled paper

ISBN 978-1-60868-810-4

New World Library
www.newworldlibrary.com

51995
9 781608 688104